PERFORMANCE
EVALUATION

PERFORMANCE EVALUATION

Proven Approaches for Improving Program and Organizational Performance

INGRID GUERRA-LÓPEZ

JOSSEY-BASS
A Wiley Imprint
www.josseybass.com

Published by Jossey-Bass
A Wiley Imprint
989 Market Street, San Francisco, CA 94103-1741—www.josseybass.com

Jossey-Bass books and products are available through most bookstores. To contact Jossey-Bass directly call our Customer Care Department within the U.S. at 800-956-7739, outside the U.S. at 317-572-3986, or fax 317-572-4002.

Jossey-Bass also publishes its books in a variety of electronic formats. Some content that appears in print may not be available in electronic books.

Library of Congress Cataloging-in-Publication Data

Guerra-López, Ingrid.
 Performance evaluation : proven approaches for improving program and organizational performance / Ingrid Guerra-López. — 1st ed.
  p. cm.
 Includes bibliographical references and index.
 ISBN 978-0-7879-8883-8 (pbk.)
  1. Employees—Rating of. 2. Performance standards.
3. Organizational effectiveness. I. Title.
HF5549.5.R3G84 2008
658.3'125—dc22

                   2007050973

FIRST EDITION

HB Printing	10 9 8 7 6 5 4 3 2 1
PB Printing	10 9 8 7 6 5 4 3

CONTENTS

Acknowledgments   xi

Preface   xiii

The Author   xv

PART ONE: INTRODUCTION TO EVALUATION

ONE: FOUNDATIONS OF EVALUATION   **3**

A Brief Overview of Evaluation History   4

Evaluation: Purpose and Definition   5

Performance Improvement: A Conceptual Framework   8

Making Evaluation Happen: Ensuring
Stakeholders' Buy-In   9

The Evaluator: A Job or a Role?   10

The Relationship to Other Investigative Processes   11

When Does Evaluation Occur?   15

General Evaluation Orientations   18

Challenges That Evaluators Face   20

Ensuring Commitment   23

Benefits of Evaluation   24

Basic Definitions   25

**TWO: PRINCIPLES OF PERFORMANCE-BASED
EVALUATION**   **27**

Principle 1: Evaluation Is Based on Asking
the Right Questions   28

Principle 2: Evaluation of Process Is a Function
of Obtained Results   32

Principle 3: Goals and Objectives of
Organizations Should Be Based on Valid Needs   33

Principle 4: Derive Valid Needs Using a
Top-Down Approach   34

Principle 5: Every Organization Should Aim
for the Best That Society Can Attain   34

Principle 6: The Set of Evaluation Questions
Drives the Evaluation Study   35

PART TWO: MODELS OF EVALUATION

**THREE: OVERVIEW OF EXISTING
EVALUATION MODELS**   **39**

Overview of Classic Evaluation Models   40

Selected Evaluation Models   42

Selecting a Model   43

Conceptualizing a Useful Evaluation That Fits
the Situation   44

**FOUR: KIRKPATRICK'S FOUR LEVELS
OF EVALUATION**   **47**

Kirkpatrick's Levels   49

Comments on the Model   54

Strengths and Limitations   55

Application Example: Wagner (1995)   56

**FIVE: PHILLIPS'S RETURN-ON-INVESTMENT
METHODOLOGY**   **61**

Phillips's ROI Process   63

Comments on the Model   67

Strengths and Limitations   70

Application Example: Blake (1999)   70

SIX: BRINKERHOFF'S SUCCESS CASE METHOD — 75
 The SCM Process — 77
 Strengths and Weaknesses — 78
 Application Example: Brinkerhoff (2005) — 79

SEVEN: THE IMPACT EVALUATION PROCESS — 81
 The Elements of the Process — 83
 Comments on the Model — 96
 Strengths and Limitations — 97
 Application Example — 97

EIGHT: THE CIPP MODEL — 107
 Stufflebeam's Four Types of Evaluation — 108
 Articulating Core Values of Programs and Solutions — 111
 Methods Used in CIPP Evaluations — 112
 Strengths and Limitations — 113
 Application Example: Filella-Guiu
  and Blanch-Pana (2002) — 113

NINE: EVALUATING EVALUATIONS — 117
 Evaluation Standards — 119
 The American Evaluation Association Principles
  for Evaluators — 120
 Application Example: Lynch et al. (2003) — 122

PART THREE: TOOLS AND TECHNIQUES OF EVALUATION

TEN: DATA — 133
 Characteristics of Data — 135
 Scales of Measurement — 137
 Defining Required Data from
  Performance Objectives — 139

Deriving Measurable Indicators 141

Finding Data Sources 152

Follow-Up Questions and Data 155

ELEVEN: DATA COLLECTION 159

Observation Methodology and the
Purpose of Measurement 160

Designing the Experiment 186

Problems with Classic Experimental Studies
in Applied Settings 188

Time-Series Studies 188

Simulations and Games 189

Document-Centered Methods 191

Conclusion 192

TWELVE: ANALYSIS OF EVALUATION
DATA: TOOLS AND TECHNIQUES 195

Analysis of Models and Patterns 196

Analysis Using Structured Discussion 197

Methods of Quantitative Analysis 199

Statistics 200

Graphical Representations of Data 210

Measures of Relationship 212

Inferential Statistics: Parametric
and Nonparametric 214

Interpretation 217

THIRTEEN: COMMUNICATING
THE FINDINGS 221

Recommendations 222

Considerations for Implementing
Recommendations 225

Developing the Report 226

The Evaluator's Role After the Report 235

PART FOUR: CONTINUAL IMPROVEMENT

FOURTEEN: **COMMON ERRORS IN EVALUATION** **239**

Errors of System Mapping 240

Errors of Logic 242

Errors of Procedure 244

Conclusion 246

FIFTEEN: **CONTINUAL IMPROVEMENT** **249**

What Is Continual Improvement? 250

Monitoring Performance 250

Adjusting Performance 253

The Role of Leadership 254

SIXTEEN: **CONTRACTING FOR EVALUATION SERVICES** **257**

The Contract 258

Contracting Controls 260

Ethics and Professionalism 262

Sample Statement of Work 262

SEVENTEEN: **INTELLIGENCE GATHERING FOR DECISION MAKING** **271**

Performance Measurement Systems 273

Issues in Performance Measurement Systems 275

Conclusion 277

EIGHTEEN: THE FUTURE OF
EVALUATION IN PERFORMANCE IMPROVEMENT   279

    Evaluation and Measurement in Performance
      Improvement Today   281

    What Does the Future Hold?   282

    Conclusion   283

References and Related Readings   285

Index   295

ACKNOWLEDGMENTS

Recognition for any achievement is usually owed to a group of people rather than any one individual alone. First, I thank Jossey-Bass and, in particular, Andrew Pasternack for his interest in my potential contributions, which was the major catalyst for this work. I also thank Seth Schwartz for his graciousness and flexibility as I encountered a glitch or two along the way. Much gratitude is owed to Beverly Miller and Barbara Armentrout for their outstanding editing and proofing work.

I thank my mentor, Roger Kaufman, who continues to push me to think critically and support my ideas with evidence. A special recognition is owed to Hillary Andrei for her invaluable support in various aspects of my evaluation work. My gratitude is also owed to Rahat Sharma for her formatting support. I am grateful as well to my students, colleagues, and clients who are constant sources of ideas and reflections. The work in this book is the product of such ideas and reflections.

Finally, I am thankful to my husband, Jorge, for being once again excited, and patient, as I embarked on yet another project.

There are excellent books on evaluation already in print. Some focus on the history and theory of evaluation, some provide a comprehensive analysis of evaluation models and approaches, and some primarily offer insights into methodology. Although this book addresses these concepts, it is not intended to replicate or refute any other work. Rather, it is organized in such a way as to illustrate evaluation in the context of performance improvement. This work is directed at the following audiences:

- Performance improvement practitioners who seek to do evaluation well, wish to become sufficiently versed in evaluation so as to work well with evaluators, or want to integrate an evaluative perspective in all phases of performance improvement, from needs assessment to implementation, to evaluation itself

- Evaluators who seek to do systemic, performance-focused evaluations with the ultimate end of improving not only programs or solutions but also the organizations and the clients, including our shared society, whose needs they are meant to meet

- Students who want a solid conceptual grounding in evaluation and a guide for applying such concepts in courses and their own work and who will generate the future evaluation and performance improvement models, in part based on concepts presented here

- Instructors who are looking for a text that addresses important foundations of evaluation and presents the models and approaches in the context of the performance improvement field

- Clients, including those external to the organization stakeholders, who wish to become better-informed consumers of and partners in evaluation efforts

If you want to more clearly understand the impact this book has had on your thinking about evaluation, then I suggest that before reading it, you respond to the questions listed below. Once you have completed reading the book, I recommend answering each of the questions again, paying close attention to how your views have changed, if at all, as a result of reading this book. This exercise is meant to support deeper reflection and insight about fundamental assumptions associated with evaluation and implications for practice.

- What is your current model or approach to evaluation? Use these questions to guide your response (if you don't have a current model or approach, think about what your basic assumptions about evaluation are):

    What aspects of evaluation are addressed by your theory?

    What are the main purposes, processes, or mechanisms associated with your model?

    Does your model target a specific setting? If so, what is it?

    With what other models (if you know of any) is your model most compatible? Explain how they are compatible.

    With what other models is your theory least incompatible? Explain what the incompatibilities are.

- In what ways has your model of evaluation been applied? Was it successful? What, if anything, would you have done differently? What were the biggest lessons you learned? Provide specific situations and examples.

The book is divided into four parts, beginning with an introduction to the foundations of evaluation, then proceeding to a collection of models chosen specifically for the reputation and applicability in the performance improvement field. Part Three looks at the tools and techniques that are common in various evaluation perspectives, and Part Four concludes with a look at continual improvement and the future of evaluation in performance improvement.

Ingrid Guerra-López is an associate professor at Wayne State University in Detroit, associate research professor at the Sonora Institute of Technology in Mexico, and principal of Intelligence Gathering Systems. She publishes, teaches, consults, and conducts research in the areas of performance measurement and evaluation, assessment and analysis, and strategic alignment. She has published four other books, including *Evaluating Impact: Evaluation and Continual Improvement for Performance Improvement Practitioners,* and is coauthor of *Practical Evaluation for Educators: Finding What Works and What Doesn't.* She has published numerous chapters in books in the performance improvement field, including the 2006 *Handbook for Human Performance Technology.* Her articles have appeared as well in *Performance Improvement, Performance Improvement Quarterly, Human Resource Development Quarterly, Educational Technology, Quarterly Review of Distance Education, International Public Management Review,* and the *International Journal for Educational Reform,* among others.

INTRODUCTION TO EVALUATION

FOUNDATIONS OF EVALUATION

This chapter defines and describes evaluation and sets the frame for this book within the principles of performance improvement. Various kinds of evaluation, as well as some closely related processes, are differentiated from each other. The basic challenges that evaluators face are laid out, and the reason that stakeholder commitment is so important is examined. The benefits of evaluation to an organization are listed. Finally, definitions are provided for some key terms used throughout the book and in the evaluation field.

In our daily lives, we encounter decision points on an almost continuous basis: Should I do this, or should I do that? Should I go right or left? Should I take the highway or the back streets? Should I buy now or later? Should I take my umbrella today or not? Life in an organizational setting is no different: We face decisions about which programs to sustain, which to change, and which to abandon, to name but a few organizational dilemmas. How do members of an organization go about making sound decisions? With the use of relevant, reliable, and valid data, gathered through a sound evaluation process aligned with desired long-term outcomes.

Unfortunately, these data are not always available, and if they are, many decision makers do not know they exist, or do not have access to them, or do not know how to interpret and use them to make sound decisions that lead to improved program and organizational performance. In fact, Lee Cronbach (1980) and others have argued that decisions often emerge rather than being logically and methodically made.

Effective leaders are capable of making sound decisions based on sound data, and evaluators can do much to influence the leadership decision-making process. Evaluation can provide a systematic framework that aligns stakeholders, evaluation purposes, desired results and consequences, and all evaluation activities, so that the evaluation product is a responsive and clear recipe for improving performance. This in essence allows the decision-making process to become clearer and more straightforward. Evaluation is the mechanism that provides decision makers with feedback, whether through interim reports and meetings or a final report and debriefing.

A BRIEF OVERVIEW OF EVALUATION HISTORY

Michael Scriven (1991) describes evaluation as a practice that dates back to samurai sword evaluation. Another type of evaluation was in evidence as early as 2000 B.C.: Chinese officials held civil service examinations to measure the ability of individuals applying for government positions. And Socrates included verbal evaluations as part of his instructional approach (Fitzpatrick, Sanders, & Worthen, 2004).

In response to dissatisfaction with educational and social programs, a more formal educational evaluation can be traced back to Great Britain during the 1800s, when royal commissions were sent by the government to hear testimony from the various institutions. In the 1930s, Ralph Tyler issued a call to measure goal attainment with standardized criteria (Fitzpatrick et al., 2004). And during the 1960s, Scriven and Cronbach introduced formative (used to guide developmental activities) and summative (used to determine the overall value of a program or solution) evaluation, and Stufflebeam stressed outcomes (program results) over process (program activities and resources) (Liston, 1999).

In 1963, Cronbach published an important work, "Course Improvement Through Evaluation," challenging educators to measure real learning rather than the passive mastery of facts. Moreover, he proposed the use of qualitative instruments, such as interviews and observations, to study outcomes. In the latter part of the 1960s, well-known evaluation figures such as Edward Suchman, Michael Scriven, Carol Weiss, Blaine Worthen, and James Sanders wrote the earliest texts on program evaluation.

In 1971, Daniel Stufflebeam proposed the CIPP model of evaluation, which he said would be more responsive to the needs of decision makers than earlier approaches to evaluation were. In that same year, Malcolm Provus proposed the discrepancy model of evaluation. In 1972, Scriven proposed goal-free evaluation in an effort to encourage evaluators to find unintended consequences. In 1975, Robert Stake provided responsive evaluation. In 1981, Egon Guba and Yvonna Lincoln proposed naturalistic evaluation on the basis of Stake's work, feeding the debate between qualitative and quantitative methods (Fitzpatrick et al., 2004).

All of this was occurring in the context of a movement to account for the billions of dollars the U.S. government was spending on social, health, and educational programs (Fitzpatrick et al., 2004; Patton, 1997). In order to address a demand for accountability, those responsible for programs soon began to ask evaluators for advice on program improvement. Thus, the initial purpose of program evaluation was to judge the worthiness of programs for continued funding.

When Sputnik became the catalyst for improving the U.S. position in education, which was lagging compared to other countries, educational entities in particular began to commission evaluations, partly in order to document their achievements. The need for evaluators soon grew, and government responded by funding university programs in educational research and evaluation. In the 1970s and 1980s, evaluation grew as a field, with its applications expanding beyond government and educational settings to management and other areas. Evaluations are now conducted in many different settings using a variety of perspectives and methods.

EVALUATION: PURPOSE AND DEFINITION

While some rightly say that the fundamental purpose of evaluation is the determination of the worth or merit of a program or solution (Scriven, 1967), the ultimate purpose, and value, of determining this worth is in providing the information for making data-driven decisions that lead to improved performance of programs and organizations (Guerra-López, 2007a). The notion that evaluation's most important purpose is not to prove but to improve was originally put forward by Egon Guba when he served on the Phi Delta Kappa National Study Committee on Evaluation around 1971 (Stufflebeam, 2003). This should be the foundation for all evaluation efforts, now and in the future. Every component of an evaluation must be aligned with the organization's objectives and expectations and the decisions that will have to be made as a result of the evaluation findings. These decisions are essentially concerned with how to improve performance at all levels of the organization: internal deliverables, organizational gains, and public impact. At its core, evaluation is a simple concept:

- It compares results with expectations.

- It finds drivers and barriers to expected performance.

- It produces action plans for improving the programs and solutions being evaluated so that expected performance is achieved or maintained and organizational objectives and contributions can be realized (Guerra-López, 2007a).

Some approaches to evaluation do not focus on predetermined results or objectives, but the approach taken in this book is based on the premise of performance improvement. The underlying assumption is that organizations, whether they fully articulate this or not, expect specific results and contributions from programs and other solutions. As discussed in later chapters, this does not prevent the evaluator or performance improvement professional from employing means to help identify unanticipated results and consequences. The worth or merit of programs and solutions is then determined by whether they delivered the desired results, whether these results are worth having in the first place, and whether the benefits of these results outweigh their costs and unintended consequences.

An evaluation that asks and answers the right questions can be used not only to determine results but also to understand those results and to modify the evaluation so that it can better meet the intended objectives within the required criteria. This is useful not only to identify what went wrong or what could be better but also to identify what should be maintained. Through appreciative inquiry (Cooperrider & Srivastva, 1987), evaluation can help organizations identify what is going right. Appreciative inquiry is a process that searches for the best in organizations in order to find opportunities for performance improvement. Here too the efforts are but a means to the end of improving performance. Although the intentions of most evaluators are just that, the language and approach used are charged with assumptions that things are going wrong. For instance, the term *problem solving* implies from the start that something is wrong. Even if this assumption is not explicit in the general evaluation questions, it makes its way into data collection efforts. Naturally the parameters of what is asked will shape the information evaluators get back and, in turn, their findings and conclusions. If we ask what is wrong, the respondents will tell us. If we ask what went right, again they will tell us. The key point is that evaluation should be as unbiased as possible. Evaluators should ask and answer the right questions, so that the data they get are indeed representative of reality.

In specific terms, before evaluators start to plan, and certainly before they collect data, they must determine why they are conducting an evaluation. Is this their initiative, or were they directed to do this work? What is the motivation for the study? What are they looking to accomplish and contribute as a result of this evaluation? Here are some general reasons for conducting an evaluation:

- To see if a solution to a problem is working, that is, delivering valued ends

- To provide feedback as part of a continual monitoring, revision, and improvement process

- To provide feedback for future funding of initiatives

- To confirm compliance with a mandate

- To satisfy legal requirements

- To determine if value was added for all stakeholders

- To hold power over resources

- To justify decisions that have already been made

Although the last two in this list are particularly driven by political agendas, in reality most reasons can be politicized; thus, it takes an insightful evaluator to recognize the feasibility of conducting an honest evaluation. An experienced evaluator will recognize, most of the time, whether evaluation stakeholders are truly interested in using evaluation findings to improve performance or are more concerned with advancing their political interests. With careful attention to detailed planning, either goal can be made to fit a data-driven and results-oriented action approach to evaluation. But if taken too narrowly—in isolation and without proper context—each has its own narrow set of problems, blind spots, and special data generation and collection issues. Perception of the purpose of the evaluation can shape and limit the data that are observed (or not observed), collected (or not collected), and interpreted (or ignored). Thus, evaluators and stakeholders must begin the planning process with a clear articulation of what decisions must be made with the results of their findings, decisions that are linked to the overall purpose for conducting the evaluation.

PERFORMANCE IMPROVEMENT: A CONCEPTUAL FRAMEWORK

The field of performance improvement is one of continuous transition and development. It has evolved through the experience, reflection, and conceptualization of professional practitioners seeking to improve human performance in the workplace. Its immediate roots stem from instructional design and programmed instruction. Most fundamentally, it stems from B. F. Skinner and his colleagues, whose work centered on the behavior of individuals and their environment (Pershing, 2006).

The outgrowth of performance improvement (also called *human performance technology*) from programmed instruction and instructional systems design was illustrated in part by Thomas Gilbert's behavioral engineering model, which presented various categories of factors that bear on human performance: clear performance expectations, feedback, incentives, instruments, knowledge, capabilities, and internal motives, for example. This landmark model was published in Gilbert's 1978 book, *Human Competence: Engineering Worthy Performance,* and was based in large part on the work Gilbert conducted with Geary Rummler and Dale Brethower at the time. Pershing (2006) declares that Joe Harless's 1970 book, *An Ounce of Analysis Is Worth a Pound of Objectives,* also had a significant impact on the field and was well complemented by Gilbert's work. Together these works served as the basis for many researchers who have contributed to and continue to help develop the performance improvement field.

Currently the International Society for Performance Improvement, the leading professional association in the field, defines *performance improvement* as a systematic approach to improving productivity and competence, using a set of methods and procedures—and a strategy for solving problems—for realizing opportunities related to the performance of people. More specifically, it is a process of selection, analysis, design, development, implementation, and evaluation of programs to most cost-effectively influence human behavior and accomplishment. This series of steps, commonly known as the ADDIE model, is the basic model from which many proposed performance improvement evaluation models stem. Pershing (2006) summarized performance improvement as a systematic combination of three fundamental processes: performance analysis (or needs assessment), cause analysis (the process that identifies the root causes of gaps in performance), and intervention selection (selecting appropriate solutions based on the root causes of the performance gaps). These three processes can be applied to individuals, small groups, and large organizations. The proposition that evaluation of such interventions should also be at the core of these fundamental processes is presented in the final chapter of this book.

This is the context in which evaluation is seen and described in this book—not as an isolated process but rather as one of a series of processes and procedures that, when well aligned, can ensure that programs and organizations efficiently and effectively deliver valuable results.

MAKING EVALUATION HAPPEN: ENSURING STAKEHOLDERS' BUY-IN

One of the most important elements of any evaluation is its stakeholders. Before we define the stakeholders, it is worthwhile to define the term *stake*. A *stake* is essentially a claim, an interest, or a share in some endeavor and how that claim or interest might be affected by anything that is used, done, produced, or delivered. The traditional view of a stake used to be limited to the financial realm (for example, stockholders), but in fact a claim or interest can be financial, legal, or moral (Carroll, 2000). Thus, a stakeholder is any individual or group with a stake in an endeavor and can either affect or be affected by the decisions and actions of the organization.

Stakeholders can be broadly categorized as internal (owners, employees, and management) and external (customers, customers' customers, the community, suppliers, competitors, the government, and the media, to name a few), and both categories can then be subdivided into various groups.

Not every individual within each stakeholder group has to participate directly in an evaluation; what is important is that those who participate are seen as representative by their group members. The greater the sense of stakeholder involvement and influence there is, the less likely it is that the evaluator will encounter resistance to the evaluation process and the findings.

While ideally evaluators will select stakeholders who will help define useful evaluation expectations, questions, and criteria, in fact, they realistically will be faced with stakeholders who have their own special interests or represent a powerful lobby. Although it is not particularly unusual for human beings to have their own special interests, evaluators should neutralize as much as possible the risk that the evaluation will become a manipulation tool for the special interests of one—or some—at the expense of others.

A vital challenge in working with stakeholders to help all be successful is to keep them focused on results and consequences rather than on politics of means. Single-issue politics from both within and outside organizations have a tremendous impact on defining objectives and selecting means. It is essential that evaluators learn enough about the specific political climate of a given evaluation to understand how it will affect the evaluation and the implementation of its recommendations. If evaluation recommendations are not implemented or are implemented improperly, performance probably will not improve, and the evaluation may have been conducted in vain.

THE EVALUATOR: A JOB OR A ROLE?

The term *evaluator* describes not only one profession or occupation, but also a given role at a particular time. Individuals conducting evaluation often wear many hats. They may be internal employees, members of the management team, faculty members, or consultants who have acquired interest and expertise in measurement and evaluation through education, training, or experience. In some cases, individuals arrive at this point by default and face an unexpected request to conduct an evaluation. They could be trainers who are charged with demonstrating the value of their training programs and departments. They may even be individuals who because of their status as a subject matter expert in some solution or program are also faced with demonstrating the value of their efforts.

Their common function is, or should be, an interim goal to document the results and impact achieved by a given solution: a program, a project, a tool, or the use of a resource. The final goal should be to use this information to make sound decisions and help the organization take appropriate action to improve performance at all levels.

Evaluators should be competent in some basic areas. Sanders (1979) proposed that at a minimum, evaluators should be able to

- Accurately describe the object (the evaluand) and context of that which is being evaluated

- Conceptualize the purpose and framework of the evaluation

- Derive useful evaluation questions, data requirements, and appropriate data sources

- Select the means for collecting and analyzing data

- Determine the value of the evaluand

- Effectively communicate results and recommendations to the audience

- Manage the evaluation project

- Maintain ethical standards

- Adjust to external factors influencing the evaluation

- Evaluate the evaluation

THE RELATIONSHIP TO OTHER INVESTIGATIVE PROCESSES

The results and consequences we want to accomplish are the primary drivers for deriving the useful questions of an organizational study. Another driver is the types of decisions that have to be made; in large part, they will determine what data have to be gathered and for what purpose. For instance, if decisions have to be made about what programs, interventions, and solutions should be continued, revised, or discontinued, then the data collection approach may take an evaluative perspective. That is, the data collected will be used to compare predetermined objectives with what was actually achieved. If the need is to make decisions about what results the organization should be targeting and, in turn, what types of programs, interventions, and solutions will help it get there, the data collection approach will take on a needs assessment perspective. Notice that in both cases, results—and gaps in results—are the primary drivers.

Table 1.1 illustrates some sample questions from both perspectives that could apply to any organization in any sector. Both approaches to data collection should be systematic and designed to answer specific questions that can be used to improve performance.

Assessors and evaluators may share data collection techniques, but the types of questions they seek to answer differ. In this sense, the roles of assessor and evaluator differ in purpose or function rather than in importance and methods.

Needs assessors help create the future by providing hard and soft data for identification of performance-based, vision-aligned missions

TABLE 1.1. Unique Perspectives of Needs Assessment and Evaluation

Needs Assessment Questions	Evaluation Questions
What value-added results should we be targeting?	How much closer did we get to reaching our vision and mission?
What value-added results are we now getting?	Did we add to or subtract value from our external clients and our shared society?
Who or what is the primary client of the results and their consequences?	Which objectives in our mission did we achieve?
How do we get from current results and consequences to desired ones?	How are we doing in comparison to last quarter? Last year?
What interim results must be accomplished and when?	Which internal results targets were reached? Not reached?
What are our options?	Which implemented programs, projects, or solutions were effective?

and building-block objectives, as well as the gaps between current and desired results. In addition, they help identify the best solutions for closing these gaps and thereby ultimately reaching the organizational vision. It should be noted that asking people what they need is not a needs assessment; this simply creates a "wants list" or "wish list" without rigorous applicability (Kaufman, 2000). *Evaluators* help to determine whether they are heading toward reaching the future they set out to create during the needs assessment process. One of the primary ways they do this is by determining the effectiveness and efficiency of the implemented programs and solutions, as well as the causal factors associated with any gaps between expected and accomplished results. Measurably improving organizational and individual performance depends heavily on these two roles and processes.

Needs Assessment Questions	Evaluation Questions
What are the most effective and efficient ways for reaching our desired or required results?	How efficient are these implemented programs, projects, or solutions?
What will it cost us to reach those results?	In which of these should we continue to invest?
What will it cost us to ignore those results?	What results do we have to justify our continued programs?
How far do we have to go to reach those results?	What should we discontinue?
Which results take priority over others?	Which projects, programs, or solutions could be successful with some modifications? Is it worth it?
Where do we have the most—and least—leverage?	Did we add or subtract value from our internal clients and employees?

Source: Guerra (2003b).

Although both assessors and evaluators collect data with regard to the results of a process or activity, evaluators collect data to determine whether results match the results expected from solutions that have already been implemented—for example, new programs, new technologies, new processes, or any other means selected to help achieve objectives. Assessors, in contrast, seek to anticipate the expected return on investment of potential interventions before they are implemented by collecting data about both current results (what is) and potential results (what should be). With these data in hand, decision makers are able to choose among competing alternatives.

So how does scientific research come into the picture? Before answering this question, let us first explore the meaning of *science*. Science is based on a series of assumptions about the world—assumptions that can be true today but false tomorrow. Scientists are always testing these assumptions, ready to change them when the findings support such a change. To this end, scientists collect data about reality and consult with other sources to ensure the reliability of the data. Results are considered basic data, later subject to repeatable observations in order to confirm findings and scientific reports. Thus, we want to make decisions and take action based on what is currently known through scientific inquiry.

Research is essentially another systematic process of inquiry, with the purpose of finding, interpreting, and updating facts, events, behavior, and theories. In this sense, research skills are a basic requirement in today's world and can be applied in just about any context, whether needs assessment, evaluation, or scientific inquiry. In fact, the heart of the data collection plan is very much the same for all of these. Following are the common elements among these three inquiry processes. These are stated generically but can be made specific to investigative contexts.

1. Important decisions that must be taken by stakeholders are identified. They lead to element 2:

2. Guiding questions, purposes, or hypotheses that the inquiry process must answer or test, which are related to element 3:

3. Key variables or results that are the central focus of the questions or hypotheses.

4. When results are not directly observable, measurable and observable indicators must be identified.

5. These indicators become the data to collect and inform the data source used.

6. The types of data sought inform the data collection tools appropriate for use.

7. The types of data sought determine the types of data analysis tools qualified to summarize and test these data.

8. The process concludes with findings, interpretations, and reporting that are supported by the data collected.

The key in the methodology is the alignment of all the elements: from adding value to all internal and external stakeholders to linking with resources and methods to deliver worthy results.

Certainly in much basic research, generalizability of findings is critical, and thus there is a strong push for controlled environments and the isolation of effects. However, the complexity of real-world evaluation does not easily lend itself to the control of variables. Perhaps evaluation overlaps more closely with applied research, where the goal of the study is the solution of real organizational problems rather than the advancement of the theoretical body of knowledge. However, both evaluation and applied research benefit from the knowledge obtained through basic research. Table 1.2 provides a side-by-side comparison of basic research, applied research, and evaluation. Although the dimensions of each process are described generally, modification of any of them is possible, thereby blurring these distinctions. For example, an evaluation report could be used as part of the literature review of a basic research study, thereby influencing what research questions are studied and how.

WHEN DOES EVALUATION OCCUR?

Having measurable performance objectives in the correct format does not guarantee that the objectives address the right things. Decades ago, people realized that focusing only on objectives could cause an evaluator to miss important data on process and environment. In the 1960s, the realization that evaluation could play a role in the development of educational programs to adjust content and process along the way to the final results gave rise to a famous distinction when Scriven (1967) introduced the terms *formative* and *summative* as well as *goal-free* evaluation. Since then, evaluators have had a term for the type of evaluation activity used to guide developmental activity in programs (*formative*)

TABLE 1.2. Dimensions of Investigative Processes

Dimensions	Basic Research	Applied Research	Evaluation
Goal	Advancement of knowledge and the theoretical understanding of relevant variables	Application of scientific knowledge to the solution of a specific, defined problem	Identification of relevant information to improve specific objects and organizations
Approach	Exploratory and often driven by the researcher's curiosity and interests	Generally descriptive rather than exploratory and conducted by educational or other institutions	Generally guided by the need to make important organizational decisions
Use	Conducted without a currently practical end in mind	Done to solve specific, practical questions	Done to solve specific, practical questions
Basis	As its name suggests, it could provide the basis for further, often more applied research	Often done on the basis of basic research or on previous valid research findings	Should be done on the basis for a needs assessment, while also considering past basic and applied research findings

and another term for evaluation that is used to comment on overall final value (*summative*).

While determining the overall value added—or potentially subtracted—by programs and organizations should be one of its key functions, formative evaluation is also quite important to the overall contributions of programs and other solutions. Moreover, formative evaluation can be designed in such a way that it continuously monitors the alignment of a program with its subsystems and suprasystems to facilitate the achievement of its ultimate value.

Formative evaluation should start at the same time as the identification, design, development, and implementation of the program or solution of interest. Some general questions include the following ones:

- Are we targeting the right objectives?

  Are they based on assessed needs (gaps in results)?

- Are the criteria measurable and soundly based?

- Are we using the right criteria to judge the effectiveness and efficiency of our solution?

- Did we identify the appropriate program or solution?

  Did we base our selection on an analysis of alternatives?

  Did we weigh the pros and cons?

  Did we weigh the costs and consequences?

- Is our design useful and relevant?

  Is it aligned with the front-end analysis findings (causes for gaps in results)?

  Is it appropriate for the ends we want to reach?

- Is the development of the program or solution aligned with its intended design?

  Is our pilot designed to capture the right data required for improvements?

  Does our prototype meet the requirements of our users?

- Is the program or solution being implemented appropriately?

Incidentally, implementation questions may also be appropriate during summative evaluation approach, where we not only look at the results and consequences but also at the factors that may have led to those results and consequences. Obviously, if the intent is to ensure the effectiveness of the solution, we want to know if we are implementing it effectively before and during implementation, not just after the fact:

- Were those affected by the program or solution included in the problem identification, solution selection, and every other stage?

- Were fears and unfounded ideas about the implications of the program or solution confronted, clarified, or disproved, as appropriate?

- Is the program or solution being implemented according to initial plans?

- Is the implementation of the program or solution flexible and responsive to the current situation (for example, challenges not previously foreseen)?

Evaluating each stage and using evaluation data to improve it will allow evaluators and stakeholders to stay on track in order to reach the short- and long-term objectives of the program or solution.

GENERAL EVALUATION ORIENTATIONS

Two common distinctions in evaluation are formative and summative. *Formative evaluation* typically occurs during the developmental stage of a program and can be used to improve the program before it is formally launched. The formative approach can also be used to improve all stages of performance improvement, from assessment to implementation, and the evaluation itself.

Summative evaluation occurs after the implementation of a program or solution and usually requires some appropriate amount of time to have transpired so that the object of evaluation has the opportunity to have the full impact required on performance at various levels of the organization. It is worth noting that summative evaluation can also be used to improve programs and solutions. Stufflebeam and Webster (1980) hold that an objectives-based view of program evaluation is the most common type of evaluation. Once the results that have been accomplished have been determined, the evaluator is well advised to identify causal factors contributing to those results. These data should provide insights as to what the drivers and barriers to the success of the program are, thereby providing the basis for recommendations for improving performance.

Another distinction often made among evaluation orientations is that of *process evaluation* versus *results evaluation.* These terms are used to describe the same processes that formative and summative approaches, respectively, take. Depending on how these are interpreted and implemented, they can also differ somewhat from their counterparts described above. For instance, the Canadian Evaluation Society uses the term *process evaluation* (also referred to as *efficiency evaluation*) to describe the monitoring of the implementation of programs. Obviously, there should be a well-planned logic model with specified results and processes, but modifications are made if a discrepancy between the program design and the actual implementation is found. For example, one might want to determine if the program is being delivered as intended, if it is being delivered to the targeted clients or participants, or if it is being delivered with the intended effort or in the intended quantity.

Process evaluation is critical in helping evaluators address the variations in program delivery. The greater the variation in program delivery, the greater the requirement is for useful data gathered through a process evaluation approach. For instance, there may be differences in staff, clients, environments, or time, to name a few variables.

Stufflebeam and Webster (1980) have argued that objectives-based program evaluation is the most prevalent type used in the name of educational evaluation. Scriven (1972) proposed goal-free evaluation to urge evaluators to also examine the process and context of the program in order to find unintended outcomes.

Results evaluation, also referred to as *effectiveness evaluation,* is used to determine whether the immediate outcomes of a program meet predetermined objectives specified by program planners; *impact evaluation* tends to refer to an evaluation that looks at not only immediate outcomes but also the long-term outcomes of a program and their interdependency. A results evaluation approach is important because it allows us to ensure and document that we are on track by gathering data that show quality accomplishments. It also helps us stay accountable and our programs to stay cost-effective by making program benefits and costs tangible.

Other evaluation approaches are associated with effectiveness evaluation. *Cost-benefit evaluation* is the translation of costs and benefits into monetary terms, which is used to compare the relative net benefits of doing one thing versus another. However, monetary terms are not always applicable, and they are seldom sufficient to appreciate costs and benefits. *Cost-effectiveness evaluation* considers alternative forms of program delivery according to both their costs and their effects with regard to producing some result or set of results. Of course, a stable measure of result should be defined. The least costly program is not necessarily the best one. And in the context of technology solutions, an additional orientation to evaluation is *usability testing,* which focuses on whether people are using the product and how well they are using it to meet required objectives.

CHALLENGES THAT EVALUATORS FACE

A common excuse for avoiding evaluation is insufficient resources to conduct one. In fact, it can often take more resources to maintain programs blindly and indefinitely than it does to conduct a rigorous and focused evaluation. The decision about whether to conduct an evaluation in the first place requires thinking about not only its cost but also the benefits it can render. Both cost and benefit categories contain monetary and nonmonetary items, and they should be honestly and carefully considered before making decisions about conducting or not conducting an evaluation.

One of the most serious challenges faced by evaluators—and probably researchers in general—is getting people to use the findings and recommendations. One study (Henderson, Davies, & Willis, 2006) cited lack of key stakeholder and consumer involvement as a factor that reflects the adoption of evidence for changes in practice. Lack of leadership support was also identified as a factor. When these two factors are combined, there is no support at all for creating and promoting change. The default stance is maintaining the status quo, even if "changing" is the logical proposition.

Limited expertise can also become a barrier. When no one, or few people, in the organization understands the benefits of evaluation or the process itself, finding a champion is difficult. Even if evaluation efforts are undertaken, these are frequently undermined by poor evaluation direction, design, findings, and recommendations. The consequences of conducting a poor evaluation can be worse than not doing one at all.

Once the expectation for improvements has been created, failure to see such improvements can severely harm the morale and trust of organizational members.

Fear and cynicism are supported not only by poor evaluations but also by past efforts to use evaluation as a means of control and intimidation. Findings—or even the mere "threat" of evaluation—have been used to point the finger at the inadequacies of programs, organizations, and human competence. In fact, even when evaluation has provided useful information for improving programs, it is not uncommon for people to disbelieve the evidence.

Another challenge is the low awareness of the utility and benefits of evaluation. People are not often short of ideas about what to do; the challenge begins with helping them articulate how they will know whether the things they have done or implemented have delivered valuable results. Our culture is one of action, so there is often a false sense of accomplishment in just doing something. Verification and documentation of desired results are often neglected and not viewed as an integral part of what we do unless there is a funding source or a mandate to do so.

Perhaps the biggest challenge—and the most important one—is helping those around us understand that every organization, program, department, function, employee, and resource must be ultimately aligned with positive results and consequences for society (Kaufman, 1992, 2000, 2006a). If what is being used, done, produced, and delivered is not adding benefit to society, it is probably doing quite the contrary. Evaluation and needs assessment are uniquely positioned tools for helping stakeholders make sound decisions about what direction to set, how best to get there, how close they have come to getting there, and what improvements must take place in order to ensure the attainment of organizational and societal ends. In fact, even the business community is embracing this reality through movements like corporate social responsibility. Milton Friedman's old paradigm about the "business of business is business" is being disputed even by the heads of top management consulting firms like McKinsey, who argues that "social issues are not so much tangential to the business of business as fundamental to it" (Davis, 2005, p. 1).

There are enormous societal needs to fill in all areas: education, physical and mental health, economic development, crime, and discrimination, to name a few. Kaufman has set out his ideal vision of "the world we want to create for tomorrow's child," which identifies the basic indicators of societal ends, and thus of needs, and has been used as the basis for strategic planning, needs assessment, and evaluation. Kaufman (2000) defines needs as gaps between what should be accomplished and what is currently accomplished:

> There will be no losses of life nor elimination or reduction of levels of survival, self-sufficiency, or quality of life from any source including (but not limited to) the following:
>
> - War, riot, terrorism, or unlawful civil unrest
> - Unintended human-caused changes to the environment including permanent destruction of the environment and/or rendering it non-renewable
> - Murder, rape, or crimes of violence, robbery, or destruction to property
> - Substance abuse
> - Permanent or continuing disabilities
> - Disease
> - Starvation and/or malnutrition
> - Destructive behavior (including child, partner, spouse, self, elder, others)
> - Accidents, including transportation, home, and business/workplace
> - Discrimination based on irrelevant variables including color, race, age, creed, gender, religion, wealth, national origin, or location
>
> Consequences: Poverty will not exist, and every woman and man will earn at least as much as it costs them to live unless they are progressing toward being self-sufficient and self-reliant. No adult will be under the care, custody or control of another person, agency, or substance: all adult citizens will be self-sufficient and self-reliant as minimally indicated by their consumption being equal to or less than their production (p. 95).

Societal ends are not defined by a single organization, and it is not expected that any one organization will accomplish them on its own. These strategic-level objectives represent the shared ambitions of the organizations, individuals, and other partners that stand for our shared communities and society.

ENSURING COMMITMENT

It is vital to get the ownership of evaluation and performance by those who define, deliver, and receive organizational objectives, products, and services. Evaluators and stakeholders must define the required contributions each will make so that they can create a solid partnership for success. Trust, understanding, and agreement on a common destination—results to be achieved—are all key to a successful enterprise. Without the commitment and participation of all of the stakeholders, the success of the evaluation will be less than it could be.

Evaluation data can sometimes be unnerving for stakeholders. Imagine the sense of loss of control when faced with evaluation: on the one hand, they want to know what issues must be resolved and how, and on the other hand, they may resort to any passive-aggressive tactic to keep the evaluator from finding out anything because they are apprehensive that the evaluation will confirm their worst fears.

Consider this situation. A manufacturer implemented a pilot program and rollout to its dealers of a state-of-the-art inventory management and automatic replenishment system. It was designed to minimize inventory (freeing up cash) while maximizing availability to customers (increased sales). The problem was that it quickly and unequivocally shed light on the very poor state of affairs at most dealers, highlighting their expensive inventories and thus discouraging the managers of those inventories from buying in or wanting to participate. Although they had very difficult jobs, they had a vested interest in maintaining the status quo because they did not want others, in particular, their bosses, to find out about their problems. A responsive evaluator would attempt to obtain buy-in from these managers with the common purpose of improving things—in a sense, becoming part of the solution rather than being the problem.

In easing these fears, which are based in part on past experiences with evaluation, the evaluator might want to consider staying away from the term *evaluation* and focusing more on describing the process, which is finding out what is working well, what should be modified and why, and then identifying actions to take that will support continuous improvement. If there is good news, it should be trustworthy. If there is bad news, it is best provided in an environment of trust and the common purpose of continual improvement. Evaluators should never withhold disappointing evidence, but must simultaneously ensure that the successes and shortfalls are based on solid evidence. Trust, common purpose, and shared destiny are keys to getting and maintaining commitment.

Creating the partnership for evaluation and improved performance hinges not only on seriously involving stakeholders but also on listening to them. Although it might be tempting to move ahead with plans and evaluations without the stakeholders' involvement and commitment, doing so risks that later they will see these worthwhile efforts as deceptive or worse. Peter Drucker (1993) had good advice when he suggested that evaluators get "transfer of ownership" of their stakeholders; people see it as their own rather than as belonging to someone else. And the best way to get such a transfer is to involve the partners in setting the objectives and sharing with them the results of any successes and shortfalls. With ways to build trust, evaluation study will be easier, recommendations and findings will have more impact, and the evaluation will stand a better chance of leading to meaningful change.

Evaluation provides the opportunity to have an open and honest relationship with the stakeholders based on performance data, not just biased opinions and perceptions. Involving stakeholders is the best way to ensure that the evaluation meets their expectations and adds demonstrable value.

BENEFITS OF EVALUATION

Conducting an evaluation requires resources, but the benefits outweigh those costs in most situations. Here are some of the many benefits to include in an evaluation proposal or business case:

- Evaluation can provide relevant, reliable, and valid data to help make justifiable decisions about

    how to improve programs and other solutions,

    what programs and solutions to continue or discontinue,

    how to get closer to organizational goals, and

    whether current goals are worth pursuing.

- Evaluation plans and frameworks provide the basis for design, development, and implementation project management plans.

- Evaluation can identify any adjustments that have to be made during and after development and implementation, so that resources are maximized.

■ Evaluation provides the means to document successes so that

the merit of decisions, department, staff, and solutions is recognized by all;

budget requirements and jobs are justified;

the quality of this work is respected by organizational partners;

the value of opinions and data is taken into account throughout the organization; and

evaluators gain credibility and competence, are granted autonomy and power along with accountability, and are seen as true strategic partners in the organization.

■ Evaluation reports can be used to disseminate and market the organization's successes to internal and external partners, such as current and prospective customers.

BASIC DEFINITIONS

Some basic definitions will help convey the concepts in this book:

Performance: The accomplishments of behavior rather than the behavior itself

Performance improvement: A systemic and systematic process for assessing and analyzing performance gaps; planning improvements in performance; designing and developing efficient, effective, and ethically justifiable interventions to close performance gaps; implementing the interventions; and evaluating all levels of results

Ends: Results sought at various organizational levels

Means: The behaviors, activities, processes, procedures, projects, and programs used to achieve results

Levels of results: Society, organization, program, department or team, individual (adapted from Kaufman, 2002)

Needs: Gaps in results (not processes or resources) at any level

Needs assessment: The process of identifying gaps in results and placing them in priority order for resolution

Stakeholders: Anyone who has an interest in the evaluation process and recommendations

Goal: A stated result that identifies a desired end

Objective: A precisely stated goal that identifies who is responsible for achieving it, what accomplishment will be delivered, under what conditions, and with what measurable criteria or metric it will be deemed as reached

Value added: The ultimate result and contribution made by an organization to society—essentially, its societal impact

KEY POINTS

- Evaluation is a systematic way to make decisions based on reliable data.

- Evaluation compares results with expectations, finds drivers and barriers to expected performance, and produces action plans for improving the programs and solutions being evaluated. It can be formative (done during the design of a program or solution) or summative (done in the context of an existing program or solution)

- The approach to evaluation presented throughout this book is based on performance improvement principles.

- A useful evaluation begins by ensuring the commitment and active participation from key stakeholders.

- Evaluators face many challenges, including involving stakeholders, convincing organizations to use the evaluation results, and convincing people that programs require evaluation. If they are not committed to the process, stakeholders can (and will) keep evaluations from being successful.

REFLECTION QUESTIONS

1. How does evaluation affect decision making?

2. How did evaluation evolve into a field?

3. When is a needs assessment more appropriate than an evaluation?

4. How can evaluators ensure commitment from their stakeholders? What happens if they neglect this step?

5. What are the most compelling benefits for conducting an evaluation?

PRINCIPLES OF PERFORMANCE-BASED EVALUATION

This chapter establishes and examines six principles that guide every high-quality evaluation. Evaluators must (1) ask the right questions. To do this, they must (2) understand the distinction between means and ends and (3) examine the goals of the organization as a function of its valid needs. (4) Needs should be validated using a top-down external approach. (5) Evaluation standards should be based on a useful and real strategic vision. (6) The set of questions derived from the first five principles drives the evaluation study.

Evaluation seeks the answer to the general question, What worked and what didn't? It should also ask at the same time, Of what value is this, and what does it contribute? Successful evaluation hinges on how the questions are framed in the context of results-oriented programs that serve an organizational and societal purpose. It also seeks to determine whether the results obtained are of value to the client organization and the society it serves.

The results and consequences of evaluation are not arbitrary. It is important not only to see whether we get the results we hope for but also to ensure that what we hope for is reflected in the means selected and that the ultimate value was added by a program, project, solution, or organizational system to our shared society. All of these are important.

Societal and organizational needs are met through organizational efforts focused on value-added outcomes. The primary focus of performance evaluation is to determine that the goals and objectives of programs are valid, as well as effective and efficient, in producing desired results internal and external to the program and organization.

Planning for legitimate programs starts by identifying desired organizational impacts on the organization's clients and market as well as on society—needs, not wants—and moves into the organization to derive strategic, tactical, and operational objectives. Thus, evaluators should look at the alignment of programs, organizational objectives, and desired external impact. All must be clearly aligned and linked. These ideas are essential threads that must be woven into the fabric of every evaluation.

Words and concepts are rigorously defined here, for evaluation should be used to measurably improve what organizations use, do, produce, and deliver. Undefined ideas and hasty selection of methods will not serve anyone well. Thus, we must be thoughtful and reflective as the pragmatic evaluation landscape is created. The journey will be worth the planning time and attention.

The following set of principles, based on Kaufman, Guerra, and Platt (2006), will be helpful to define and determine what worked and what did not.

PRINCIPLE 1: EVALUATION IS BASED ON ASKING THE RIGHT QUESTIONS

Evaluation is based on asking and answering the right questions, which depend on the view and scope of the investigation. A fundamental assertion in this book is that the scope of evaluations must be wide enough to question the legitimacy of the proposed programs as well as their effectiveness and efficiency. Some of the evaluation criteria that we will use to referee the system will follow from an examination of how well stakeholders (and the organizational system) have addressed the external impact desired for clients and society. We start by examining some typical sets of questions that relate to this point of view.

Societal String

- What is the role of the organization in our society?

- What are the ultimate results sought?

- Are the results of benefit to society?

- What should be accomplished by the organization as a whole?

- How should it be accomplished?

- What are the conditions under which it will be accomplished?

- What resources will be invested in the organization on the way to reaching the desired accomplishments?

Process String

- How will this program be implemented?

- What is the timeline for deliverables?

- What resources will be used?

- What are the limits of the influence of the evaluation?

- What other departments or programs will have an impact on the deliverables?

- How will results be measured?

- How will the program performance be managed?

- How will we secure the right people for the job?

Decision String

- Which program will yield the best return?

- What is the least-cost method that meets the objectives and criteria?

- How can unnecessary expenses be reduced?

- How long before the program can be expected to fully deliver desired results?

- Should we look into different alternatives?

- What new programs should be implemented?

System String

- What is the ultimate purpose of our organizational system?

- What are the boundaries of the system?

- Are all subsystems working for the greater system?

- What is the flow of inputs, throughputs, and results?

- What is the communication flow?

- What is the resource flow?

- Are there points of failure in the system?

- What is the critical path to reach each objective?

- Do all objectives add up to a coherent system goal and overarching objective?

Different points of view produce different sets of questions. Customers, policymakers, shareholders, executives, managers, administrators, employees, and other stakeholder subgroups all have their own viewpoints. As evaluators, we also have a point of view and a set of questions to ask that are related to how we conduct our evaluation study. We must also be aware of the unconscious or conscious questions that all stakeholders ask. What they ask or do not ask will be expressed in the performance that we are going to evaluate. One of our tasks as evaluators is to ensure that all stakeholders are seeking to answer the same set of questions about what worked and what did not. If the program and the organization are to move toward their goals, we must find out what is bringing about value and what might be improved. While we are talking about some fundamental basics about educational evaluation, it is vital that evaluation be used only for fixing and improving, never for blaming.

There are some subtle differences in the four sample question sets above as compared to most conventional approaches. The first set implies a duty to society, a requirement to add value to customers and to our shared society. It is interested in legitimacy. The second set is concerned with getting on with the job without considering alternatives. It is interested only in efficiency. The third set implies consideration of alternatives, with cost as a possible factor in reaching decisions. It is primarily interested in cost-efficiency and cost-effectiveness. The last set asks how things fit together to make a functional system. It is interested in effectiveness and possibly efficiency.

Related sets of questions hang in the background for every situation that we encounter when doing educational evaluation. It is our job to tease out the appropriate strand of the question structure that is represented by the existing situation, along with stakeholder expectations and requirements. If after we have completed our investigation, we can identify one or more gaps between intended results and existing results, these gaps will be the basis for the recommendations we make.

As evaluators, we have a prime set of questions that serve these purposes:

- To identify the legitimacy of the enterprise: How well are needs being met, or did they take the time to determine valid needs?

- To measure how effective and efficient the solutions are (methods, means, activities, programs, projects, activities): Is the organization getting the results it intended these solutions to deliver?

- To determine how the evaluation study should be implemented: What are the objectives, methods, resources, and schedule?

- How do we interpret and report findings and recommendations that are credible and useful?

From these questions, we can choose a more specific set for a specific evaluation target:

- Does the executive or decision-making team show evidence of effectiveness in meeting the needs of clients and society?

- Is the system effective at the organizational level?

- Does the project or system get useful results efficiently?

- What objectives in the mission did the organization achieve?

- What objective in the mission did the organization miss or ignore?

- How do employees perform? Are their achievements aligned with market requirements?

- Did the system and its efforts add value to the organization's communities and shared society?

- What value-added results did employees accomplish as a result of the target program?

- Was what was achieved worthwhile?

- Are methods, techniques, and tools effective? Efficient? Appropriate?

- What should the organization keep, change, or stop?

- What value did the organization add for internal and external stakeholders?

- What results does the organization have to justify its continued programs, projects, and activities?

- What are the recommendations for this organizational system? What should the group do next?

The locus of decision making and the driving force in organizations is found at the organizational level. It is important that evaluators understand the role and functional behavior of organizations. The alignment within the organization and the alignment of the organization with its external market and societal demands are essential for educational success and thus are prime areas of focus for evaluators.

PRINCIPLE 2: EVALUATION OF PROCESS IS A FUNCTION OF OBTAINED RESULTS

Two concepts that often get blurred in organizations (and in life) are *what* and *how* or, stated another way, *ends* and *means. Ends* are results, accomplishments, and consequences, and *means* are the ways, methods, and resources that can be used to accomplish ends.

Evaluation compares results (and consequences) with intentions. Useful evaluations focus on ends and not just on means. Evaluation results provide data and information for making useful decisions relative to the merit and worth of what the organizational system has used, done, produced, and delivered, which is called *valuation.*

The abundant guides to program evaluation—often with self-contained criteria such as number of participants, program completers, costs, and the like—do have a place, but they are not in and of themselves sufficient. It also must be shown that these criteria lead to desired program and organizational results. Linking what we use, do, produce, and deliver to external clients is an essential holistic framework that is missing from most conventional planning and evaluation.

The most sensible way to select any means is on the basis of the ends to be accomplished. As basic as that sounds, most educators mix means into their objectives and thus blur this distinction. Objectives (performance, learning, or any other type) should never have the means or resources stated as part of the objective. When this mistake is made, the group is selecting the solutions before having clearly identified the problem. This can be dangerous, to say the least. Executives, administrators, managers, supervisors, and every other organizational member must learn to differentiate between ends and means and to link them only after the ends are established.

PRINCIPLE 3: GOALS AND OBJECTIVES OF ORGANIZATIONS SHOULD BE BASED ON VALID NEEDS

Valid and useful objectives come from a proper needs assessment, which should never be confused with a wants or wish list. Needs are gaps in results (between what should be and what is), not gaps in resources or methods. They are collected at three levels of results and consequences: societal, organizational, and departmental or individual. And they are prioritized by determining the financial and other costs of meeting them—closing the gaps in results—compared with the comparable costs for ignoring them.

By viewing a need as a gap in results and collecting real and objective data, we can demonstrate the costs to meet the need (usually when this half is reported alone, the program or system gets cut) as compared with the costs to ignore the needs (thus shifting the responsibility to the decision makers if they decide to make the cut).

Real needs can be met by linking to useful means and resources, such as programs and solutions that drive the organization toward desired results. When a group says, "We need . . .", they often cut off all consideration of other possible ways to obtain the desired results. This assumes that the methods, solutions, or programs the group rushes into will meet the need, that is, will close the gaps in results. If a group first focuses on identifying required results and then establishes the gap between those results and its current results, it will identify a legitimate need. Finally, the group should consider all alternatives for best meeting such needs.

PRINCIPLE 4: DERIVE VALID NEEDS USING A TOP-DOWN APPROACH

We live in a complex society that is multicultural, diverse in many ways, and full of competing interests. How do we sort out these issues? What is their impact? The answers lie in identifying the common good in terms of results and carefully dealing with competing issues, using a disciplined process to arrive at justifiable goals and objectives that will make a positive contribution to customers and the shared society.

An organizational *vision* is the ultimate result an organization seeks to obtain; it is tied to the strategic level of an organization. The vision concerns the long-term, external impact on clients and society and is the starting point for planning. The organizational *mission* is a more immediate and operational result that the organization commits to deliver, perhaps in the next year or two. This is tied to the tactical level of the organization and is the basis for the operational planning and processes that go on at the level of the functions or departments. No one can develop good operational plans without a strategic plan that clearly defines strategic objectives. By the same token, a department, program, or team cannot create its own strategic plan; however, it can and should develop operational plans that are clearly linked to the strategic objectives of the organization.

If we are going to conduct a serious evaluation—compare results with intentions—then it is vital to make sure that we are evaluating and measuring the right things. To do this, we have to think and act in order to deliver societal value added. There is no sense in trying to achieve something that is not useful in the first place or, worse, is wrong.

PRINCIPLE 5: EVERY ORGANIZATION SHOULD AIM FOR THE BEST THAT SOCIETY CAN ATTAIN

Real and useful evaluation hinges on linking what we use, do, produce, and deliver to adding value to society. Starting with a useful vision tied to long-term positive external impact ensures that we all can align our unique contributions. Why should a group care about strategy, alignment, measurability, and objectives? Because the survival of their organization depends on it. If this sounds hard to believe, review the Fortune 500 list of companies; see how many thought they were at the top of the world one year or a few years and then dropped off the list, never to reach it again. The drop-off rate is about 80 percent. The formula for getting to the top is not the same as the one for staying at the top. Customers eventually figure out which organizations have their benefit in mind and which care only about the bottom line. Think for a moment about the types of organizations that earn your loyalty and business. Most consumers have the same criterion: organizations that provide quality products and services that truly meet their needs, from the most basic to the most specialized.

Chapter Seven provides examples of useful visions and the types of missions they can help create and deliver.

PRINCIPLE 6: THE SET OF EVALUATION QUESTIONS DRIVES THE EVALUATION STUDY

Just as the organizational system should strive to be in alignment with the needs of the organization's customers, the evaluation efforts should be aligned with the questions that stakeholders must answer. The organization will have objectives at the strategic, tactical, and operational levels. The evaluation team, which will include representatives of the decision makers and other stakeholders, should develop evaluation questions related to each objective and activity relevant to the program or solution under evaluation.

The evaluation team must formulate a set of study objectives based on evaluation questions. This set of questions determines which activities will be undertaken and which methods will be used to observe, gather, and record data.

The team then monitors the process, keeping an eye on the goals and activities. The criteria for evaluation must be based on the desired organizational results and take into account all that is known about effective programs and solutions relevant to the systems or projects being evaluated.

The set of evaluation questions developed as a result of this wide view will be comprehensive and ensure that the findings and recommendations will be based on a complete data set.

KEY POINTS

▪ The purposes of a performance-based evaluation include determining if the goals and objectives of programs are valid and if they are effective and efficient in producing desired results internal and external to the program and organization.

▪ A useful evaluation hinges on the usefulness of the evaluation questions asked; these questions must be aligned to the results that the organization values.

▪ Evaluation should be used for fixing and improving, never for blaming.

▪ Evaluating the usefulness of the organization's systems and programs to its external clients is essential, yet it is missing from most conventional evaluations.

▪ Evaluation questions should have a direct relationship to preestablished program and solution objectives produced by a sound needs assessment. This ensures that they will be aligned to the questions that stakeholders must answer.

REFLECTION QUESTIONS

1. What makes a program or solution legitimate from a performance perspective?

2. How can organizations distinguish means from ends?

3. Why should an evaluator be concerned with the societal impact of a program or solution?

4. What happens if evaluations are driven by something other than the organization's real needs? What happens if the evaluation does not answer the stakeholders' questions?

2

MODELS OF EVALUATION

OVERVIEW OF EXISTING EVALUATION MODELS

This chapter briefly reviews six classic evaluation models that are not considered in detail in this book. It then establishes the five models discussed in the following chapters in Part Two. Finally, it offers guidance on how to select an appropriate evaluation model for a given evaluation task, including a list of conceptual questions and a list of reflective questions that can be asked about any evaluation.

The professional literature on evaluation and its many contributors and concepts is extensive, and excellent sources of evaluation models already exist (Fitzpatrick, Sanders, & Worthen, 2004; Stufflebeam & Shinkfield, 2007). The selection presented in this chapter is not meant to replicate or refute such works. Instead, it provides a review of some of the seminal evaluation models and approaches that fit within the field of performance improvement.

OVERVIEW OF CLASSIC EVALUATION MODELS

Many worthwhile models that will not be covered here can certainly be applied (and in fact already may have been) in any number of contexts, including performance improvement. Before examining the evaluation models covered in the upcoming chapters, this chapter mentions some worthy evaluation approaches without studying them in detail.

Objective-Based Evaluation: Tyler (1949)

Over the course of Ralph Tyler's more than sixty-year career, he influenced education at all levels, including curriculum, testing, evaluation, and educational policy. Directly and indirectly, he influenced many noteworthy developments such as objective-referenced testing, objective-based program evaluation, mastery learning, achievement test construction, item banking, the taxonomic classification of educational outcomes, and cooperative test development (Madaus & Stuffleman, 1989). Objective-based evaluation describes whether students have met their goals, with the results informing how to handle a new instructional strategy (revise, adopt, or reject). One noted weakness of this approach is that the evaluator may overlook unexpected outcomes or benefits of instruction beyond the original goals.

Consumer-Oriented Evaluation: Scriven (1967)

This approach is focused on meeting consumer needs and societal ideals more than achieving the developer's objectives for a given program. Scriven made a major contribution to this approach with his distinction between formative and summative evaluation. He proposed that summative evaluation enables administrators to decide whether the entire finished curriculum, refined by the use of formative evaluation, represents a sufficiently significant advance on the available alternatives to justify the expense of adoption by a school system (Fitzpatrick et al., 2004). Scriven proposed a set of seminal criteria for evaluating any education product, titling it a Key Evaluation Checklist (Scriven, 1991, 2002). He continues to revise this checklist and uses it as part of a data-reduction process, where large amounts of data are obtained and assessed and then synthesized in an overall judgment of value (Stufflebeam & Shinkfield, 2007). Scriven's checklist also addresses meta-evaluation.

Discrepancy Model of Evaluation: Provus (1971)

For Provus, preestablished objectives were the basis for evaluation; however, he also emphasized the importance of providing data about the consistency of (or discrepancy between) what was planned and what was actually executed. The model has four basic phases: establishing objectives, collecting evidence of compliance with the standards, identifying any discrepancies between preestablished objectives and what was accomplished, and identifying and starting corrective actions. This model lends itself to a self-evaluation framework and a systematic approach to improvement. This model is the theoretical foundation for the Impact Evaluation Process (Guerra-López, 2007a).

Goal-Free Evaluation: Scriven (1974)

This approach compensates for inherent weaknesses in a goals-oriented approach by providing an unbiased perspective of ongoing events. Here, the evaluator purposely remains uninformed of the program's predetermined goals and looks for all effects of a program regardless of its developer's intended objectives. If a program is meeting its intended purpose, the evaluation should confirm that. In addition, the evaluator will be more likely to find unanticipated effects that goal-based evaluators could miss because of the specificity of their search. Stufflebeam and Shinkfield (2007) indicate that goal-free evaluation provides important supplementary information, expands the sources of evaluative information, is effective for finding unexpected information, is cost-efficient, and is welcomed by clients.

Responsive/Client-Centered Evaluation: Stake (1975)

Based on Ralph Tyler's conception that evaluators should compare observed outcomes to intended outcomes, Stake's approach expanded evaluation focus to include background, process, standards, judgments, and outcomes. Although his philosophy of evaluation first appeared in the literature in 1967, his formal proposal of this approach, named *responsive evaluation,* was not published until 1975. In this work, he broke away from Tyler's perspective of examining whether intentions had been realized, instead assuming that intentions would change and calling for continuing communication between evaluator and stakeholders for the purposes of discovering, investigating, and addressing important issues (Stufflebeam & Shinkfield, 2007).

Utilization-Focused Evaluation: Patton (1997)

Closely linked to decision-oriented theory, this approach to evaluation is concerned with designing evaluations that inform decision making. Although many authors have contributed to this approach, Stufflebeam and Shinkfield (2007) credit Michael Patton as the most prominent figure (1980, 1984, 1997, 2003). In his 1997 book, *Utilization-Focused Evaluation,* Patton fully articulated his approach to evaluation. Here he defined a utilization-focused program evaluation as one done "for and with specified intended primary users for specific, intended uses" (p. 23).

SELECTED EVALUATION MODELS

Our in-depth discussion begins with Donald Kirkpatrick's four levels of evaluation (1959), one of the most widely known models in the training and performance improvement fields. Its four component levels are reaction, learning, behavior, and results. One of its major appeals to trainers and clients has been its simplicity, although this simplicity has also attracted criticism.

The next model discussed is Jack Phillips's Return-on-Investment (ROI) methodology (1997a), based on Kirkpatrick's framework. It starts with Kirkpatrick's four levels. Then Phillips presents an elaborate methodology for calculating the ROI of training solutions. One of the key steps in this approach is to isolate the effects of training in order to attribute direct costs and benefits to the training program under evaluation. This model has been received with mixed reviews about its strengths and inherent limitations.

The discussion then turns to Robert Brinkerhoff's Case Success method (1981), which addresses some of the limitations encountered by Kirkpatrick's and Phillips's models. Its approach is based on finding extreme cases of success and failure in using new skills and tools obtained from training and other performance programs to achieve valuable organizational accomplishments.

Next, Ingrid Guerra-López's Impact Evaluation process (2007a), the most recently published of the models covered here, is presented. It is based on a reiterative process flow that allows evaluators and stakeholders to focus on three levels of alignment: between the evaluand and the ultimate impact on external outcomes for clients and society, among all performance improvement steps, and among all the impact evaluation process steps.

The next model discussed is Daniel Stufflebeam's CIPP model (1967), which has four distinct evaluation foci: content, inputs, process, and products. It reaches beyond the traditional evaluation model to incorporate elements of assessment, planning, implementation, and other phases relevant to the success of an evaluand, overlapping in this sense with the impact evaluation process.

Finally, Part Two closes with a chapter on meta-evaluation, the evaluation of evaluations. It helps evaluators and evaluation stakeholders explore inherent biases of evaluation projects.

SELECTING A MODEL

There is no one best model. The utility of evaluation models, as with any other type of model or tool, depends entirely on the situation at hand. What works in one organization does not necessarily work in another, and what worked yesterday will not necessarily work in the same way today. Stufflebeam and Webster (1980) analyzed thirteen alternative evaluation approaches in terms of their adherence to the definition of an educational evaluation: one that is designed and conducted to assist some audience to judge and improve the worth of an educational endeavor. Their analysis resulted in three categories of evaluation studies: politically oriented, or pseudo-evaluations; question oriented, or quasi-evaluations; and values oriented, or true evaluations. They provided strengths and weaknesses for each in order to offer evaluators a variety of frameworks and perspectives.

The most important part of choosing a responsive model is that we clearly identify the requirements of the situation and use that as the criterion for selecting an evaluation model. Popham (1975) has said that comparing evaluation approaches in order to select the best model is usually a waste of time. He argues that instead of focusing on similarities and differences, evaluators should become sufficiently proficient with the evaluation models to decide which is the most appropriate for the situation. Moreover, he has argued for an eclectic approach: selectively drawing from various models the concepts that are most helpful. Following Popham's advice, we might find it useful to borrow the most relevant bits and pieces of various models to form an evaluation plan. This approach can be taken for every evaluation. Cronbach (1982) also supports this view and states that evaluation design must start from a blank slate at each new undertaking, addressing the countless decisions to be made in each situation.

CONCEPTUALIZING A USEFUL EVALUATION THAT FITS THE SITUATION

Nevo (1981) revised a list of questions initially proposed by Stufflebeam (1974) in an effort to conceptualize evaluation and its key dimensions. The revised list remains applicable today:

- How is evaluation defined?

- What are the functions of evaluation?

- What are the objects of evaluation?

- What kinds of information should be collected regarding each object?

- What criteria should be used to judge the merit or worth of an evaluated object?

- Who should be served by the evaluation?

- What is the process of doing an evaluation?

- What methods of inquiry should be used in evaluation?

- Who should do evaluation?

- By what standards should evaluation be judged?

Some reflective questions will help formulate a model for a specific evaluation. Note that this list is not exhaustive but rather is a starting point:

- What are the characteristics of the evaluation task?

- What is the object of evaluation (the evaluand)?

- At what stage of conception (planning, design, development, implementation, maintenance, evaluation) is the evaluand?

- What are the limitations and constraints of the evaluation effort?

- Which evaluation models best lend themselves to address these characteristics?

- What are the pros and cons of each model with regard to the evaluation task?

- Is blending these approaches to create a unique model for this situation more feasible and responsive to the evaluation task than using one of them as it stands?

You may find it useful to keep these questions in mind as you read through the following chapters.

KEY POINTS

- Several historically and currently important evaluation models were not selected for detailed discussion in this book.

- The evaluation models presented in the chapters in Part Two have been selected based on their place in the performance improvement field.

- There is no perfect model of evaluation; there is only the most useful one for a given situation. Frequently this will be a combination of models and approaches. One approach to identifying an existing model or combination of models to suit a specific evaluation is to ask a set of conceptual and reflective questions and make a decision guided by the answers to those questions.

REFLECTION QUESTIONS

1. What are some important models of evaluation that are not covered in detail in this book?

2. What is the main criterion for including evaluation models for detailed coverage in this book?

3. You have just been asked to take the leadership in an evaluation effort in your organization, but you do not know much about evaluation. How will you go about figuring out which evaluation model or conceptual framework (or combination of models and frameworks) will fit your purpose?

KIRKPATRICK'S FOUR LEVELS OF EVALUATION

This review defines and describes the four levels of Kirkpatrick's model and identifies some of its strengths and weaknesses. It then describes some criticisms and variations designed to meet those criticisms. Finally, it reviews and analyzes a sample application of the model.

Developed in 1959 by Donald Kirkpatrick as part of his dissertation research, Kirkpatrick's four levels of evaluation (1959) is a well-accepted evaluation framework in the industrial and organizational psychology arena (Cascio, 1987). It has been used primarily to evaluate traditional instructor-led training programs and consists of evaluating four distinct general areas in sequential order (Figure 4.1):

1. *Reactions:* Focuses on participants' opinions about the training, processes, and results, asking primarily how much participants liked the training program

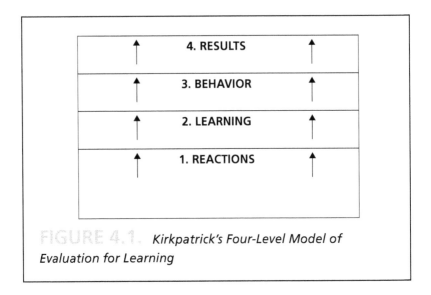

FIGURE 4.1. *Kirkpatrick's Four-Level Model of Evaluation for Learning*

2. *Learning:* Focuses on the degree to which learning actually took place, asking what knowledge the participants gained from the training program

3. *Behavior:* Focuses on the linkage between learning and workplace performance, asking what changes in the participants' work performance can be attributed to the training program

4. *Results:* Focuses on bottom-line results, asking what the impact of the training program was on the performance of the organization

According to Kirkpatrick's model, evaluation should always start at level 1 and then, as time and budget allow, move sequentially through levels 2, 3, and 4. Information gathered during each level informs the next levels. Consequently each succeeding level represents a more precise measure of success, requiring a more rigorous focus. However, there are no data or other forms of evidence that clearly suggest that the four levels are actually positively (or otherwise) correlated or that one causes the other (Alliger & Janak, 1989). For example, it is conceivable that people can dislike a training and yet learn the material. In addition, some psychologists have argued that people are not good at reporting their own experiences of learning (Hofstadter & Dennett, 1981).

Research shows that most training evaluations occur at the reaction level (Bassi, Benson, & Cheney, 1996; Saari, Johnson, McLaughlin, & Zimmerle, 1988). This is perhaps attributable to the fact that reaction information can be readily obtained through participant questionnaires, and most trainers are quite comfortable with developing and implementing questionnaires. Knowledge tests too are somewhat familiar tools of trainers and can be readily applied, particularly when participants are still in the training environment. Once participants get back to the job, it becomes more difficult to gauge how the training program has affected their performance, because participants are in an environment outside the influence of the trainer and their performance is subject to many other variables, such as environment, feedback, tools, and incentives, as the performance improvement literature tells us (Gilbert, 1978; Rummler & Bache, 1995; Rummler, 2004). Almost always missing is level 4, which measures the return on investment of the training programs. Here we again face the challenge of multiple factors that may be affecting results. Clearly the task of isolating the effects of training can be daunting.

KIRKPATRICK'S LEVELS

Level 1 Evaluation: Reactions

Evaluation at this level measures how participants react to a training program, with the driving question being "Did they like the program?" This level is often referred to as a "smile sheet" because the data are often gathered through a questionnaire that asks general questions about the various program elements, often requesting responses through Likert scales that can range from 1 (extremely dissatisfied) to 5 (extremely satisfied).

While some doubt the utility of such instruments, Kirkpatrick (2006) argues that every program should be evaluated at least at this level because it is a measure of customer satisfaction. If participants leave unsatisfied, he argues, they might tell others, including their bosses, and this could bear on decisions about the training program in the future.

Let us not forget that the point of conducting any type of evaluation at any level is to enable evaluators to make informed decisions about improving performance—that of the program as well as that of the participants. Thus, the utility of a smile sheet ultimately depends on whether the items in that questionnaire will render useful and specific information about how to improve the program. Asking participants whether they like the instructor, the course, or the classroom facility will reveal little about how to improve these if required. However, questions based on measurable, observable, and specific events or behaviors will. The following sample questions can help maximize the utility of a smile sheet (Guerra, 2005):

- Is the information that is presented relevant?
- Is the information that is presented necessary?
- Is the information that is presented sufficient?
- Are the instructional materials complete?
- Is more background information required?
- Is there anything that can be removed without affecting desired performance?
- Are additional tools, information, or practices needed to ensure desired performance?
- Is the order of instruction appropriate for learning?
- Were the advanced organizers (for example, section headings, section overviews, or concept maps) helpful?
- Is the content targeted appropriately to match the audience?
- Which sections need additional time? Which could be shorter?
- Which exercises add to the learning? Which are unnecessary?
- Are the materials clear and easy to teach from?
- Are the exercises engaging for the learners? Do they add to the learning?
- Is there enough learner participation?

An instrument like this is particularly useful in the context of a formative evaluation, where the participant responses will be used to improve the development of the training program.

Kirkpatrick also argues that when reactions are positive, so are the chances for learning. And if learning is improved, then the chances for a change in behavior are also improved, and so on, until results are positive.

Level 2 Evaluation: Learning

Assessing at this level moves the evaluation beyond learner satisfaction and focuses on the extent to which students have increased their skills, knowledge, or desired attitudes. To determine the extent of learning that has occurred as a result of a training program, level 2 evaluations often test participants before the training program (pretest) and after training has been completed (posttest). The difference between these two test results is said to be attributable to the training program. However, this attribution cannot be made with absolute certainty because often the pretest itself may have an impact on performance on the posttest, even if the performer did not fully (or even in part) participate in the training program. For example, items on the pretest may prompt the performers to look for the answers on their own rather than attend a time-consuming training program. Figure 4.2 shows how these two data points can be illustrated to easily communicate the findings to stakeholders.

The validity of such tests depends to a great extent on how closely matched the test items are to the actual objectives of the training program, and to what extent the content and instructional strategies adequately meet those objectives. Measurement at this level is said to be more rigorous and, as before, requires the evaluator to measure the right things in the right way. Poorly designed tests can render invalid data,

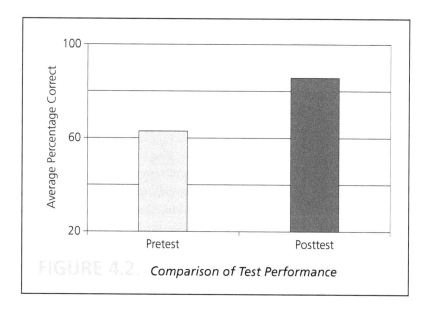

FIGURE 4.2 *Comparison of Test Performance*

leading to false interpretations and conclusions, which in turn can lead to poor decisions about programs and how to proceed with performance improvement.

Level 3 Evaluation: Behavior

This level measures the change that has occurred in the behavior of learners due to the training program. Evaluating at this level attempts to determine whether the skills, knowledge, or attitudes obtained from the training program are being applied on the job. For many trainers, this level represents the ultimate test of a program's effectiveness. However, measuring at this level is often difficult because changes in behavior can occur at any point from immediately after the training has been completed, to a few weeks, to months, and potentially beyond. One obvious consideration here is when and how often to conduct evaluation at this level, because measuring at the wrong time can lead to inaccurate findings, interpretations, and conclusions. Moreover, Foxon's transfer of training model (1993) outlines transfer as a series of stages: (1) intention to transfer, (2) initiation of transfer, (3) partial transfer, (4) conscious maintenance, and (5) unconscious maintenance.

Brinkerhoff (1988) notes that many high-order skills, such as emergency flight procedures, cannot be safely or economically performed on a regular basis. In such cases, evaluators should recognize that transfer is not easily observed or measured in a workplace context and that the nonuse of target skills does not imply a training failure.

As with any other level and any other evaluation approach, evaluators must take special care to measure valid indicators, that is, indicators that truly represent and measure the behaviors of interest. Depending on the specific behavior, appropriate observation methods should be selected. While Kirkpatrick recommends using surveys where respondents (for example, performers, supervisors, subordinates, or other appropriate sources) are asked if their behavior or the behavior of others has changed, these methods are quite subjective. What people say they do does not automatically translate into what they actually do. The evaluator is well advised to use multiple sources of data to confirm any results.

As training expenditures have grown over the years, so has research on the transfer of training to the job. Foxon (1993) contends that transfer of training depends greatly on motivation, among other variables (for example, leadership support), and she makes a distinction between the motivation to learn and the motivation to transfer what has been learned. She cites Noe's proposal (1986) that motivation to transfer is the intention of the learners to use the new skills and knowledge on the job and is influenced by learners' self-efficacy (that is, their confidence in their ability to use the new skills), the perceived relevance of these skills and knowledge to their work, their ability to recognize work situations where the learned material would be appropriate, and their belief that using the new skills will improve their job performance.

Here, Kirkpatrick's notion that if learning occurred, the probability of transfer is high becomes problematic. The level of concern is increased by the lack of evidence correlating the four levels of his evaluation model.

Level 4 Evaluation: Results

This level, often referred to as the bottom line, measures the success of the training program in terms of organizational or departmental performance indicators that the organizational leadership cares about—for example, production quality, costs, reduced complaints, sales, or profits. These are the organizational results that the training program ultimately is to affect, yet this level is almost always left out of training evaluation efforts. Although it is difficult to isolate the effects of training on the bottom line, documenting any evidence of this sort of impact is key to justifying the existence and costs of such programs. Perhaps this is one major reason that training programs and departments are the first to get cut when budgets are tight; there is not sufficient evidence of the value they add to organizational results. Studies of the actual returns from training programs suggest that not more than 10 percent of training expenditures actually result in transfer to the job (Baldwin & Ford, 1988). In a billion-dollar industry, those figures are astonishing.

Kirkpatrick (1994) suggests that one reason trainers do not evaluate at this level is that they do not know how to measure results and compare them to the cost of the training program. Another reason he cites is that many in the organization do not think measurable results can be attained, and in fact, trainers do not feel pressured to create bottom-line value. However, Kirkpatrick (1994) also asserts that the days of living without proof of impact are about over.

One important consideration here, as with level 4, is to allow sufficient time to transpire in order to see an impact on bottom-line results. As with levels 2, 3, and 4, a baseline should be established so as to

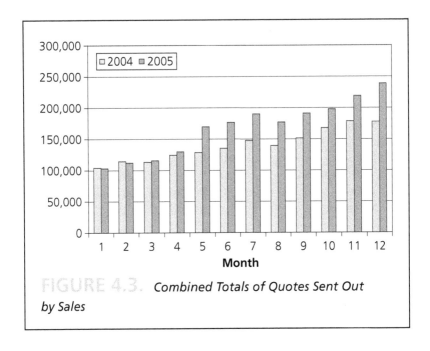

FIGURE 4.3. *Combined Totals of Quotes Sent Out by Sales*

provide context for the posttraining measurement. Figure 4.3 provides an illustration of how one might represent the pre- and postprogram results.

COMMENTS ON THE MODEL

Holton (1996) criticizes the four-level model as simply a taxonomy with no causal relationships among the various levels. Alliger and Janak (1989) acknowledge the simplicity of Kirkpatrick's four levels but fault his causality attribution, focusing on rejecting three critical assumptions: (1) training directly causes change, (2) each level is causally linked to the next highest level, and (3) correlations between levels are positive. They agree that levels 3 (behavior) and 4 (results) usually suggest a causal relationship, but argue that other variables are just as influential in performance improvement. In particular, they cite the influence of motivation, attitudes, and environmental context (support factors) as alternative causes of behavioral change.

Bates (2004) criticizes its lack of formative and summative components for improving instruction, and Dick and King (1994) propose combining the third and fourth levels with traditional formative evaluation as a solution.

In response to the idea that nontraining solutions are also valid and require evaluation, Kaufman and Keller (1994) propose a variation of Kirkpatrick's four levels. Their model adds a fifth level, societal impact, and redefines the remaining levels to include performance data for the availability, efficiency, and quality of organizational resources. Their expanded model enables consideration of the value and worth of training resources, as well as the broader social consequences. Moreover, they emphasize strategic evaluation planning to anticipate unintended consequences to the organization and to society alike. Kaufman and Keller's levels are redefined as follows:

1. Enabling/reaction

2. Acquisition

3. Application

4. Organizational outputs

5. Societal outcomes

Another well-known variation of Kirkpatrick's four levels of evaluation is Phillips's ROI, the topic of Chapter Five.

STRENGTHS AND LIMITATIONS

Below are some strengths and limitations commonly associated with Kirkpatrick's model:

Strengths

- Simple to conceptualize

- Provides a framework that easily helps people think about measuring training

- Provides four basic categories of training success indicators: reaction, learning, relevant on-the-job behaviors, and organizational results

- Popularity could help promote evaluation within the organization

- Created specifically for training interventions and thus may be perceived as a reliable approach to evaluation by training departments

Limitations

- Simplicity can lead to misunderstandings and overgeneralizations.

- The model was created specifically for training interventions and thus does not fully address all important indicator categories of performance improvement interventions in general.

- Levels are not actually hierarchies, and there is no evidence to suggest they are correlated; they may merely illustrate a different focus or perhaps even steps in a larger evaluation scheme.

- Level 1 and 2 measurement instruments (for example, question-naires and tests) are often poorly designed and lead to inaccurate interpretations and conclusions.

- The model usually is not applied in its entirety. Evaluations stop at level 1 or 2, leaving decision makers to make decisions based on incomplete data sets.

- Value added beyond the organization itself is ignored.

APPLICATION EXAMPLE: WAGNER (1995)

Despite limited and conflicting evidence about their effectiveness, out-door management training (OMT) programs such as ropes courses are used frequently. In addition, proponents of these programs and their skeptics are equally impassioned. Proponents of OMT argue that the sessions prepare managers and employees to deal with change and that they are appropriate for all employees within an organization; skeptics argue that OMT is at the very least a waste of time and at the worst can be evidence of managerial malpractice.

One such program was designed and developed by Chris Rowland of Rowland/Diamond in New Hampshire. The OMT was a one-day ropes course for the U.S. Navy installation in Indiana. In the spring of 1989, Rowland contacted R. Wagner and Tim Baldwin (then at Indiana University) to evaluate the effectiveness of the program. The six-year effort began with benchmarking and literature review that sought to answer the question, How are OMTs evaluated? This study yielded surprisingly few results. Those that were found were perceived to be flawed in their methods; for example, some relied on exceedingly small samples (three or four participants) from which to generalize their find-ings. This led the evaluation team to conduct an evaluation of the OMT using a traditional training evaluation framework: Kirkpatrick's. The study is reported in Wagner (1995).

Methodology

Organized around Kirkpatrick's levels, the evaluation sought to answer the following general questions:

Reaction: How do the participants feel about the program? Is it providing customer satisfaction?

Learning: To what extent did participants change their attitudes, improve their knowledge, and increase their skills?

Behavior: To what extent did participants change their on-the-job behavior?

Results: "What final results occurred? This includes such factors as increased sales, improved quantity of production, improved quality, reduced costs, reduction of accidents, reduction in turnover, increased profits and return on investments (p. 4)."

Based on team-building literature, the initial evaluation emphasized evaluation of two types of behaviors: individual (self-esteem, control, and faith and confidence in peers) and group oriented (cohesiveness, clarity, homogeneity, problem solving, and overall group processes). It used a pre-post design, and data were collected using either a five-point or a seven-point Likert questionnaire. The evaluators added a control group to mitigate potentially erroneous conclusions drawn as a result of the pre-post design. Because this evaluation was conducted in a corporate environment, random assignment to control groups was not feasible, so assignments were made using stratification and matched based on potentially important differences such as gender. In addition, post-questionnaires asked participants not only to self-report a behavior or attitude but to justify it by providing an open-ended response explaining why and providing an on-the-job example. Additional methods included open-ended interviews with participants, on-the-job observation, 360-degree evaluations, and participant journals (for multiday OMT programs). The use of journals created two notable problems for the evaluation: It required processes for ensuring that journals were completed regularly throughout the training, and it increased the amount of raw data included in the evaluation, thus increasing the time, resources, and skills required for analysis and interpretation.

Findings

Work group functioning improved significantly, but individual behavior variables showed no significant changes. In addition, intact work groups (versus newly formed teams) benefited significantly, with no important differences between those who volunteered for training versus those who were required to attend. Work groups that were gender balanced (as opposed to female or male dominated) benefited more significantly. When supervisors attended training with subordinates, the only significant finding was that subordinates liked the training more. The outdoor setting for the training had no effect, and changes in group effectiveness between the first and second year were attributed to increased facilitator skill (as a result of facilitator training).

In 1992, the evaluation had begun to take on a meta-analytical approach (including more than thirty organizations and five thousand participants in OMTs) and began to evaluate similar programs in countries throughout the world. Findings from these evaluations suggested not only that team building was occurring but that changes in the overall culture of the organizations were exhibited.

Issues

One limitation inherent in this application is the nature of the findings on team building and organizational culture. To what extent are these "higher-level" issues related to the subject matter of OMT? To what extent are they related to starting at level 1? An additional limitation is that although Wagner uses Kirkpatrick as a framework, his opinion about how it hampered or helped the evaluation is missing.

Additional Application

McLean, S. (2003). They're happy, but did they make a difference? *Canadian Journal of Program Evaluation, 18*(1), 1–23.

KEY POINTS

- Kirkpatrick's four levels of evaluation begin with reaction and move sequentially through learning, behavior, and finally results.

- The most commonly used level of evaluation is Kirkpatrick's first level: reaction.

- Although the sequential and causal relationship among the four levels is essential to the model, existing research does not establish the truth of these relationships.

- The third and fourth levels are difficult to measure reliably.

- Kirkpatrick's model of the four levels of evaluation, well known in the performance improvement field, has received much criticism.

REFLECTION QUESTIONS

1. What has made Kirkpatrick's four levels of evaluation so appealing for so many years?

2. Are Kirkpatrick's critics misinterpreting the intent of the model, or are the criticisms of the four levels well founded?

3. Is Kirkpatrick's model missing anything important? If so, what are the implications of these missing variables?

4. Can Kirkpatrick's four levels of evaluation be adapted to minimize its limitations and maximize its utility? If so, how? If not, why not?

PHILLIPS'S RETURN-ON-INVESTMENT METHODOLOGY

This review of Phillips's return-on-investment (ROI) approach explains the fifth level, which Phillips added to Kirkpatrick's model, and identifies some of the strengths and weaknesses of the ROI approach. The chapter then examines criticisms of the model and variations designed to meet those criticisms, and it reviews and examines a sample application of the model.

Jack Phillips (1997a, 1997b) popularized the return-on-investment (ROI) evaluation process within the training and performance improvement arenas. This approach is commonly known as "level 5," adding a new dimension to Donald Kirkpatrick's four levels of evaluation. This methodology measures the return on investment of programs and solutions, particularly those relating to training and human performance, using

Kirkpatrick's four levels as required preceding levels that help establish a chain of effect.

The main drive of Phillips's methodology is to measure the monetary benefits of training and development programs against their costs. One key attribute of the model is that it addresses and provides guidance for the isolation of the effects of training on the bottom line through a mathematical formula designed to calculate a percentage return on the total costs of the program:

$$\text{ROI (\%)} = \frac{\text{Net Program Benefits}}{\text{Program Costs}} \times 100$$

Measuring ROI has become an increasingly important area for training and performance improvement practitioners who seek to demonstrate the business value of their efforts. Phillips has said that his methodology, driven by economic forces, demonstrates that the value of training and education can help prevent the arbitrary or impulsive cutting of training budgets. This methodology can give training departments credibility. When they can document the monetary impact they have on bottom-line figures, the potential exists to alter traditional management perceptions of training.

Phillips (1997b) warns that for the ROI process to be useful, it must balance feasibility, simplicity, credibility, and soundness. He also identifies some common barriers to ROI implementation: costs and time, lack of skills, faulty needs assessment, fear, lack of discipline and planning, and false assumptions.

Cresswell and Lavigne (2003) caution organizations that adopt an ROI methodology not to extend the level of detail of the analysis beyond what is required to make the decisions at hand. This recommendation is based primarily on the fact that significant resources are often required to carry out a successful ROI analysis.

One recommendation, suggested by Corcoran (1997), is based on a process followed by American Express that requires projects to be categorized into strategic, required, or ROI. Strategic projects are those that help the organization get closer to where it wants to be in the long term. Estimating the ROI on these sorts of projects can be inappropriate because the return may not be seen for a long time, and thus focus may be best kept on the intangible benefits. Required projects are those that allow the organization to stay alive, such as those related to safety, government regulations, and payroll. The benefits of these projects are already obvious, and the emphasis is to carry out the project in the most cost-effective manner. Finally, ROI projects must undergo a thorough evaluation and require a resulting ROI of 30 percent prior to approval.

In sum, not all projects may be appropriate for a traditional ROI evaluation. Initial consideration should begin during project planning rather than after implementation.

PHILLIPS'S ROI PROCESS

The Phillips ROI process begins with data collection after the program has been implemented and ends with calculating the ROI (Phillips, 1997a). As with Kirkpatrick's model, data should be collected at levels 1, 2, 3, and 4 so that, accepting Kirkpatrick's sequential analysis, the chain of impact occurs as participants learn and apply skills and knowledge that affect business results. Those levels were described in Chapter Four; this chapter therefore focuses on how Phillip's fifth level, ROI, is measured.

Collecting Postprogram Data

Data collection is the heart of this process. In some cases, postprogram data are collected and compared to preprogram data or expectations. These data should include both hard (for example, production or cost) and soft data (such as attitudes). These data can be collected with a host of methods: questionnaires, observations, interviews, focus groups, program assignments, action plans, performance contracts, and performance monitoring. Some of these common methods (questionnaires, observations, interviews, and focus groups) are addressed in Chapter Twelve. The following methods are less commonly used:

> *Program assignments,* which are simple short-term projects. Participants complete an assignment on the job using the skills and knowledge they learned during the program

> *Action plans,* which are developed in training programs and implemented on the job after program completion. A follow-up of the plans provides documentation of the training program's level of success

> *Performance contracts,* which are developed when the participants, their supervisors, and the instructor all agree on specific outputs

> *Performance monitoring,* which is useful when various performance records and operational data are examined for improvement

Isolating the Effects of Training

This key component of the ROI process is not part of Kirkpatrick's model. Here, specific tactics are discussed to help determine the amount of output performance that can be directly related to the program. This is a critical step, because many things within and outside the organization have an impact on performance, and attributing any portion of bottom-line results to any program is a challenging task.

Following are specific strategies for isolating the effects of training:

- *A control group.* One group receives the training, and a similar group, the control group, does not. Special care must be taken to ensure that the groups and their circumstances are similar, with the only distinction being whether they receive training. The difference in performance of the two groups is attributed to the training program. This is one of the most effective methods for isolating the effects of training when it is properly planned and implemented.

- *Trend lines.* These are visual aids used to project the values of specific performance indicators if training had not occurred. The projection is compared to actual data after training, and the difference represents the estimate of the impact of training. Extraneous variables have to be accounted for if this method is to be reliable, and the effects of training must be isolated. If there are additional variables that have an impact on those projections, the observed differences cannot be attributed solely to the training program being evaluated.

- *Forecasting models.* If mathematical relationships between input and output variables are known, this is an appropriate approach. Here, the output variable is predicted with the use of a forecasting model. The model runs on the supposition that no training has been conducted. The actual performance of the variable after the training is then compared with the forecast value, which results in an estimate of the training impact. Again, the soundness of the findings depends on the soundness with which the forecasting model has been applied.

- *Participant estimations.* The participants are provided with the overall observed improvement, on a pre- and postprogram basis, and asked to estimate the percentage of the improvement that they believe is related to the training program. Although this approach is relatively easy to implement, it is strictly subjective and can lead to incorrect conclusions.

▧ *Leadership estimations.* This method follows the same approach as participant estimates, but the respondents here are supervisors or senior management rather than the participants.

▧ *Expert estimations.* This follows the same approach and logic as participant and leadership estimations. Using the estimation approaches together may serve as an additional step to corroborate one group's responses; however, they do not cease to be subjective data.

▧ *Accounting for other influencing factors.* When feasible, other variables are identified and their impact estimated or calculated, leaving the unexplained portion of the improvement to be attributable to the training program under evaluation.

▧ *Customer estimations.* In some cases, customers can provide their perceptions of the extent to which training has influenced their decision to use a product or service. This approach has limited applications, but it is of particular use with customer service and sales training.

Converting Data to Monetary Values

After level 4 data are estimated, they are converted to monetary values and compared to program costs. To do this, a value must be placed on each unit of data connected with the program. Here are ways to make these conversions:

▧ *Output data* are converted to profit or costs savings. Here, output increases are converted to monetary value based on their unit of contribution to profit or cost reduction. Most organizations track such figures already.

▧ The *cost of quality* is estimated, and quality improvements are directly converted to cost savings. This value tends to be readily available in organizations.

▧ *Participant wages and benefits,* where appropriate, can be used as a value for time. This is particularly important because many programs focus on improving time required to deliver accomplishments.

▧ *Historical costs* are used if they are available. In this case, organizational cost data are used to establish the specific value of an improvement.

- *Experts,* if available, can be used to estimate the value of an improvement. Here the credibility of the estimate depends on the expertise and reputation of the expert. The expert can be from outside or from within the organization.

- *Databases* may be available to estimate the value or costs of data items. Databases from all sectors can provide important information for these values. The challenge is finding databases that are relevant for the purpose at hand.

- *Participants* can estimate the perceived value of data items, provided they are qualified or capable of doing so. As with all other perceptual data, this is a subjective measurement.

- *Leaders* can provide their estimations.

- *Human resource development staff* can be a good source of estimates, provided they remain relatively unbiased.

Tabulating the Costs of the Program

On the other side of the cost-benefit analysis equation are the program costs. Estimating these costs depends on ongoing monitoring. Here are some of the elements to consider:

- Costs to design and develop the program, perhaps prorated over the expected life of the program

- Costs of all program materials, including those provided to the instructor and participants

- Costs of the instructor, including preparation, facilitation, and other time on task

- Costs of the facility where training was offered

- Travel, lodging, and meal costs for participants, if applicable

- Salaries and employee benefits of the participants who attended the training

- Administrative and overhead costs of the training function, allocated efficiently and accurately

- Costs associated with a needs assessment—if one was conducted—as well as the evaluation

Two considerations here are key:

- Consider the standard cost variables used by other departments in the organization in their ROI estimations. These comparisons should be as equitable as possible when leadership compares the ROIs of various programs across different departments.

- When in doubt, err on the side of conservativeness. Include all the fair costs you can, so that your efforts to perform an honest ROI are obvious.

Calculating the Return on Investment of the Program

The ROI is estimated by using the program benefits and the costs. The cost benefit ratio (CBR) is the program benefits divided by the costs:

$$CBR = \frac{\text{Program Benefits}}{\text{Program Costs}}$$

The ROI uses the net benefits divided by program costs, with the net benefits essentially being the program benefits minus the costs:

$$ROI\ (\%) = \frac{\text{Net Program Benefits}}{\text{Program Costs}} \times 100$$

Identifying the Intangible Benefits of the Program

Most training programs have intangible, nonmonetary benefits that should also be considered—for example, increased job satisfaction, increased organization commitment, improved teamwork, or reduced conflict. These too can be expanded into measurable performance indicators and precisely quantified and measured.

COMMENTS ON THE MODEL

This ROI process, like that of Kirkpatrick's model, has received wide attention, but the literature on the model consists primarily of applications and conceptual pieces by Phillips himself. In contrast, the literature about Kirkpatrick's model is balanced between research and application pieces by various authors, and that model has been used as the conceptual framework for numerous studies.

Although Phillips popularized this methodology in the training and performance improvement field, the concept of ROI and its formula variations have long been a part of the accounting and finance fields. In fact, even within training, other models for estimating training ROI have been proposed. One example is the return on training investment model proposed by Doucouliagos and Sgro (2000) for the National Centre for Vocational Education Research, Australia's principal provider of vocational education and training research and statistics. The authors propose a four-step model.

Step 1 is to collect data on the following categories:

- A measure of performance

- A measure of the training

- The costs of training

- The benefits arising from training

Doucouliagos and Sgro state that for most organizations, the major difficulties in the data collection process are collecting benefits data and measuring benefits. If some of the appropriate data are unavailable, the evaluation process is necessarily restricted. The costs of training are usually well known and easily identified, but the same cannot be said for benefits. Often it may be necessary to seek cooperation from areas within the organization other than the training function for data on benefits, and often some of the benefits cannot be quantified.

Once the data are collected, step 2 in the evaluation process is to compare pretraining performance or behavior to posttraining performance or behavior. Evaluation here consists of investigating these components:

- The direction of change in the target performance measure or behavior

- The magnitude of the change

- The statistical significance of the change

- The economic significance of the change

In step 3, multivariate analysis, evaluation involves exploring the extent to which interventions other than training contribute to changes in behavior and performance. This important step helps to determine the extent to which training on its own has had an impact. This step is not always possible because the necessary data are often unavailable. Nevertheless, the authors highly recommend conducting this step whenever feasible.

The final step is to compare the costs of the training to the benefits derived from the training, that is, calculating ROI. This comparison is usually expressed as a cost–benefit ratio and ROI. The analysis can be undertaken at a single point in time or over a number of time periods. In the latter case, this can involve net present value and discounted cash flow analysis.

Doucouliagos and Sgro affirm that evaluating training must use these four steps, although it is not necessarily easy. Wherever possible, all four steps are recommended to derive plausible estimates of the impact of training. The measures of the impact of training are by necessity only estimates. As many researchers note, conclusive proof will rarely be found about any organizational intervention. Rather, analysts compile credible evidence about the impact of training. This evidence must satisfy a number of requirements: The data used must be of sufficient quality, the techniques applied must be scientifically valid, and the analysis should address the possibility that training may not be the only factor behind changes in performance.

One critical difference between this training ROI model and that of Phillips is the use of rigorous statistical techniques to estimate the impact of various factors along with training. Phillips, in contrast, relies heavily on subjective self-reports to estimate the isolated impact of training. This is perhaps one of this model's limitations. Brinkerhoff (2005) criticizes this attempt to isolate the effects of training as a clear violation of performance systems logic, since performance is affected by many factors and never by training alone.

Finally, Bates (2004) argues that ROI as a measure of impact confounds short- and long-term factors that may lead to changes in performance; in addition, financial measures are self-serving and divert attention away from the goal of improving learning. He adds that ROI evaluations damage the ability of organizations to develop training systems capable of continuous improvement. Bates has also argued that decision makers who use this approach could potentially harm programs if ROI considerations outweigh stakeholder needs. In such cases, decision makers violate the principle of beneficence: the goal that evaluations should benefit stakeholders through program improvement.

STRENGTHS AND LIMITATIONS

The model is considered to have the following strengths and limitations.

Strengths

- It provides an elaborate methodology for estimating financial contributions and returns of programs.

- It provides an additional dimension to Kirkpatrick's four basic categories of training success indicators: return on investment.

- It provides an evaluation approach familiar to many executives across different departments.

- Created primarily for training and development interventions, it may be perceived as a reliable approach to evaluation by training departments.

Limitations

- Its elaborate methodology may be intimidating to trainers who are not used to dealing with such formulas.

- It may be perceived as too time-consuming and expensive.

- It was created specifically for training and development interventions and thus does not fully address all important indicator categories of performance improvement interventions in general.

- As with Kirkpatrick's four levels, its levels are not actually hierarchies, and evidence to suggest they are correlated is lacking. They merely illustrate a different focus, or perhaps even steps in a larger evaluation scheme.

- Heavy reliance on subjective estimations may lead to incorrect conclusions about program success.

APPLICATION EXAMPLE: BLAKE (1999)

Blake's dissertation, "Development of a Plan to Measure Return on Investment for Educational Programs at Providence Hospital," applied Phillips's ROI framework within the context of Providence Hospital, a private, Catholic, nonprofit, tertiary hospital in an urban setting. As in many other organizations, the training function at Providence Hospital was viewed as a cost center; although the training programs showed a high level of both participation and satisfaction, their impact on the hospital's bottom line was unmeasured. In a climate of cost reduction, the educational programs were in the precarious position of an unjustified expense and a potential area for further cost cutting.

Methodology

This case used an applied research methodology to plan ROI: information gathering, plan development and field testing, and implementation. Early stages of information gathering involved benchmarking ROI practices of similar hospitals owned by the parent organization. This was achieved by interviewing educational directors about methods used to evaluate training program costs, cost-benefit ratios, and return on investment. Based on the findings of these interviews, the author conducted interviews with senior leaders, examined pertinent literature, formed a committee, and conducted focus groups to develop criteria, tools, and a plan for implementing ROI at Providence Hospital.

Initial work led to the development of three documents to support the evaluation of ROI: (1) a program analysis planning sheet, (2) an ROI worksheet, and (3) an ROI analysis tool. These tools were field-tested with five of the hospital's educational programs over a one-month period. These tools incorporated standard thresholds for cost-benefit ratios and ROI (1:1.25 and 25 percent, respectively), based on Phillips (1997a). In addition, standards were set for calculating program costs (for example, overhead, benefits, wages, program materials, and refreshments) based on mean values in each category.

The educational director assigned individual instructors within the department to perform the ROI evaluation. These instructors were trained to use each tool, and calculations were verified by two separate instructors.

Findings

Table 5.1 provides an overview of the findings. The evaluation team noted several challenges related to measuring ROI of the educational programs: (1) determining a time period for expecting results, (2) being unable to establish a single set of ROI criteria suitable in all situations, (3) pinpointing a comprehensive and relevant set of effects related to each educational program, and (4) identifying alternative factors related to the results (but unrelated to the educational programs).

TABLE 5.1. Overview of Findings

Educational Program Title	Primary Result Targeted by Educational Program	Total Costs	Total Benefits	Net Benefits	Cost/ Benefit Ratio	ROI Period
Aseptic Technique in the Delivery Suite	Cesarean section infection rate	$1,084	$8,800	$7,716	1:8	712 percent, 5 months
Reducing Saphenous Surgical Site Infections	Surgical site infection rate	$2,789	$74,667	$71,878	1:26.77	2,577 percent, 4 months
Reflections	Lost revenue related to patient dissatisfaction and costs of complaint investigation	$10,800	$7,388	$3,412	1:1.46	46 percent, 12 months[a]
Registered Nurse Orientation	RN turnover rate	$441,116	$197,984	−$243,132	1:0.46	−55 percent, 12 months[a]
Computer-Based Training for Report Express	Reduced manual payroll adjustments	$24,695	$5,158	−$19,537	1:0.21	−79 percent, 6 weeks; projected: 81 percent, 24 months

[a]These periods have been extrapolated from the original application worksheets.

As applied research, this project sought to develop a usable ROI framework. Thus, once field tests were completed and the tools modified to make them more usable, additional data were collected (albeit from a small and nonrandom sample, $n = 3$) to evaluate the overall process and plan that was developed. As a result, the team concluded that the plan met established criteria; that its purpose, objectives, activities, and methods were valid, appropriate, worthwhile, and useful; and that it was a reasonable method for determining the value of educational programs at Providence Hospital. Of note, of all of the items addressed in this summative evaluation, only one resulted in a majority of respondents demonstrating a less positive attitude. This was item 12: "The plan produces findings that are believable"; 33 percent strongly agreed and 66 percent agreed.

Additional Applications

Engel, S., & Kapp, K. (2006). Finding ROI to ensure training dollars. *RMA Journal, 88*(11), 27–32.

Galvin, T., & Johnson, H. (2003). BEST return on training case studies. *Training, 40*(11), 24–28.

Marlatt, K., & Oliver, J. (2002). Maximize your ROI. *Credit Union Management, 25*(8), 19–24.

Simington, C. (1998). Stetnor Resource Centre: Measuring learning in earnings. *HR Focus, 75*(5), 11–13.

KEY POINTS

- Phillips's return-on-investment approach builds on Kirkpatrick's four levels of evaluation by adding a fifth level: return on investment.

- One distinguishing feature of Phillips's approach to ROI is the isolation of the effects of the training program.

- Although Phillips popularized ROI evaluation in the training and performance improvement field, many variations of ROI estimation can be found in other fields.

REFLECTION QUESTIONS

1. Under what circumstances would Phillips's ROI methodology be best applied?

2. What is Phillips's model missing? What are the implications of these missing variables?

3. What are the benefits and limitations of the alternate ROI model described by Doucouliagos and Sgro (2000) as compared to Phillips's model?

4. How could Phillips's ROI process be adapted to minimize its limitations and maximize its utility?

BRINKERHOFF'S SUCCESS CASE METHOD

This review of Brinkerhoff's success case method explains how and why this qualitative model relies on seeing training in a broad context and then focuses on the most and least successful participants in a given training or other solution. The chapter identifies some of the strengths and weaknesses of the SCM approach and looks at criticisms and variations designed to meet those criticisms. It reviews and analyzes a sample application of the model.

Brinkerhoff's views on evaluation (1981) closely resemble Stake's responsive evaluation model (1975) and, to a lesser extent, Patton's utilization-focused evaluation (1997). Brinkerhoff believes that if evaluations reflect the purposeful requirements of stakeholders, the likelihood increases that the information gathered will be used.

The success case model (SCM) was developed to address frustrations with more traditional evaluation approaches. Brinkerhoff felt that Kirkpatrick's four-levels-of-evaluation model (1976) was not suitable because it does not include investigations beyond training factors; it thus ignores the complete performance environment. He also felt that evaluation approaches based on experimental design frameworks can be cumbersome and require time, resources, and expertise beyond the scope of the typical professional setting (Brinkerhoff, 2005).

Brinkerhoff proposed the SCM as a simple approach that can be implemented in its entirety in a short time frame. It is intended to produce concrete evidence of the effects of training in ways that organizational leaders and others find highly relevant and credible. He relates verifiable incidents of training participants who applied learning content to carry out behaviors that could be demonstrated to have an impact on valuable organizational results. One critical underlying assumption is that the impact of training is inevitably a function of the interaction of training with other factors in the performance system. The SCM does not attempt to isolate the effect of training, since doing so, Brinkerhoff (2005) argues, "flies in the face of everything we know about performance-systems thinking and the inseparability of learning and performance" (p. 88).

Brinkerhoff (2005) emphasizes that if training has worked, it is due to the contributions of various parties in the performance management team. The SCM identifies these factors so that credit and feedback can be provided accordingly. If training is shown not to have worked, the SCM data will identify the weaknesses in the performance system and provide feedback to those who can resolve the problems. At its core, the SCM can be used to demonstrate to stakeholders what worked, what did not, what worthwhile results have been achieved, and what can be done to improve performance in the future.

In addition, Brinkerhoff (2005) suggests that an evaluation framework that responds to organization-wide training success factors should focus on three primary questions:

- How well is our organization using learning to facilitate required performance?

- What is the organization doing to facilitate required performance improvement from learning? What should be continued and strengthened?

- What is the organization doing, or not doing, that impedes required performance from learning? What should be changed?

These driving questions should be part of an evaluation plan with the overall purpose of building organizational capability to increase the performance and business value of training investments. Implementing this approach requires that evaluation focus on factors in the larger learning-performance process to engage and provide feedback to several audiences.

THE SCM PROCESS

Brinkerhoff's SCM combines analysis of extreme groups—as opposed to the average-performing group—with case study and storytelling. The main purpose of a success case study is to find out how well an organizational initiative such as a training program is working. This approach is meant to identify and explain the contextual factors that differentiate successful from unsuccessful adopters of new initiatives. Brinkerhoff (2003, 2005) cites a study that identified the factors that explained why some trainees were able to use their new training to accomplish worthwhile results while others were not: support from supervisors, access to certain databases, and access to training soon after being assigned new business accounts.

Brinkerhoff (1983, 1988) argues that training alone is never sufficient to improve performance and emphasizes the importance of managerial support and collaboration in building intentionality, which he defines as a clear focus on and commitment to a strategic subset of learning and performance objectives (Brinkerhoff & Apking, 2001). Moreover, Brinkerhoff criticizes other training evaluation models, stating that virtually all of them are construed conceptually, as if training were the only object of the evaluation.

The success case study process has two fundamental elements. First, all participants are surveyed, usually with a brief questionnaire, to determine by self-report how much they are using the new methods and tools a recent initiative intended them to use. They are also asked what accomplishments these methods and tools are helping them achieve.

Survey respondents are sorted to select those few who self-report as most and least successful. Then the evaluator selects a random sample from the most and least successful so that they can be interviewed and a deeper understanding of the impact of the evaluand can be gained. Specifically, the evaluator asks the most successful participants

- Exactly what was used, when, how, where, and why
- What results were accomplished

- How valuable the results were (for example, in dollars)

- What environmental factors enabled their application and results

The unsuccessful participants are asked

- What barriers they encountered

- What specific factors they attributed to being unsuccessful

- Whether anything else helps explain why they were not able to benefit from the program

The SCM results are communicated through stories that convey the most illuminating examples of success the program has achieved.

The SCM differs from more quantitative methods in that it does not seek to learn about the typical participant in a program. It purposely seeks the best performer a program is producing to help determine if the value a program is capable of producing is worthwhile, and whether it is likely to do the same for a greater number of participants. Similarly, it seeks the worst producer to help determine what barriers keep the program from wider success. The method generates a success story that is intended to be a verifiable account of how a person used a new skill or tool and what the worth of that skill or tool is.

STRENGTHS AND WEAKNESSES

The SCM has the following strengths and weaknesses.

Strengths

- It takes into account the specific experiences of participants in the training.

- Its simplicity increases the probability that evaluation will be conducted.

- It takes into account the causal factors for success and failure.

Weaknesses

- It relies exclusively on qualitative methods and self-reports.

- It does not account for the majority of experiences, only the extremes.

- Stakeholders can see it as insufficiently rigorous.

APPLICATION EXAMPLE: BRINKERHOFF (2005)

As part of a description of the processes and utility of SCM, Brinkerhoff discusses a specific case of SCM in application at SimPak Computers (a pseudonym for an information technology vendor). At SimPak, service technicians were assigned to clients and were held responsible for keeping these clients' systems working well and the clients satisfied. However, the research and development (R&D) function at SimPak was very active and released upgrades and new technologies and services frequently. This meant that service technicians had to be retrained frequently so that they had the most current knowledge required to ensure that their clients' systems worked well and the clients were satisfied.

SCM was applied to evaluate a residential training presented over a two-week period; the objective was that the service technicians would be able to install and initialize SimPak's newest and largest server, as well as additional equipment that allowed communication with other databases. The most critical skill, initialization, was a complex process that required several hours. In addition, the training was believed to be affected by contextual issues related to limited class availability, the fact that participants were nominated by regional leaders, tension between the sales and service divisions, and shared accountability of the program between the technical division and the training department.

Methodology

After getting information about program goals from stakeholders, the evaluation team decided to evaluate the course over a ten-month period, which encompassed twelve classes and 172 participants. The SCM does not require explicit in-depth understanding of complex course content; however, an impact model of how the technical skills would be applied was deemed necessary and therefore developed. Data were collected using a brief e-mail survey and keyed through a participant's name to existing data, such as client and geographical region information. It is unclear whether the e-mail questionnaires were anonymous. In addition, the potential issue of response bias was addressed by following up with a sample of nonrespondents in a telephone interview.

Findings

Of the 172 participants surveyed, 127 responded to the questionnaire (74 percent response rate). Of these respondents, 61 percent indicated having used the learning from this course at least once in their job, and

39 percent indicated never having used it. Because only one (out of twelve) of the random sample of nonrespondents surveyed by telephone indicated having applied learning from the training, the evaluation found a response bias, and thus the 39 percent nonuse rate was probably underreported. During the nonrespondent telephone interviews, the team uncovered the reason for lack of use: Although trained how to initialize one particular server, many technicians did not have clients who had purchased these servers. As alluded to by the contextual issues, regional leaders assigned technicians to training. Presumably because of limited class availability and long waiting lists, they nominated a technician for training just in case a client in their region purchased the server. As a result of these findings, the course itself remained unchanged. SimPak's leaders did modify enrollment practices and institute coverage practices in the event that a client requested installation of the server, but no technician in the region was trained to install it.

KEY POINTS

- The success case method relies on detailed evidence of one successful training participant in order to provide rich data about what contributed to the success of the participant.

- An underlying assumption of the SCM is that the training impact is inevitably a function of the interaction of training with other factors in the performance system.

REFLECTION QUESTIONS

1. In what context would the SCM approach to evaluation be most appropriate? What types of stakeholders would be most open to this approach?

2. What is the reason that the SCM focuses on the most successful and least successful participants in a training? Do you think this approach is productive? Why or why not?

3. How could the SCM be used with a group of stakeholders who rely on hard facts and figures?

THE IMPACT EVALUATION PROCESS

This review of Guerra-López's impact evaluation process describes the seven reiterating steps of the model. The chapter identifies some of the strengths and weaknesses of the approach and acknowledges that the newness of the model works against having a significant body of criticism and response. After the model is examined, strengths and limitations are examined, and a sample application of the model is reviewed and analyzed.

The impact evaluation process (Guerra-López, 2007a) is the most recently published evaluation model of those covered in this book. It was the culmination of the author's research, applied work, and teaching. One of the underlying ideas is that everything we do is aligned to some greater purpose (whether we are conscious of it or not and whether we are aligning it well or not), and evaluation is no different. The most prominent influence on the model comes from Roger Kaufman's work (1992, 2000, 2006a, 2006b) with needs assessment and strategic planning. Guerra-López worked on various projects related to needs assessment and strategic planning with Kaufman. Her contributions and experiences eventually led her to develop a focus on measurement and evaluation.

Kaufman's organizational elements model (1992, 2000, 2006a, 2006b) provided the differentiation of the three basic levels of results, as well as the ever-important distinction between means and ends. With this as the overarching conceptual framework for the impact evaluation process, the evaluand is always considered a means to an end, with the end manifesting itself in three levels of results: *strategic* (long-term organizational results that ultimately benefit clients and society, often stated in terms of a vision), *tactical* (short-term missions that operationalize organizational vision into more immediate organizational achievements), and *operational* (the building block objectives that together make it possible to reach the organizational mission). The idea that any evaluand must ultimately add value to the strategic level in the long term, but that in the short term the goal is to begin to align and measure the operational and tactical results, is key to establishing a chain of impact. In this sense, establishing impact refers to the extent that the evaluand helped the organization get closer to its strategic long-term goals.

Scriven's consumer-oriented evaluation approach is consistent with this view, in that Scriven (1991) argues that rather than accepting a developer's goals as given, the evaluation must judge whether achieving these goals would contribute to the welfare of clients and consumers. Regardless of the products and outputs, Scriven holds that the evaluators must also identify outcomes and determine their value as they relate to the consumer's needs.

If a needs assessment was conducted and done well, there is a high probability that the evaluand will in fact add positive and measurable value to the organization and its customers through its various levels of results. In other words, the evaluand should have been selected in the light of needs (that is, gaps in results) prioritized (based on the cost and consequences associated with meeting the needs versus ignoring them) at the operational, tactical, or strategic levels, and the pros and cons associated with each alternative considered for closing such gaps. Incidentally, the solution alternatives come directly from a need or causal analysis, the process by which root causes of the identified needs are found (Kaufman, 2000). Consistently, Scriven (1991) also calls for identifying and ranking the alternative programs or solutions that are available based on the relative costs and effects, and in consideration of the needs identified through a needs assessment based on societal value added.

If the evaluand was the best alternative for closing the gap, then one evaluation hypothesis is that the evaluand should have helped eliminate or reduce such gaps in results or performance. The basic evaluation question would then be, Did solution X contribute to the reduction or elimination of performance gap X? This is the major thrust of the Provus discrepancy evaluation model (1971). In addition, the impact evaluation process is influenced by decision-oriented theory and Patton's utilization-focused evaluation (1997), an approach to evaluation concerned with designing evaluations that inform decision making.

It is worth noting that much as instructional systems and performance systems are based on systems theory concepts, the impact evaluation process is based on a systemic approach to evaluation and performance improvement. Traditional science and research have been heavily based on studying independent variables: The focus of evaluation has been to study the impact of one variable over the system in order to understand what is going on with the system. However, as we look around in organizations and programs across sectors, it is obvious that there are no purely independent variables. In fact, all variables are interdependent, and the more complex the system is, the more obvious the interdependencies become (Gharajedaghi, 1999).

Understanding the interdependency of factors that have an impact on human, program, and organizational performance requires a shift from a pure analysis (taking apart that which we seek to understand in order to explain the behavior of the separated parts and extrapolate an explanation of the whole) to synthesis (looking at system components and their interdependencies in order to understand their impact on the whole). In other words, performance improvement professionals and evaluators alike must look at the entire performance system and understand that any impact observed is rarely ever attributable to one solution or one cause alone. It is responsible, ethical, and pragmatic to look for and communicate the whole story.

THE ELEMENTS OF THE PROCESS

Evaluation at its core may be straightforward, but the situations in which it is applied can be complex and at times make evaluation daunting. The impact evaluation process is primarily directed at individuals who want

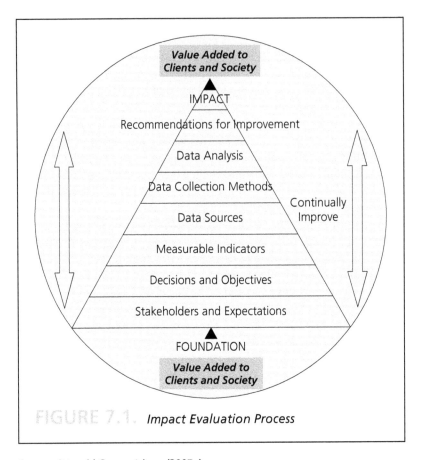

FIGURE 7.1. *Impact Evaluation Process*

Source: © Ingrid Guerra-López (2007a).

a clear map that guides them through the process and helps them keep a pragmatic focus. The idea is that with a well-articulated plan, the actual evaluation process will be simpler and more straightforward.

The impact evaluation process consists of seven elements. Although they are conveyed in sequence here, they can be considered reiteratively. The basic steps and approach are illustrated in Figure 7.1, which reflects the nested relationship among the seven elements of the process, with stakeholders and external impact on society as the basis for everything done in an evaluation.

Step 1: Identifying Stakeholders and Expectations

The process begins with the evaluator's identification of the key stakeholders involved. In the stakeholder group are those who will be making decisions throughout the evaluation process or directly as a result of the evaluation findings. Those with the authority to make critical decisions are often the ones who finance the evaluation project, but if the funders are different people or groups, they too should be included. Also important are those who will be affected by the evaluation—either in the process or potentially as a result of the findings. Including this group will make the implementation of the evaluation plan easier, particularly during the data collection stage. There may also be other stakeholders important to the situation. The driving question for identifying stakeholders is, Who is or could be affected by the evaluation or could potentially affect the evaluation in a meaningful way.

Each stakeholder group will have its own set of expectations. Some of these expectations might overlap, and some will be particular to the vantage point and respective interests of a given group. Relevant expectation areas include specific evaluation questions to be answered, time frames, final report content and format-related issues, and data or observation access, among others. One common element that should tie these individual expectations together is the organizational vision, which should be based on the external impact on the society. Otherwise each stakeholder group might end up pulling in separate directions, leaving the organization no better (or even worse) than it was before.

This process presumes that if the evaluator does not clearly identify the expectations and requirements of stakeholders, it is nearly impossible to meet those expectations and requirements. Even if the evaluation technically was a good one, it will not add any value if it was misaligned to stakeholder expectations. Evaluation data and results that are not relevant, and thus not used, waste everyone's time and resources.

It is critical to understand how a successful evaluation—and evaluator—will be judged by stakeholders. Here are some general questions that should be answered before proceeding:

- What decisions do the stakeholders wish to make as a result of the final deliverable?
- What is expected of the evaluator?
- What is expected of the evaluation project?
- How will the evaluator's performance be judged?
- What will the communication process be? With whom? How often? Through what medium?

What will be expected of stakeholders? For example, what type of support will they provide to the evaluator: feedback, data collection assistance, administrative, or something else?

What will be the impact of applying the evaluation results or not applying them?

Also critical is aligning stakeholder expectations with external societal demands. Although not all stakeholders might see the link easily, it is the evaluator's responsibility to clarify those linkages. It is not a matter of whether such linkages exist for this particular organization; instead it is how well the evaluator can clarify and communicate those linkages and consequences. This is the only way all of the stakeholders can see clearly where their organization is headed and how the programs or solutions being evaluated help or hinder that journey.

These expectations then become the basis for the contract, whether verbal or written, and should explicitly articulate what is expected of the evaluator and stakeholders. If anyone feels they are unreasonable, this is the time to discuss them and come to a consensus. After the evaluator has completed what in his or her own mind is a successful evaluation is the worst time for such a discussion.

Step 2: Determining Key Decisions and Objectives

Another important early step is to identify the decisions that will have to be made using the evaluation findings. Asking the stakeholders to think carefully about these decisions early in the process will help the evaluator focus on the important issues and lead to useful data (Watkins & Guerra, 2003). For instance, a decision might be whether to roll out a new incentive program to other branches of a bank after its implementation in one of the branches. This decision would be based on a number of criteria, one of which might be whether the performance goals were reached. Another might be whether the goals were accomplished within the required time frame. Yet another might be whether the benefits of the new incentive program outweighed the costs. Was there an unintended effect on other parts of the performance system? As you can see, these issues are pertinent to determining the net worth of the intervention.

The discussion about the decisions that must be made is also about the objectives that must be reached. All organizations have objectives, both external and internal, and everything within the organization should contribute toward those objectives (Guerra, 2005). The relative worth of any program or solution is primarily contingent on whether it is helping or hindering the achievement of organizational performance objectives and external contributions.

While some stakeholders may not provide the evaluator with the specific results they expect, they will offer clues about the relevant effects they are expecting, even if these are about means rather than results. The evaluator's task here and throughout the entire process is to be the educator and facilitator and approach the conversation from the standpoint, If we were to accomplish that, what would the result be? This line of inquiry should continue until key results have been identified. Another key source for identifying the specific performance objectives of the solution is to look at past needs assessment reports, if there are any. These reports should include the initial problem, why this solution was recommended, and what specific objectives it is supposed to meet.

With these decisions and objectives clarified, the overarching questions that will drive the evaluation process, as well as the purpose of the evaluation, should also become clear, well articulated, and ready to be agreed on.

The evaluator will not always start out with a clear purpose. Sometimes the decisions that have to be made are broader (for example, to continue to fund a program), and sometimes they start out with specific questions (for example, the impact the program is having on employee retention or the return on investment of this program). Whatever form the initial information is in, the evaluation will be more effective if the important details are clarified before proceeding.

Sound decisions should be primarily driven by relevant (related to results of interest), reliable (trustworthy), and valid (a true measure of what is measured) data, and these data should come from measurable indicators of the results sought, which in turn are related to the questions that need to be answered.

Guiding evaluation questions come from various perspectives and stakeholder groups. As we will discuss later, each stakeholder group represents a unique point of view based on where in (or out of) the organization the members view the issues. It is important that the evaluator identify a comprehensive and representative list of questions. However, often not all questions will be within the scope of this evaluation effort. The key is to obtain consensus among the stakeholders (or the individuals representing them) as to what the most critical questions are, and thus what this evaluation study commits to deliver. Evaluators who cannot obtain consensus on a set of questions will be far less likely to obtain consensus about the usefulness of the evaluation report.

Data collection should be systematic and designed to answer specific questions that can be used to improve performance. Good data can be used to prove the value of the program or solution without simply relying on opinions about what seems to be working and what seems not to be.

Different perspectives lead to different questions, and different questions lead to different findings, so the list of questions should be comprehensive. This does not imply that the list should be long; rather, the questions should come from a systemic perspective that considers the entire performance system, including its ultimate purpose, its subsystems, and their interactions.

Ultimately all of the questions must be related to the desired results, whether they are stated in those terms from the outset or not. Part of the evaluator's job is to help create the linkages between the stakeholders' initial questions and the results to which they are inherently (and sometimes covertly) related. All organizations have an ultimate result or results that they want to reach. To make that possible, numerous building block results have to be accomplished. Everything else that the organization does or uses must contribute to those, or it is wasting valuable and limited resources.

First, the ultimate goal for the organization to reach is about its ideal impact on the community and society, and it is stated through an organizational vision. Kaufman (2006a, 2006b) stresses that all organizations, public and private, share a vision to add value to all of society and strongly suggests that each organization should define a shared and measurable ideal vision based on creating the kind of world that all stakeholders want to create for tomorrow's child. Watkins (2007) makes this observation:

> Objectives at the societal level are neither defined by a single organization, nor is it expected that any one organization will accomplish them on their own. Strategic objectives are the shared ambitions of the individuals, organizations, groups, and other partners that represent our shared communities and society (e.g., no loss of life nor elimination or reduction of levels of survival, self-sufficiency, or quality of life from substance abuse, disease, discrimination, etc.). To define their mission, organizations then identify from these strategic intentions (which inherently aligns organizational Outputs with societal Outcomes) (p. 29).

Based on all organizations having the same societal value-added vision, each organization decides on what parts of the ideal vision it commits to deliver and move ever closer toward. Thus, each organization can derive its responsive mission. For instance, a financial institution's ideal vision-related mission might be striving to "ensure the continued success of our organization while we improve the quality of life of the community by providing, demonstrating, and achieving equal opportunity and unbiased access to both financial solutions and a working environment, without regard to irrelevant variables such as race, color, religion, ethnic background, gender, and sexual orientation."

While many organizations have already derived a mission and a vision, the approach suggested here builds on what has already been done and encourages a shift from statements of purpose isolated from the shared community to statements in alignment with it. For useful evaluation to take place, expectations of the evaluation partners should be aligned with the ideal vision and a related mission: The ultimate purpose of the organization relates to long-term success based on meeting the needs (not just wants) of external stakeholders and thus adding social value.

In a formal needs assessment or evaluation process, this would be used as the basis for deriving relevant measurable indicators of quality of life and other ideal vision elements (as we will see later in this book). It is particularly important that all those involved in planning, executing, and evaluating at all levels of the organization understand this. Nonetheless, the language used to articulate this ideal vision may not always include the details.

Ideal vision is about the ideal ultimate destination for a shared society, not about what the organization commits to deliver by the end of next year. As such, its primary purpose is to guide the organization and all its members toward a common, long-term, strategic destination. Thus, the first general question to ask from an evaluation perspective is, How much closer to the ideal vision and our mission did we get as a result of the solutions we implemented? From this general question would stem other vision- or strategy-driven evaluation questions, for example, How well are we meeting the needs (not just wants) of our clients?

As the organization aligns its mission with the ideal vision, the next level of organizational results is expressed through organizational missions. These are essentially the primary organizational-level results through which the organization ultimately seeks to reach the ideal vision.

Hence, the mission should be derived from the vision. To continue with the previous examples, a sample mission for a financial institution might be "We will ensure 100 percent customer and employee satisfaction, free of any discrimination lawsuits, grievances, or complaints (including not meeting fiduciary responsibilities), while moving to reach full market share." Notice how the elements of this mission are directly linked to the ideal vision while targeting more specific results. Thus, the general evaluation question to ask at this level is, What mission results did our solution help us accomplish? Other specific evaluation questions stem from this level, for example, Did the solution we implemented have an impact on our profits?

Since the mission is what the organization will use as its standard of success, Kaufman (2000) suggests striving for perfection by using ideal target figures rather than limiting the organization to a target that could aim below its potential. The goal is to encourage organizational members away from mediocrity and closer to ideal organizational results than perfection.

Finally, there are a number of internal building block results that, when properly linked, deliver the mission. These internal results are sometimes delivered by individual units, cross-sectional special teams, or individuals. Focusing on the financial institution case, here are some examples of building block results.

For Increasing Market Share

- Increase customer retention by at least X by the end of the fiscal year.

- Increase customer referrals by at least Y by the end of the next fiscal year.

- Increase profitable service areas by at least Z by the end of the next fiscal year.

For Increasing Customer Satisfaction

- Increase at least X in annual customer satisfaction survey ratings.

- Decrease customer complaints or grievances by at least Y.

- Decrease discrimination lawsuits filed by customers or potential customers against the institution by at least Z.

- No client of the bank will become bankrupt due to being given a loan or financial assistance that was inappropriate for that client's survival.

Note that customer retention and referral may also serve as an indicator of customer satisfaction.

For Increasing Employee Satisfaction

- Decrease undesired turnover rate by at least X.

- Decrease absenteeism rate by at least X.

- Increase scores of employee satisfaction surveys by at least Y.

- Eliminate filed discrimination lawsuits filed by employees against the institution.

As you can see, these building block results themselves can be broken down further into other building block results. The specific figures targeted should be derived from a needs assessment process. The means used to achieve them will depend in great part on the causal factors that contribute to the fact that these indicators are at less than desirable levels. The general question at this level would be, What internal results did our solutions help us accomplish? Related questions might be, Are we meeting the established criteria for reaching those results? and What other impact did the solution have on our subsystems results?

It is essential to tie stakeholder questions to important results you will measure at the various levels. There will undoubtedly be questions about means (types of questions about being better, faster, or bigger, for example), and these should not be dismissed; rather, they should be linked to specific results through useful questions. This could be an opportunity for the evaluator to educate stakeholders about how to create value chains. The guiding question in this case might be, If it is faster, what measurable benefit has it added for the organization, external stakeholders (including society), and our internal stakeholders? This type of discussion should help the stakeholders come to their own conclusions about what is truly important. It is imperative that evaluators help them focus on the results and consequences of the solution, as that is what speaks to its effectiveness. The means associated with it speak about its efficiency, and that is not enough.

Step 3: Deriving Measurable Indicators

Sound decisions are made on the basis of relevant, reliable, and valid data related to desired results and the related questions to be answered (Guerra, 2003b). Therefore, the heart of an evaluation will be gathering the data required to answer the questions that guide the inquiry. People often end up making judgments based on wrong or incomplete data, particularly when they try to force connections between inappropriate data and the decisions that must be made. This is a mistake made by reliance on existing data for answers simply because the data are already there (Kaufman, Guerra, & Platt, 2006).

Indicators are observable phenomena linked to something that is not directly observed; they are useful for providing information that will answer an evaluation question. Results are not always neatly and directly observed. A number of indicators or, to borrow Gilbert's term (1978), performance requirements can be relevant when results are measured. For instance, profit is a result that has various metrics that collectively indicate its level; examples are monies collected, monies paid out, and assets. Indicators for customer service include referrals, repeat business customer retention, length of accounts, and satisfaction survey scores. (Chapter Ten elaborates on how to identify performance indicators.)

Step 4: Identifying Data Sources

With a list of specific indicators in hand about which data to collect, evaluators must determine where to find those data. Often the answer is right in the organization where the evaluation is taking place. Existing records about past and current performance may already be available, collected by different parties in the organization and for different reasons (Guerra, 2003b, 2003c). The best place to start is here, as it could make the process much more efficient.

The access we have available to data today is unprecedented. Telecommunications and other technologies can be used to link to reports, documents, databases, experts, and other sources to a degree never before possible (the Internet is an efficient vehicle for linking to these). Companies, government agencies, and research institutions, national and international, publish a variety of official studies and reports that can prove to be valuable sources of data.

The sources the evaluator selects depend on the type of data sought. Other sources may be experts, employees, and leadership. As with other elements of the evaluation planning, these are discussed in detail in later chapters. Additional guidance for finding data sources is provided in Chapter Ten.

Step 5: Selecting Data Collection Methods

The right data collection methods and tools are a function of the data required, just as the data collected are a function of the methods selected.

When evaluators limit the data they collect by employing a narrow set of observation methods based on the way it has always been done or personal preference, problems arise (Kaufman et al., 2006).

The fundamental consideration in selecting appropriate data collection tools is the data required. If you seek hard data such as sales figures, for example, do not use a survey to get people's opinion of these sales figures. Rather, review relevant sales reports. Conversely, if you are interested in attitudes, there are a number of ways to get them (interviews, focus groups, and surveys, among others). There is extensive literature about these and other data collection methods. The evaluator should make the selection based on the pros and cons of the possible approaches, specifically with regard to important criteria such as appropriateness of the instrument for the required data, time, characteristics of the sample, comprehensiveness of the tool, previous experience with tools that are being considered, and feasibility, among others (Guerra, 2003b, 2003c; Witkin & Altschuld, 1995). The secret ingredient for successfully collecting valid and reliable data is alignment of data type, data source, data collection tools, and, later, data analysis procedures.

Chapter Eleven looks at how to select and create data collection instruments.

Step 6: Selecting Data Analysis Tools

A number of quantitative analysis techniques are available; selecting the appropriate technique depends on not only the scale used to measure the data but also the specific purpose of our analysis. Is the intent to show the relative position of an individual in a group (measures of central tendency)—for example, which salesperson stands apart from the rest of the team? Or is it to describe the shape of a data set (measures of variability)—for example, whether the sales figures are generally consistent for this branch, or whether individual salespeople's figures vary significantly from one another? Or is it to show relative ranking—for example, how Jane's performance scores stack up against those of others in her group?

There is more to evaluation than data collection. Considerable planning should take place before the actual data collection, as well as analysis, synthesis, and interpretation of the data that will take place after the information has been collected. The analysis of data in the evaluation effort is the organization of data to discover patterns used to support hypotheses, conclusions, or evaluative claims that result from the evaluation study (Kaufman et al., 2006) and therefore provide useful information to make good decisions.

One basic purpose for statistics in evaluations is that they enable us to sensibly and clearly summarize large amounts of data. There are two basic categories of summary statistics. One is the measure of central tendency: the mean, median, and mode. These measures present, in one simple figure, a summary of characteristics of an entire group, such as the average sales figures of agents or the average number of calls resolved by a customer service agent.

The other category under summary statistics is dispersion, or variance: How much variability exists? One of the most frequently used measures of dispersion is the standard deviation. This reveals how much each individual score or figure in the group is dispersed. For example, a large standard deviation for the average attendance call center agents means that absenteeism varies greatly from person to person in that group of employees. One key insight provided by W. Edwards Deming and Joseph Juran about quality is that there is variability in everything we do. Performance improvement aims to reduce variability so that all performers reach the required or desired performance criteria.

Another purpose for statistics is that they can be used to determine the relationship between two or more events (for example, profit and holidays) or scores or items that represent these events. Earlier in this chapter, the importance of synthesis in order to understand the interdependencies among variables was underscored. When data are analyzed, the relationship between two or more items will likely be important. The term used for this relationship in quantitative techniques is *correlation,* which represents the degree to which the items are related and is expressed in terms of a coefficient (ranging from -1 to $+1$). A positive correlation between two items means that as one item or score increases, so does the other item or score. For example, high achievement in school might positively correlate with effective note-taking techniques. A negative correlation between two scores (represented by a negative coefficient) means that as one item increases, the other decreases.

It is important to remember that *correlation* does not mean *causation.* That is, a relationship between two variables does not automatically indicate that a change in one caused a change on the other. One alternate possibility is that a third variable caused a change in the two considered. Again, the evaluator is strongly encouraged to look at the data in the context of the entire performance system, accounting for a complete (or as complete as feasible) list of factors that could have affected the performance indicators of interest.

Statistics also show how to compare the differences in performance between two groups. When performance improves after a human performance improvement intervention, a likely question is, Is the performance of the group receiving the intervention different from that of the group that did not?

Qualitative data (sometimes called *soft data*) are also subject to analytical routines. Qualitative observations can be ordered by source and by impact. Checking the frequency of qualitative observations will begin to merge qualitative into quantitative data (sometimes called *hard data*). Continually reflecting on and searching for patterns within the data even while the data collection process is continuing can help evaluators adjust and refocus their data collection to render useful information. Chapter Thirteen provides a detailed discussion of both qualitative and quantitative recommendations and provides additional references.

Both qualitative and quantitative data sets should be obtained from valid data sources. Once that is done, the information is examined to make sure it is relevant to each issue or evaluative question in the study.

Whatever statistical tools are chosen, the evaluator must be sure that they are the right vehicles to answer the evaluation questions. Different questions call for different analyses, as do different levels of measurement. Use the right tool for the job.

Whereas data analysis focuses on organizing and summarizing information, the findings begin to highlight the most important elements, thereby engaging in the process of turning data ("the mean is 18") into information ("the average number of items sold per day by the sales clerk in this store is about 18"). The findings begin to personalize and make meaningful the numbers that the analysis rendered, but the evaluator is not yet interpreting what that means.

Interpretation attaches meaning to organized information in order to draw plausible and supportable conclusions. Scriven (1991) emphasizes that evaluators must arrive at defensible judgments rather than simply measuring objectives. In this sense, data analysis deals with the facts, while interpretation is related to value judgments. Because this is an innately subjective process, careful attention and effort should be placed on ensuring fairness, openness, and as much objectivity as is realistic under the circumstances.

Even the fairest and most well-meaning evaluators will be biased to some extent. Our perceptions are formed by our experiences, preferences, values, and habits (for example, noticing some details while being unaware of others). Thus, it is helpful to clearly articulate the rationale for interpretations by linking them back to the findings, which are, of course, based on the data analyzed. This alignment is critical throughout the evaluation process: The data collected are relevant and valid indicators of the results sought, which are related to important evaluating questions to answer so that stakeholders can make sound decisions about how to improve performance.

Step 7: Communication of Results and Recommendations

The importance of effective communication cannot be overstated. A rigorous evaluation does not speak for itself. The evaluator may have indeed implemented a flawless evaluation in theory, but it will be worthless if it does not communicate the importance and purpose of the evaluation process and associated activities throughout and the data-supported findings and action that must be taken as a result. If people are not moved to action as a result of the evaluation, the main objective—to create positive (though not necessarily comfortable) change—has not been met. Communicating with key stakeholders throughout the evaluation process keeps them aware of what the evaluator is doing and why, which increases the amount of trust they place in the evaluator and his or her efforts. In addition, it allows stakeholders the opportunity to participate and provide valuable feedback. By the time the final report and debriefing come along, they should not see these products as something imposed on them but rather as something that they helped create. With this type of buy-in, their resistance to the findings will likely be lower.

Things to consider in the communication are medium, format, language, and timing, all of which are discussed in a later chapter.

COMMENTS ON THE MODEL

Because of the newness of the impact evaluation model, little research has been conducted to date using this framework. However, several conceptual pieces have been published (Guerra-López, 2007a, 2007b, 2007c, 2007d), and two case studies are in preparation. The framework has been applied in evaluation projects with educational, business, and health care partners.

STRENGTHS AND LIMITATIONS

The model is considered to have the following strengths and limitations.

Strengths

- A strong focus on aligning performance toward ultimate desired impact

- A strong focus on alignment of all evaluation steps

- Detailed guidance for conducting an evaluation in its entirety, from establishing partnerships to ensuring that recommendations are implemented

- A focus on finding the performance indicators appropriate to the evaluand rather than restricting the focus to predetermined performance indicators such as reaction, learning, or behaviors

- Appropriate for evaluating any range of programs and performance improvement interventions.

- A goal of alignment with other important performance improvement processes (for example, a needs assessment), while recognizing them as separate

Limitations

- Steps in the process could be perceived as linear.

- The linkage to external contributions and environment could be seen as irrelevant by some organizational members.

APPLICATION EXAMPLE

The Visionary Corporation (TVC) is a leading global provider of integrated information solutions to business and professional customers. It provides must-have information and uses technology and applications that allow its customers to make better decisions faster. The TVC Sales EZ Maximizer tool (SEZM) was created to improve sales representatives' productivity through better access to data, as well as speed to transact business. TVC wanted to know if its efforts were paying off. The evaluator was tasked with helping stakeholders determine whether they should continue using the tool or try something else.

The evaluator was internal to the organization, a full-time employee of TVC, and received the request from her boss, the head of the TVC learning and performance department. However, this was not the direct client. The direct client, who was pushing (and paying for) the evaluation, was the new senior vice president of sales operations.

Methodology

In talking with her client, the evaluator identified many stakeholders for the organization and the evaluation project: sales reps, who used the tool to create quotes; the technology department, which had developed the software; the finance department, which was managing the funding of the project; the order entry department, which used quotes to enter orders; the learning and performance department, which had implemented the program; managers who were decision makers on development and changes; and TVC's clients. All of these stakeholders' interests were represented on the evaluation committee.

The committee sought to determine whether the investment of money, time, and effort was worthwhile. This required developing a clear picture of the alignment between the SEZM tool and the operational, tactical, and strategic objectives of the organization. Based on these objectives and TVC's vision and mission, the evaluator developed measurable and relevant indicators.

When discussing the strategic level, stakeholders expressed that they wanted SEZM to allow them to be responsive to their external clients. Members of the evaluation committee agreed that if these clients received fast and accurate quotes, this would be an indication of TVC's responsiveness to clients, which would contribute to continued customer satisfaction (measured, for example, through customer attitudes, length of time for active accounts, and activity in the account), as well as continued increases in profits and market share. At the tactical level, the SEZM tool provided the opportunity for an increase in sales. TVC wanted to track the total sales volume, overall sales dollars, items sold per client, and sales dollars per client. At the operational level, the lead evaluator found that the standardized SEZM quoting tool was intended to cut down on the time it took for sales reps to create quotes. This in turn would allow reps to increase contact with clients, which would increase the number of quotes requested by and sent to clients. Because clients were also able to access the tool using TVC's online interface, the number of orders submitted and their accuracy were important.

Supporting the process level, the SEZM would reduce the number of order errors made, as well as the time wasted on identifying and resolving mistakes. Table 7.1 illustrates the relationship between results and relevant indicators.

These key performance indicators became the central focus of the evaluation. To make this process precise and account for other factors that might have affected performance, the lead evaluator wanted to compare each indicator to preestablished measurable criteria. However, since a formal needs assessment was not completed prior to SEZM's implementation, the lead evaluator worked with the evaluation committee to determine how much of an improvement was required to consider SEZM worth the investment. The executive team used historical data, forecasting records, and their own experience and expectations to come up with feasible targets.

Sales and revenue reports were used to study figures before and after the implementation of the SEZM quoting tool. Special sales reports also allowed the lead evaluator to measure client satisfaction, looking at increases in client account activity. Production and performance reports were helpful in identifying an increase in the number of quotes and order accuracy, as well as a decrease in time spent on resolving order errors. Also consulted were industry reports to establish relative market share, profit and loss sheets to establish net profits, and customer sales reports to analyze sales figures and customer account activity.

A customer survey was conducted to collect data about the perceived benefits of customers' use of SEZM, in particular how it helped TVG be more responsive to clients' requirements. The questionnaire was brief and consisted of five questions, which were approved by the evaluation committee and measured on a five-point Likert scale (1 = *never* to 5 = *always*). All questions focused on observable and measurable behaviors, which prompted the respondents to provide thoughtful responses about their actual experiences. For example, one of the questions was, "When I used SEZM to obtain quotes, I obtained all the information required within five seconds of submitting the quote request form." The questionnaire was administered to a stratified random sample during a period of two weeks using the same interface that hosted SEZM. After submitting an order, every other client was taken to the survey home screen, which included an explanation of the purpose of the survey, the time required to complete it, assurance of anonymity, and a 5 percent discount off their next order if they completed the questionnaire.

TABLE 7.1. **List of Relevant Performance Indicators**

Level	Result	Related Indicators
Strategic	Continuously having the largest portion of market share	Indicator 1: Continued customer satisfaction Indicator 2: Continued increase in market share Indicator 3: Continued increase in profits
Tactical	Increase sales	Indicator 1: Overall sales volume increased by using SEZM Indicator 2: Overall sales dollars increased by using SEZM Indicator 3: Sales volume per client Indicator 4: Sales dollars per client
Operational	Increase sales reps' productivity	Indicator 1: Number of sales calls sales reps attend to is increased Indicator 2: Number of sales quotes sent by reps is increased
	More purchase requests are received from clients	Indicator 1: Number of purchase requests sent directly by potential customers is increased
Process		Indicator 1: Increased order accuracy with the use of SEZM Indicator 2: Decrease in time fixing order errors

In order to gather the required information for the evaluation, members from the departments that use SEZM (sales, sales management, and order entry departments) were chosen to participate in nominal groups. The facilitator asked the participants to share to what, if any, extent SEZM had reduced the time required to track and fix order errors and how SEZM had contributed to their productivity. The facilitator wrote down the responses on flip chart paper. Responses ranged from having significantly increased the time available to focus on sales, to not having much of an impact at all on what they did, to having a negative impact on productivity due to systems' downtime or not having the full functionality required to meet all client requirements. After jotting down responses during each session, the facilitator, with the participation and consent of the participants, ranked all responses.

Findings

In analyzing the data from profit reports and industry market share reports, the evaluation committee found no significant increases in market share or profits after implementing SEZM. This was somewhat expected given the short performance period (about one year).

The customer satisfaction survey was a relatively useful activity, with a 52 percent response rate. Since the responses were based on a Likert scale, the median response was estimated as a measure of central tendency. In addition, the percentage of respondents selecting each of the response options for a given item was estimated.

Sales revenue report figures were carefully analyzed by looking at the total number of overall sales, as well as total number of sales per individual account. In addition, because they were dealing with real numbers (money and number of sales), the mean, or average, for each account was estimated as the measure of central tendency. The current totals and averages were compared to the totals and averages obtained prior to the implementation of the SEZM. The prior period of time consisted of the same months during the previous year; it was confirmed that no other major initiatives that might have affected those results had taken place during that time.

The evaluation committee found a net increase of 13 percent in overall sales from the previous year (prior to SEZM's implementation), almost twice as much as the trend in the past six years (average yearly sales growth had been 8 percent). The average number of transactions per account had also increased over the previous year, by about 7.5 percent. This too reflected an increase over the previous six-year period, albeit a more modest one: Average increase in account activity from year to year has been roughly 5 percent.

Performance records revealed a consistent increase in productivity among the sales reps. The total number of sales calls before and after SEZM's implementation was compared, and an increase was found, as well as in the number of quotes sent out by the sales force.

No data were available to determine whether order accuracy had increased, and thus, the nominal groups were instrumental in gauging employee perceptions about SEZM's role in its effect on order accuracy and the time they spent fixing order errors. There was consensus about SEZM's positive contribution toward increasing order accuracy and decreasing time spent on order errors, though initially, almost all participants indicated that the transition to the tool was not smooth.

For the first two to three months of implementation, employees had to maintain their regular workload while learning to use the new tool. As a result, their numbers fell in the beginning and made it difficult for them to accept the new tool; in fact, some did not use it at all for the first few weeks (during the transition, they could use the old way or the new tool to submit orders). In addition, not everyone received training on how to use the tool before they began using it. Some were told to start using the tool even before they were scheduled for the training, which in some cases took six to eight weeks. Most viewed the transition period as uncoordinated and unnecessarily difficult, with some saying they almost gave up using SEZM because of this. A few raised other issues, such as system downtime, which prevented a quick response to their clients. The system did help, but only when it was up, and there was no contingency plan in place for when the system was down. A couple of other participants indicated that the tool itself was "too inflexible and you can't adapt the fields to submit additional information a client was looking for." One factor that helped them bear with the limitations was that those who had mastered the use of the tool attested to its great utility and ease. Others stated that their manager's flexibility throughout the process was invaluable.

During one of the last debriefing meetings of the evaluation committee, it became obvious that although it was essential for the SEZM tool to contribute to strategic results, it was too soon to see the impact of the tool on long-term strategic results. The data collected about market share, profit, and customer satisfaction were considered the first official measurement at one point in time, which would become part of a collection of periodic measurements used to monitor these indicators.

One key recommendation was that any shifts in these indicators must be considered in the context of the range of factors that may have had a potential impact. One indicator that supported the utility of the tool was customer attitudes, as measured by the brief questionnaire. Most of the clients surveyed, 82 percent, said that the SEZM tool met their requirements consistently and promptly, and nearly 76 percent indicated that they preferred this quote method over the previous one. With all items on the questionnaire obtaining favorable responses by at least 55 percent of respondents, stakeholders were confident that the tool was meeting client requirements. Stakeholders agreed to monitor satisfaction annually and adapt the questionnaire instrument to reflect any new changes to the quoting process.

An increase in sales figures also supported the hypothesis that the SEZM tool was having a positive impact on the organization. After all, the previous year had seen double the increase in sales over the previous six years. However, one stakeholder, the senior vice president for sales and marketing, pointed out that this increase could not be interpreted out of context, specifically, industry figures and trends. He presented his own set of data to the rest of the group, which indicated that the industry as a whole had seen a remarkable increase in sales over the past year, an increase almost as high as what TVG had seen. Thus, TVG's increase could not be solely attributed to the implementation of SEZM. The group agreed that although other indicators appeared to support SEZM's positive impact, they would be conservative and agree that its impact on sales was inconclusive.

One recommendation that stemmed from this point is that sales figures and account activity would continue to be monitored not only by the sales department but by every other department. Any department implementing any changes or new tools, processes, or ways of doing things would inform other departments and jointly track the impact of these on sales in the short and long runs. As one member of the group put it, "There are simply too many factors at play for one person or department to track. We have to track the right things at the right time. If we don't have the data to prove our investments are paying off, they may not be paying off." The industry trend also provided a context for the salespeople's performance data. While an increase in quotes sent out had been seen for most of the sales force, the senior vice president and the team saw this in the context of industry growth. At the very least, it appeared that the tool allowed the sales force to keep up with the growing demand for services and, in turn, quotes.

For a fuller view, the performance data were reviewed in conjunction with the nominal group technique data. The data seem to suggest that SEZM was a useful tool for salespeople as well as the data entry people. Most stakeholders were a bit troubled by the glitches in the implementation process and attributed them to poor planning on the part of management and those in charge of implementing the tool. Further discussion revealed that no one project manager had been responsible for overseeing all aspects of the implementation. They reached the conclusion that this could have potentially sunk the whole SEZM initiative; fortunately, it had not done so, but this mistake should not be repeated with the implementation of future initiatives. One specific suggestion was to distinguish between a sponsor role and project manager role, with the latter being ultimately responsible for the success of the project (setting objectives and milestones, balancing resources, and so forth) and the former being responsible for delivering all required resources to the project manager, including material and human resources, as well as the required authority to get the job done. Another suggestion was that a project protocol, standardizing key elements of a successful implementation project, be designed, distributed, and applied throughout the organization. The stakeholder group also suggested that systems' downtime be addressed as a priority, because every minute the systems were down meant a lost sale.

The employee data suggested the tool was very helpful and overall a better way to create and submit quotes. They also indicated that in the employees' estimation, it had contributed to an increase in their productivity because they did not spend anywhere near the amount of time they used to spend tracking and fixing order errors. Overall the data seemed to suggest the SEZM tool was worth the continued investment, at least until the next set of data suggested otherwise. The data also revealed some ways to improve the tool itself and the implementation of future initiatives.

One key result of this process was that stakeholders either suggested or agreed that various indicators continue to be tracked before definite conclusions about perceived solutions' impact were drawn.

KEY POINTS

- The impact evaluation process incorporates a focus on adding value to external clients and society.

- The defining characteristic of the model is alignment: between data collected and evaluation questions, evaluation and needs assessment, expectations and deliverables, and throughout the entire evaluation and continual improvement process.

- The model is action-based and targets the implementation of recommendations that lead to improved performance.

- The model is very new; thus, a full body of criticism and response to it has not yet been developed.

REFLECTION QUESTIONS

1. How can the impact evaluation process be integrated with each of the phases of performance improvement to ensure continual feedback throughout (for example, as part of a formative evaluation process)?

2. What are the key differences between the impact evaluation process and the previous evaluation models discussed in this section? How do these differences enhance the evaluation of programs and performance improvement initiatives so that they enhance organizational performance and external contributions?

3. Under what circumstances would the impact evaluation process be an appropriate starting point for a new evaluation? Under what circumstances would you want to start with a different approach?

CHAPTER 8

THE CIPP MODEL

*This review of the CIPP (context, input, process, products)
model developed by Daniel Stufflebeam presents the
four aspects of the model. It then touches on some of the
strengths and weaknesses of the approach and offers a brief
analysis of a sample application.*

The CIPP, proposed by Daniel Stufflebeam (1967), is a framework intended to guide formative and summative evaluations of projects, programs, personnel, products, institutions, and systems. This acronym denotes the model's basic concepts, which focus on evaluating an entity's contexts, inputs, processes, and products.

Like other evaluation models, it was created in response to the limitations that traditional experimental design, objectives-based evaluation, and standardized achievement tests face in evaluation programs that inevitably exist in dynamic social settings (Stufflebeam & Shinkfield, 2007). The earliest formal documentation of the model is offered in *Educational Evaluation and Decision Making* (Stufflebeam et al., 1971), the product of an evaluation study committee appointed by Phi Delta Kappa in 1969 (Stufflebeam & Shinkfield, 2007).

The model's underlying purpose is to provide evaluation clients with timely and valid information that allows them to identify areas for development and improvement. In the context of a formative evaluation, the CIPP asks, What should be done? How should it be done? Is it actually being done? and finally, Is it succeeding? In a summative perspective, it asks in hindsight, Were important needs addressed? Was the effort well guided? Was service designed and executed as required? Did the effort succeed? (Stufflebeam, 2003).

According to the CIPP model, evaluation is the systematic investigation of the value or merit of an evaluand, where *merit* refers to the intrinsic quality or excellence, regardless of its utility, and *worth* refers to something's intrinsic quality and its extrinsic value, especially its utility in meeting targeted needs. Stufflebeam views evaluation as a functional activity oriented in the long term to stimulating and aiding efforts to strengthen and improve the ability of organizations to recognize that some programs or solutions can be found to be unworthy of attempts to improve them and should be terminated. Assisting in the dissolution of unnecessary, corrupt, or hopelessly flawed efforts, evaluations serve an improvement function through assisting organizations to free resources and time for worthy programs and solutions.

STUFFLEBEAM'S FOUR TYPES OF EVALUATION

Stufflebeam suggests (2003) that the CIPP model is intended for use in internal evaluations conducted by an organization's evaluators, self-evaluations conducted by project teams or individual service providers, and contracted or mandated external evaluations.

The CIPP model allows the evaluator to focus on four distinct but related activities, mainly the specific evaluation of each one of four areas: context, inputs, processes, and products. Evaluation of each of these areas can be conducted individually, sequentially, or in parallel, depending on the situation. The basic idea is that these evaluations complement the information requirements of the stakeholders rather than replace existing information or reports.

Context

Context evaluation focuses on guiding the future direction of the enterprise. During this evaluation, needs are assessed, opportunities are identified, and priorities for the future are determined. The purpose of this evaluation focus is to set objectives and determine priorities.

Input

Input evaluation centers around identifying and choosing the best programs or solutions for reaching prioritized goals by considering competing action plans, staffing plans, and budgets for their feasibility and potential cost-effectiveness to meet targeted needs and achieve goals. The basic idea is to ensure linkages between the means selected and the ends desired. The purpose of this evaluation focus is to create or improve plans.

Decision makers use input evaluations in choosing among competing plans, writing funding proposals, allocating resources, assigning staff, scheduling work, and ultimately helping others judge an effort's plans and budget. Stufflebeam (2003) argues that input evaluation is the most neglected yet important type of evaluation.

In fact, when you read the two initial evaluation focuses in this model, you may have recognized some similarities with an investigative approach presented in Chapter One: needs assessment. Context evaluations are analogous to needs assessments, as both are meant to identify needs and opportunities in order to help decision makers define and prioritize their goals. The CIPP's input evaluations also overlap with specific functions within a needs assessment, particularly as defined by Kaufman (1992, 2000). For instance, Kaufman's methods-means analysis is a technique used in the context of a needs assessment to identify the best methods and means to address each of the identified needs, looking at pros and cons, including potential costs and consequences of each alternative considered. Both Stufflebeam and Kaufman suggest that these functions are among the most critical in creating and improving performance, even though Stufflebeam considers these types of evaluations, and Kaufman a different but related process: needs assessment.

Process

Process evaluation provides guidance about the implementation of selected means. The implementation is tracked so as to improve it by ensuring the implementation is going as planned while the entire implementation process and associated costs are documented. The purpose of this evaluation focus is to monitor performance.

Products

Product evaluation provides feedback with regard to maintaining, improving, or abandoning that which is being evaluated. The initial needs should

TABLE 8.1. CIPP Applicability in Formative and Summative Evaluations

Formative/Proactive	Summative/Retroactive
Context: Direction for identifying needed solutions and choosing and prioritizing goals (based on assessing needs, problems, assets, and opportunities)	*Context:* Comparison of priorities: goals to assess needs, problems, assets, and opportunities
Input: Direction for choosing a program or other solutions (based on assessing alternative methods and means, and resource allocation plans), followed by examination of the work plan	*Input:* Comparison of the program's tactics, design, and budget to those of critical competitors and the targeted needs of beneficiaries
Process: Direction for implementing the work plan based on the monitoring and judging activities and periodic feedback	*Process:* Complete description of the actual process and record of costs; comparison of the designed and actual processes and costs.
Products: Determining outcomes and side effects in order to provide direction for continuing, modifying, adopting, or terminating the program or solution (based on assessing)	*Products:* Comparison of outcomes and side effects to targeted needs and, as feasible, results of competitive programs; interpretation of results against the effort's assessed context and inputs

be used as the standard for determining whether results are satisfactory. The purpose of this evaluation focus is to judge accomplishments and make decisions.

In long-term evaluations, the product evaluation component may be subdivided into evaluation of impact, effectiveness, sustainability, and transportability (Stufflebeam, 2003). These product evaluation subparts ask the following questions:

- Were the right beneficiaries reached?

- Were their targeted needs met?

- Were the gains for beneficiaries sustained?

- Did the processes that produced the gains prove transportable and adaptable for effective use elsewhere?

Like the impact evaluation process described in Chapter Seven, the CIPP proposes that all performance improvement efforts should begin with identifying and prioritizing organizational needs. These serve as the primary solution selection criteria, as well as the ultimate determination of an evaluand's worth (whether it helped solve important needs). In fact, both models can be used not only for the summative perspective of evaluation but also for the formative perspective. Table 8.1 compares the CIPP's formative (proactive) and summative (retroactive) applications.

ARTICULATING CORE VALUES OF PROGRAMS AND SOLUTIONS

In the evaluation's definition, the term *value* refers to the range of ideals held by stakeholders and society. The CIPP model calls for the evaluator and client to identify and clarify the values that will guide particular evaluations. Stufflebeam (2003) suggests that all evaluations should begin with the clear articulation of core values associated with any program or solution. Each of the four types of evaluations (context, input, process, and product evaluation) has a reciprocal relationship with a particular evaluative focus: goals, plans, actions, and outcomes:

- The goal-setting focus elicits questions related to a context evaluation, which provides information for validating or improving goals.

- Planning improvement efforts bring forth issues related to input evaluation, which provides judgment of plans and guidance for improving those plans.

- Program actions produce questions for process evaluation, and this evaluation provides judgments of activities along with feedback for improving staff performance.

■ Obtained results and side effects relate to product evaluation, which ultimately provides judgments of outcomes and identifies performance improvement recommendations. These relationships stem from grounding evaluations in core values.

In a sense, these values are integrated into Kaufman's ideal vision (1992, 2000, 2006a, 2006b), which he holds should be the basis for planning and performing any endeavor—for example, helping students become self-sufficient citizens, eliminating all work-related accidents, or eradicating discrimination based on irrelevant variables. From these ultimate outcomes flow building block outputs (for example, graduation) and products (promotion to the next grade level). Like Kaufman, Stufflebeam has also suggested that evaluators take into account a set of relevant societal, institutional, program, and professional and technical values when assessing programs or solutions.

These values then form the basis for evaluation criteria, providing the compass that informs stakeholders and evaluators about whether the program or solution is helping the organization move closer to the ultimate accomplishments it values. This is the basis for deriving evaluation questions, related results, and the measurable indicators that will form the basis for data collection and determine the data collection instruments as well as the analysis techniques appropriate for each of the data sets (Guerra-López, 2007a).

METHODS USED IN CIPP EVALUATIONS

Stufflebeam suggests that a wide range of qualitative and quantitative methods be considered and recommends applying triangulation procedures to confirm information. Evaluators must address a number of evaluation complexities—for example, limited time and resources; the impracticability of laboratory-style controls; unavailability of validated data collection instruments that meet the exact criteria specified; and, often, not enough time or expertise to create a well-designed, tested instrument. Evaluators must operate within such constraints and still do their best to ensure that the data collected truly represent reality. This model advocates engaging multiple observers and informants with different perspectives, designing one's own instruments as required, finding relevant data, using multiple procedures, cross-referencing qualitative and quantitative findings, supporting arguments over time, and sharing the evaluation for review by a variety of stakeholders.

STRENGTHS AND LIMITATIONS

The CIPP model has the following strengths and limitations.

Strengths

- The model was not designed with any specific program or solution in mind; thus, it can be easily applied to multiple evaluation situations.

- Its comprehensive approach to evaluation can be applied from program planning to program outcomes and fulfillment of core values.

- The model is well established and has a long history of applicability.

Limitations

- The model could be said to blur the line between evaluation and other investigative processes such as needs assessment.

- It is not as widely known and applied in the performance improvement field as other models.

APPLICATION EXAMPLE: FILELLA-GUIU AND BLANCH-PANA (2002)

In response to a growing body of research illustrating a negative correlation between employment and repeat offenses by ex-convicts, a medium-sized Spanish prison implemented the Guidance Program for Job Search (PORO) to prepare inmates for gainful employment. Based on individuals' judicial situation, PORO assigned prisoners to one of three levels of guidance. The program content was organized around four core areas: (1) job skills and competency, (2) where to search for jobs, (3) practical aspects of job searching (for example, interviewing and preparing a résumé), and (4) worker rights.

Methodology

Stufflebeam's CIPP model was used to perform an evaluation of this program for the years 1995 to 1998. Data about inmates' and instructors' feelings and opinions were collected through interviews and questionnaires. In addition, inmates were surveyed in a pre-post design to determine their rate of adjustment on the job. The evaluation employed both experimental ($n = 145$) and control ($n = 51$) groups, but judicial requirements prevented randomly assigning the participants. Evaluators

TABLE 8.2. **Measured Indicators**

Area	Indicators
Context	Gender, age, length of sentence, occupational specialty, level of formal education, entry job skills, and professional self-esteem
Input	Operational, material, and human resources
Process	Self-reported workload of instructors (for example, preparation and instruction), inmates' motivation and attitudes toward usefulness and desirability
Products	Efficacy, effectiveness, efficiency, unexpected outcomes

compared these groups at an initial stage by analyzing the prequestionnaires, at a final stage by analyzing the postquestionnaires, and by a combination of the two. Table 8.2 illustrates the indicators that were measured based on the CIPP framework.

Findings

Participants were predominantly male (89 percent), between the ages of twenty-five and thirty-five, and serving less than four-year sentences. Inmates participated in occupational training in mechanics, graphic arts, dressmaking, carpentry, building, binding, and computing. Although there were no significant differences in level of formal education, entry job skills, or professional self-esteem between groups at the initial stage, the authors report that program participants illustrated significant gains in job adjustment knowledge and professional self-esteem. However, it is difficult to discern what items were used and whether appropriate statistical methods were applied to arrive at this conclusion.

The authors of this application contended that these benefits are worth the required resources. In general, instructor activities aligned well with the employment department's guidelines and favored practical work over theoretical or preparatory activities (by a factor of two to one). Overall, inmates became more enthusiastic throughout the program and viewed it as both useful and desirable. In terms of product evaluation, early data suggest that the program is effective. Only 30 percent of the experimental group and 41 percent of the control group were "in freedom," that is, out of prison, when the evaluation was conducted, yet of those in the experimental group who were free (n = 43), 50 percent were already employed.

The authors believe that Stufflebeam's CIPP evaluation model was particularly suitable to this situation, given the "personal and situational factors" of a prison environment (p. 67).

Additional Case Applications

Chiang, P. L. W. (1996). *Assessing the effectiveness of five-year mechanical engineering technology programs of junior colleges in Taiwan, R.O.C.: An application of the CIPP evaluation model.* Unpublished Ed.D. dissertation, Florida International University.

Hsieh, W. -K. (1999). *Assessing the effectiveness of two-year banking and insurance technology programs of junior colleges in Taiwan, Republic of China: An application of the context input process product (CIPP) evaluation model.* Unpublished Ed.D. dissertation, Florida International University

Nicholson, T. (1989). Using the CIPP model to evaluate reading instruction. *Journal of Reading, 32*(4), 312–318.

Schultz, A. K. W. (1991). *An evaluation of a nursing clinical advancement system.* Unpublished Ed.D. dissertation, University of Rochester.

KEY POINTS

- The CIPP model consists of four types of evaluations with different foci.

- Context evaluation could be said to be analogous to needs assessment, the first step in the basic performance improvement model.

- Like Kaufman and Scriven, Stufflebeam suggests that evaluators take into account a set of relevant societal, institutional, program, and professional and technical values when evaluating programs or solutions.

REFLECTION QUESTIONS

1. Refer back to Chapter One's formative evaluation questions based the performance improvement process or traditional

ADDIE model (Guerra, 2003a). How does the CIPP, as presented here in Chapter Eight, overlap with the proposed approach?

2. How do the first two types of CIPP evaluations relate to Kaufman's needs assessment approach?

3. What are some similarities and differences between the CIPP model and other models already addressed in Part Two of this book?

EVALUATING EVALUATIONS

This chapter addresses meta-evaluation, that is, evaluation of an evaluation. Meta-evaluations help identify and address inherent biases in evaluation design. They can take place alongside an evaluation or after it, and they can be either formative or summative. The primary model for meta-evaluation is Standards for Evaluation of Educational Programs, Projects, and Materials, *developed by the Joint Committee on Standards for Educational Evaluation. The American Evaluation Association has also published a set of principles for evaluators. An example in which the* Standards *were employed in a meta-evaluation concludes the chapter.*

Where human beings are involved, there are likely to be biases. Biases can be found even in the most basic, scientific research. For example, the questions that are asked and studied can be a function of the personal interests of the researchers. Thus, what is known about a particular topic is known because someone or some group chose to go down that path of investigation, not necessarily because that is all there is to know about it or because that was the most critical path of investigation in that area of study.

Evaluations also can be influenced by the personal experiences and persuasions of the people making decisions about how and when to conduct them. From choosing the evaluation questions, to the results, indicators, and activities that would be appropriate for answering such questions, and even to the analysis tools—all of these factors influence evaluation conclusions. At times, the purpose of an evaluation can, most likely at a covert level, be a simple political exercise rather than an honest and open invitation to improve a program or performance solution. Politicization of an evaluation can potentially lead to sabotaging activities such as blocking access to relevant, reliable, or valid data or discarding findings and recommendations that do not confirm the claims of a special interest group.

Evaluating evaluations, or conducting a meta-evaluation, is perhaps one of the most important things to do to confirm the fidelity of any evaluation endeavor. Establishing a mechanism by which to establish the validity of work is a common practice in various fields, from accounting to medicine, teaching, and other service professions. It is a professional obligation of evaluators and performance improvement professionals. Meta-evaluation can help the customers of an evaluation decide whether to accept and implement evaluation conclusions and recommendations.

As with most other evaluations, this does not have to begin after the evaluation has been completed; rather, it can be done as a parallel process, helping evaluators use relevant and timely feedback to improve the overall evaluation process. In fact, Scriven (1968) notes that meta-evaluation can be formative, assisting the evaluator in designing and conducting a sound evaluation, or summative, giving the client an independent account of the technical competence of the evaluator and the evaluation report.

Stufflebeam and Shinkfield (2007) define meta-evaluation as

an evaluation to help detect and address problems, ensure quality, and reveal an evaluation's strengths and limitations. It is the process of delineating, obtaining, and applying descriptive information and judgmental information—about the utility, feasibility, propriety, and accuracy of an evaluation and its systematic nature, competent execution, integrity and honesty, respectfulness, and social responsibility—to guide the evaluation and report its strengths and weaknesses. Meta-evaluation is a professional evaluation of evaluators (p. 705).

They say that the role of a meta-evaluator "can be extended to assessing the worth, merit and probity of all that the profession is and does, evaluation services, use of evaluation, evaluation training, evaluation research, and organizational development" (p. 705).

Stufflebeam and Shinkfield (2007) propose a set of essential qualifications for meta-evaluators:

- Knowledge of alternative sets of professional standards for evaluations, together with an ability to choose and apply standards that fit particular evaluation assignments

- Methodological expertise, along with a comprehension of the evaluand

- Experience and competence to fulfill clients' needs for meta-evaluation

- Honesty, integrity, and respect for individuals and society

- Skills in negotiating formal meta-evaluation contracts

- Ability to communicate and collaborate effectively with other meta-evaluation stakeholders

EVALUATION STANDARDS

Although meta-evaluation has perhaps been around almost as long as evaluation, evaluators began to discuss it formally only in the 1960s (Fitzpatrick, Sanders, & Worthen, 2004). Some of the most noted early work includes that of Scriven (1967, 1974), Stake (1970), and Stufflebeam (1968). Most evaluators were in favor of evaluating the quality of an evaluation and directed adopted meta-evaluation as a guide or standard to be in partnership with the consumers of evaluations, so that evaluations that were wasteful and added little value could be avoided. As the criteria and lists for judging the quality of an evaluation increased, so did confusion among evaluators and consumers of evaluation about which was indeed the most useful guide.

In 1975, Daniel Stufflebeam, through Western Michigan University's Evaluation Center, led an initiative to develop a comprehensive and universal set of standards directed specifically at educational evaluations. This initiative was overseen by the Joint Committee on Standards for

Educational Evaluation. As a result, the *Standards for Evaluation of Educational Programs, Projects, and Materials* (Joint Committee, 1981) was published (Fitzpatrick et al., 2004). The *Standards* have been updated (1994) and are currently used in multiple settings, providing a common language and set of rules for dealing with a variety of evaluation issues.

The *Standards* can be used as a comprehensive framework for meta-evaluation. They can be consulted during the planning stages of an evaluation, the implementation stage to monitor progress, and during a final audit of an implemented evaluation. The thirty standards fit into four categories: utility, feasibility, propriety, and accuracy. A listing of these standards is provided in Table 9.1. For more detailed information, consult the updated *Standards* (1994).

The *Standards* are intended for educational and training evaluands and do not address evaluands outside those two fields. In evaluating other performance improvement interventions and related meta-evaluations, evaluators and meta-evaluators are advised to use the *Standards* as one source of potential criteria but also to consider external criteria appropriate for their situations and contexts.

Stufflebeam and Shinkfield (2007) caution that the *Standards* were developed expressly for the United States and Canada. The Joint Committee recommended that other countries consider what standards are useful to them.

THE AMERICAN EVALUATION ASSOCIATION PRINCIPLES FOR EVALUATORS

The American Evaluation Association (AEA), perhaps the best recognized professional association for evaluators, was created in 1986 as a result of a merger between the Evaluation Network and the Evaluation Research Society. At the time, both entities supported the work of other organizations in the creation of evaluation guidelines, though they did not officially endorse any of them. Eventually it became apparent that guiding principles for evaluators were important, and in 1992, the AEA board created a task force to develop such principles. The following list of principles was offered in 1994 and revised in 2004 (American Evaluation Association, 2004):

- Systematic inquiry: Evaluators conduct systematic, data-based inquiries about whatever is being evaluated.

- Competence: Evaluators provide competent performance to stakeholders.

TABLE 9.1. Program Evaluation Standards, 1994

Utility Standards. Intended to ensure that an evaluation will serve the information needs of the intended users

U1. Stakeholder Identification
U2. Evaluator Credibility
U3. Information Scope and Collection
U4. Values Identification
U5. Report Clarity
U6. Report Timeliness and Dissemination
U7. Evaluation Impact

Feasibility Standards. Intended to ensure that an evaluation will be realistic, prudent, diplomatic, and frugal

F1. Practical Procedures
F2. Political Viability
F3. Cost Effectiveness

Propriety Standards. Intended to ensure that an evaluation will be conducted legally, ethically, and with due regard for the welfare of those involved in the evaluation as well as those affected by its results

P1. Service Orientation
P2. Formal Agreements
P3. Rights of Human Subjects
P4. Human Interactions
P5. Complete and Fair Assessment
P6. Disclosure of Findings
P7. Conflict of Interest
P8. Fiscal Responsibility

Accuracy Standards. Intended to ensure that an evaluation will reveal and convey technically adequate informa-tion about the features that determine the worth or merit of the evaluand

A1. Program Documentation
A2. Context Analysis
A3. Described Purpose and Procedures
A4. Defensible Information Sources
A5. Valid Information
A6. Reliable Information
A7. Systematic Information
A8. Analysis of Quantitative Information
A9. Analysis of Qualitative Information
A10. Justified Conclusions
A11. Impartial Reporting
A12. Metaevaluation

▨ Integrity/honesty: Evaluators ensure the honesty and integrity of the entire evaluation process.

▨ Respect for people: Evaluators respect the security, dignity, and self-worth of the respondents, program participants, clients, and other stakeholders with whom they interact.

▨ Responsibilities for general and public welfare: Evaluators articulate and take into account the diversity of interests and values that may be related to the general and public welfare.

APPLICATION EXAMPLE: LYNCH ET AL. (2003)

This case study was intended to demonstrate how the *Standards* were used to guide a descriptive meta-evaluation and to help identify the strengths and weaknesses of the evaluation being meta-evaluated. A single case was examined: evaluation of the Interdisciplinary Rural Health Training Program (IRHTP).

Funded by federal and local sources, the IRHTP was established in 1994 in rural eastern North Carolina. Its purpose is to encourage the recruitment and retention of health care professionals in rural areas through student participation in a community-based interdisciplinary curriculum. The curriculum has several components: case conferences (for example, a medical and pharmacy student team presents a treatment plan for their patient), interdisciplinary community site visits (for example, a student team works at a nursing home), skill-building sessions (such as communication skills), community projects, peer teaching, education about health care disciplines, and community resources and agencies. This graduate course is implemented one day each week, and students earn credit for participation. For the remainder of the week, students participate in discipline-specific courses. On-campus course directors identify the students who may participate in the IRHTP, which is available also to health professions students at other universities. Several hundred students from nine institutions throughout North Carolina have participated to date.

Methodology

The Curriculum Planning Committee conducted the meta-evaluation following a completed evaluation cycle for a four-month semester of the IRHTP. Although the IRHTP was implemented in three sites, the meta-evaluation addressed evaluation only at the best-established site, where the curriculum and evaluation process were most stable. A goals-based model of evaluation (Patton, 1987) was used to assess the extent to which thirteen curriculum goals had been attained. The sample consisted of twelve students who were in the following disciplines: advanced nursing (two students), health education (one student), medicine (two students), nutrition (one student), pharmacy (three students), social work (one student), and R.N. to B.S.N. nursing (two students). In the group were eight women and four men, with a mean age of thirty years six months.

Findings

Meeting Utility Standards Of seven utility standards, those most relevant to evaluating the IRHTP are discussed.

Stakeholder Identification The stakeholders were campus faculty, students, community members (including preceptors and patients or clients), program staff, and funding agencies. All of these groups were represented in the executive council, which reviewed the evaluation plan and gave final approval. Specific evaluation planning was conducted by the Curriculum Planning Committee, which did not include community preceptors, patients or clients, or students. These stakeholders may have added perspectives on the meaningfulness of the evaluation; students would have been the best judges of the feasibility of the evaluation. Therefore, their absence was a shortcoming, and this utility standard was not fully met.

Information Scope and Collection This standard requires collecting information broad enough to answer key questions and meet stakeholder needs. Because the curriculum planning committee was composed of faculty who represented eight disciplines, there were diverse ideas about the types of information needed. For instance, medical and nursing faculty were interested in obtaining data about the health of patients or clients involved in the program, and the social work faculty member was interested in students' cultural awareness and their knowledge of community resources. In addition, program administrators were interested in collecting data relevant to expectations specified by funding agencies. Without input from students and preceptors, however, the potential scope of information obtained may have been narrowed. To establish a mechanism for obtaining information about program processes and unplanned program effects, the evaluation planners agreed that informal exchanges through e-mail and conversations would be documented as sources of data about program events. Still, the absence of process-oriented objectives and the unsystematic method for assessing unplanned effects could be viewed as weaknesses of the evaluation.

Values Identification Values identification pertains to explicating the bases for judgments used to interpret findings. In effect, such values were reflected in the outcome objectives, the majority of which were educational. In other words, the curriculum planning committee implicitly agreed that the IRHTP program would be worthwhile if students demonstrated positive educational gains, students enjoyed the program, students planned to live and work in rural areas, and the program improved the health of the community.

Evaluation Impact This standard refers to the application of evaluation findings. The evaluation had two effects. First, positive findings provided a data-based rationale for maintaining selected curricular components and encouraged IRHTP staff to disseminate information at national presentations and continue to seek funds for the curriculum. Unsatisfactory outcomes prompted several changes. For example, opportunities for interactive discussion of interdisciplinary care among students were increased, lectures and independent reading assignments were decreased, and assessment paperwork was reduced. Consequently it was reasonable to conclude that this standard had been met.

Meeting Feasibility Standards Two feasibility standards were relevant in this case.

Political Viability By obtaining input (through the curriculum planning committee) from all course directors who supervised participating students, diverse evaluation interests were addressed so that the plan was politically feasible on campus. Although conjoint planning helped to prevent dominance by any single specialty, it also was important to get buy-in from those accountable to the funding agencies. Political issues emerged when students complained to their course directors about the demanding nature of the evaluation. These issues were examined during committee meetings and addressed in subsequent changes to the curriculum. In many collaborative ventures, pride of ownership is a political barrier to progress, and the IRHTP was no exception. Although the School of Medicine initiated the IRHTP, leadership conflicts emerged and were addressed to some extent by eliciting and responding to the ideas and concerns of all committee members and by making sure the curriculum was representative of several disciplines.

Cost Effectiveness This standard addresses issues such as the efficiency of the evaluation and whether benefits exceeded costs. The evaluation data have served many purposes. The information has been used to improve curriculum content and assessment; communicate the impact of the curriculum to funding agencies, course directors, community members, and other stakeholders; and help disseminate information about the curriculum at national meetings. The main costs associated with the evaluation have been in terms of personnel. Key personnel included the off-campus site coordinator, the on-campus curriculum coordinator, a data entry assistant, a Web page designer, and an evaluation consultant. Apart from the data entry assistant, who was hired solely for that purpose, evaluation activities were integrated into the employment responsibilities of the other personnel, which helped simultaneously to provide adequate resources for the evaluation and absorb much of the human resource cost. In addition, existing physical resources were made available and were adequate for the evaluation.

Meeting Propriety Standards The four most relevant propriety standards are discussed.

Service Orientation The question that examines this standard is, How does an evaluation meet the needs of those it is designed to serve (in this case, the students, community, and society)? The evaluation data have been used to improve the curriculum, thereby meeting some of the students' educational needs. Whether the curriculum has helped students in subsequent employment is unknown, and this should be addressed by the evaluation. Assessing the impact of the program on individual patients or clients or on the community has been challenging due to the difficulty of isolating relationships between the curriculum and the community. One reason is the status of students as apprentices who require supervision: For legal reasons, students may not independently provide services to patients or clients. Consequently, interactions between patients or clients and the interdisciplinary student team cannot be separated from other services received by patients or clients.

Mechanisms to measure the effects of community projects completed by students were often omitted from planning. For instance, the effects of health fairs, a typical community project, on community awareness about specific health conditions was not measured. Another social goal of the curriculum is to increase the distribution of health care providers in rural communities. This is being evaluated by tracking the practice locations of program participants. Problems have been encountered in this process; for instance, it is sometimes difficult to locate former students due to name changes that occur with marriage or their reluctance to provide this information.

Rights of Human Subjects There were several components to respecting and protecting the welfare of human subjects. Rules of the institutional review board provided information about the legal and ethical precepts pertinent to conducting research with human participants. An application to evaluate the IRHTP was submitted and approved by the institutional review board. Apart from case conference summaries and diaries, which are course requirements, participation in the evaluation was voluntary. Student confidentiality has been maintained by reporting data in the aggregate and refraining from the use of individuals' names. Although patients and clients are not evaluated, their names are coded on all evaluation material. Data have been used for scholarly purposes only.

Complete and Fair Assessment It is somewhat difficult to ascertain the extent to which evaluation of the IRHTP has been complete and fair. Although all of the outcome objectives were fully addressed, it could be argued that the evaluation was incomplete. For example, it would have been easier to explain negative findings if the evaluation report had provided more information about discrepancies between the actual curriculum and the planned curriculum. Regarding fairness, the possibility of biased reporting could not be ruled out because the evaluation team was internal. Fairness was probably enhanced by focusing the report on objectives developed by the curriculum planning committee, reporting both positive and negative findings, addressing data versus evaluator opinions, and presenting alternative explanations for results.

Conflict of Interest This standard states that conflict of interest, which occurs when an evaluation is influenced by personal or financial interests of the evaluators or when a stakeholder has an inappropriate interest in an evaluation, should be addressed openly. In this case, the potential for conflict of interest existed for at least two reasons. First, an internal evaluation team conducted the evaluation, increasing the probability that close working relationships among the evaluation team and program personnel would influence the evaluation report. Although this possibility cannot be ruled out, it was probably mitigated by the involvement of diverse faculty in evaluation planning. Many of the planners represented different divisions and schools within the campus and were previously unknown to the evaluation team. Second, procurement of funds for continuation of the IRHTP will likely depend on attaining positive evaluation results. This condition could predispose the evaluation team to focus on program strengths and achievable outcomes. The impetus to improve the program through identification of program weaknesses, however, may have helped to attenuate this bias.

Meeting Accuracy Standards The six most relevant accuracy standards are discussed.

Context Analysis To help identify variables that may affect the program, this standard requires examining the context in which a program operates. This information is important also in assessing the extent to which program implementation and results can be generalized to other settings. This standard was relevant to the evaluation due to the unique geographical location of the program and the off-campus, community-based nature of the intervention. Program implementation depended greatly on community support of the IRHTP. Personnel at community health care facilities had to be willing to precept students, and the hospital, long-term care facilities, and local human service agencies had to be receptive to site visits by the interdisciplinary student team. In addition, preceptors had to be willing to release students for (and encourage them to participate in) interdisciplinary activities. Because the community advisory council was composed of community members, progress in this area was related directly to the commitment of group members and their relationships with one another. Although many of these issues were not addressed in depth in the evaluation report, they were discussed in great detail at many team meetings and recognized as key influencing variables. In addition, the site coordinator's role as a member of both the community and the IRHTP team was helpful in providing insight into community events. The complexity of these events and the rapidity with which they occurred made this aspect of the evaluation particularly challenging.

Valid Information This standard requires assessments to yield valid data. Due to the dearth of established instruments to evaluate interdisciplinary curricula, new instruments had to be developed. Although relatively small sample sizes have precluded factor analysis of data, validity may be inferred from other evidence. Evidence for validity based on content may be inferred because the assessments were reviewed by expert faculty, tailored to curriculum goals, and field-tested with students in the health professions. Evidence for validity based on learner responses could be inferred from positive findings; for example, there was a statistically significant increase in knowledge scores from pretest to posttest using the Knowledge of Health Care Disciplines Questionnaire ($p < .05$). In addition, multiple assessment methods, which strengthen validity (Brewer & Hunter, 1989), were used: journals, Web-based threaded discussions, case conference summary forms, and questionnaires. The possibility that results were influenced by weaknesses associated with self-reports, such as social desirability, respondent fatigue, or resentment at having to complete assessments, cannot be ruled out. Exit interviews, however, which are conducted with all students, have been used to help ascertain threats to the validity of assessment data. Interview results generally supported data obtained from the other assessments.

Reliable Information This standard pertains to the consistency of information obtained from a data collection procedure. For the closed-ended questionnaire items, inter-item reliabilities (Cronbach's alpha) were calculated with a sample size of twelve and ranged from .68 to .87. The evaluator and a graduate assistant conducted content analysis of qualitative data for the same sample. Inter-observer reliabilities ranged from 0.81 to 1.0 and were calculated by the following formula:

Number of agreements ÷ Number of agreements and disagreements

Analysis of Quantitative Information Several types of quantitative data were collected: student demographics, duration and frequency of participation in the program, student knowledge of the education and roles of members of the health care team, knowledge of community agencies and resources, opinions about living and working in small communities, opinions about working as part of a health care team, and feedback about the program. Descriptive statistics were used to summarize demographic information, degree of student participation, end-of-course feedback, and the proportions of students who demonstrated changes in opinions and knowledge. The last allowed analysis of change per individual. Paired t-tests were used to assess mean changes in knowledge and opinions from the beginning to the end of the curriculum.

Analysis of Qualitative Information Several types of qualitative data were collected. Student reports of their interdisciplinary experiences were obtained from journals completed weekly. Comments and suggestions related to case presentations were obtained from Web-based threaded discussions. Information about interdisciplinary team recommendations for cases was collected from case conference write-ups. Data from these three sources were analyzed using content analysis guided by definitions developed by a subgroup of the curriculum committee. Data regarding program activities were obtained from diaries completed by the on-site coordinator, meeting minutes, e-mail, notes of other communications, and participant observation. These sources of information were helpful in confirming information obtained directly from students. Also, the content and number of community projects completed by students were documented.

Justified Conclusions This standard requires that the rationale for conclusions be articulated so that stakeholders can assess the extent to which the conclusions are warranted. Also, alternative explanations for findings should be discussed. With regard to the IRHTP, the main conclusions alluded to the effect of the curriculum on students and thereby addressed a key purpose of the evaluation. The data to assess the effect of the curriculum on the community or patients or clients were inadequate. The possibility of alternative reasons for the findings could not be ruled out and was therefore also discussed in the evaluation report. The findings could have been influenced, for instance, by the relatively small sample size, inadequacies of the assessment approaches, or characteristics unique to the student cohort, and readers were cautioned to consider the influence of such variables. Examining several sources of data and implementing mechanisms for checking data congruence, however, strengthened the credibility of evaluation findings. Given the specific context of the program, the unique features of the community in which it was implemented, and the small number of student participants, it was not feasible to draw any conclusions about the generalizability of the results.

KEY POINTS

- Evaluations are subject to human error and biases.

- *Meta-evaluation* refers to the process of evaluating an evaluation in order to ensure quality, accuracy, appropriateness, and utility.

- The Program Evaluation Standards are the criteria by which evaluations are evaluated.

- The American Evaluation Association publishes a list of principles for evaluators.

REFLECTION QUESTIONS

1. Must all evaluations be evaluated?

2. Is there any value to evaluating meta-evaluations?

3. How would you ensure that the Program Evaluation Standards are responsive to an evaluation conducted outside the United States and Canada?

TOOLS AND TECHNIQUES OF EVALUATION

DATA

This chapter defines data and establishes the relationship between data and information. It explains how to distinguish between hard and soft data and between qualitative and quantitative data. The four scales on which data can be measured are explained. Finally, the need for collecting relevant, reliable, and valid data and many methods for doing so are examined.

A central premise of evaluation and improving performance is that complete and relevant data are used to make interpretations and recommendations about how to improve performance. Unfortunately, one common mistake is to force connections between data that are already available and the evaluation questions. Although there is absolutely nothing wrong with using data that are already available (in fact, it is good practice to do so) if they are relevant and suitable for answering the study questions, the fact is that in many cases, they are not relevant or appropriate, and often not complete either. In addition, the logical order of things is frequently reversed. That is, people look at the data they have available, then ask questions they can answer with those data. What they overlook are the important questions that do not naturally stem from the data—questions that should be asked and answered, yet for which there are no current data to do so.

For purposes of evaluation, *data* can mean any documented record of something—an event, a performance, a result—that took place during the period under study or at some other time but is relevant to the evaluation. Data are what an investigator wants to collect in order to answer the evaluation questions he or she has agreed to answer. Data could include account retention rates, production rates, incident reports, content mastered and applied from training or other human resource development efforts, questionnaire results, observation notes, opinion polls, profit and loss statistics, deaths, injuries, bankruptcies, successful lawsuits, awards, and the like. These all meet the definition of data: they can all be documented; they all could take place in the flow of events under study, or they could be relevant to the study by some chain of logic or rationale. However, all data will not carry the same weight in reaching conclusions, and some data may be misleading due to bias of one kind or another.

How does information relate to data? *Information* is data that can lead to successful decisions. In other words, useful data inform sound decisions. For example, average sales dollars and average sales volume per sales region are data that can be put into the context of decisions that have to be made by management. Let us say that an evaluation recommendation at one organization indicated that consolidating some of the smaller sales regions would improve sales while reducing sales operation costs. The decision for management would be determining which regions to consolidate. Now let us say that the stakeholder group agreed that one of the criteria for making the decisions would be average sales dollars and average sales volume per region. These data would be translated into information when the decision makers determine which sales regions have the lowest sales and therefore constitute the best candidates for consolidation.

This chapter looks at some things to consider about data in order to improve success for all of the functions of the organization and to find out what is adding value and what is not. As you review each of the following, look at them in the context of what your organization (or an organization you might evaluate) is doing now and might do in the future, and how you can use performance data to ensure success.

CHARACTERISTICS OF DATA

Sound decisions are directly related to the appropriateness of the data used to make them. Thus, data must meet three critical characteristics:

- *Relevant:* Directly related to the questions (overarching and specific) that must be answered

- *Reliable:* Rigorously measured, trustworthy, and consistent over time

- *Valid:* True indicators of the results we want to measure; measure what we should be measuring

Recognizing and ensuring these characteristics is essential, but it is not necessarily easy. In evaluations or other investigations of any kind, pieces of information flow in many directions. How can you separate the relevant, reliable, and valid from the irrelevant, misperceived, misinterpreted, or inappropriate indicators that people have relied on in the past? Many people involved in data collection (either as sources of information or a helping hand in the data collection process) often do not know what is relevant and what is not. It is imperative that the evaluator subtly educate to create an environment and framework within which the possibilities of capturing relevant, reliable, and valid data are high.

Hard Data

Hard data deal with more than just numbers and measurement; they are independently verifiable through external sources (Kaufman, Guerra, & Platt, 2006). Numbers alone do not make data "hard"; hard data must consist of verifiable facts. For instance, although questionnaire responses can be expressed as numbers, as is done with Likert scales, this alone does not make the data hard, because they are not said to be based on independently verifiable facts. Hard data often consist of measurement data that quantify relevant performance; however, if you are going to perform statistical operations of numerical data, you must consider the scale of measurement used. If you gather nominal data and use a statistical routine that assumes interval or ratio scales (discussed later in this book), errors in interpretation will result. If possible, make evaluation measurements using interval or ratio scale terms because on those scales, statistical treatment is possible and the verifiable measurable results can be appropriately interpreted.

Soft Data

Soft data are attitudes and perceptions that by definition are not independently verifiable. These are typically expressed as opinions, although they also can be expressed as numbers, as in the case of Likert scale questionnaire items. Although they are important, the fact that they are individual and private to people (even if they are in consensus with those of others) means that there is no way to verify them independently. How can you establish that what someone feels (or says he or she feels) is not accurate? One way to enhance the utility of soft data is to triangulate the data with other data through multiple sources. It is particularly desirable to identify appropriate hard data to support the preliminary evidence of soft data.

For instance, suppose that a customer service survey yielded a nearly perfect score. While some would say that the data indicate that customer satisfaction is at its highest level ever, in fact, all that the evidence establishes is that the people who were surveyed were satisfied or chose to say they were satisfied. They described themselves as satisfied, but are there other indicators that they are active, loyal customers? Let us then include in our set of evidence customer retention statistics, length of time of active accounts, accounts closed within a defined time period, and total sales per account. We could possibly observe that these indicators are quite shy of desired objectives and expectations, regardless of the results of the customer survey. The point here is that opinions about satisfaction are different from observable behaviors that are indicative of satisfaction. The results of the survey do not seem to be positively correlated with the other financial indicators with which it had historically been assumed to correlate.

While things like representativeness of sample and quality of the questionnaire could have altered the survey results, even a well-designed and well-implemented survey (and its data collection instrument) will still yield opinions. And we all know that our own opinions can be in direct contrast to our behavior.

Qualitative and Quantitative

Two related and essential terms that refer to both data and the techniques used to collect them are *qualitative* and *quantitative*. The qualitative technique requires careful and detailed observation and description, expressed through descriptive narrative rather than figures (McMillan, 1992). Some appropriate ways to collect these types of data are observations, interviews, surveys, reviews of existing documents, and case studies. Quantitative techniques are used to establish facts numerically based on observed performance and consequences, to predict, and to show causal relationships. These types of data can be collected with tests, customized measures, and instruments, to name a few possibilities. Once again the distinction should be made clear, and yet it is often blurred.

For instance, Likert-scale surveys, where respondents are asked to select a response ranging from perhaps *strongly disagree* to *strongly agree* or from *never* to *always,* often have numbers associated with each response option. These numbers are then used to make mathematical computations, such as calculating the average response. Yet these numbers are merely symbols of a qualitative judgment; they do not represent actual quantitative data. Even if the soft data are quantified with an appropriate descriptive statistic, such as the median score, we are still dealing with opinions.

The distinction between qualitative and quantitative does not have to be a yes or no, either-or, for the evaluator. Starting an evaluation with qualitative observation may help arrange the unforeseen issues that develop in any study. In addition, qualitative data can be supplemented with quantitative information. In fact, with a little work, qualitative data can be converted to or expressed as quantitative data, providing a straightforward basis for interpretations. For instance, qualitative opinions can be gathered and counted. Just think of the importance of polling in election years, when the quantitative statistics based on qualitative opinions often are the basis for campaign decisions.

SCALES OF MEASUREMENT

One key consideration in collecting data is using the appropriate level of measurement. There are four levels of measurement, and each possesses unique characteristics:

- *Nominal:* essentially used to name

- *Ordinal:* to convey rank order

- *Interval*: to convey equal intervals in addition to conveying rank

- *Ratio:* in addition to all the previous characteristics, involves an absolute zero point

Nominal and ordinal data are usually associated with qualitative data, and interval and ratio data are referred to as quantitative data. Table 10.1 illustrates the unique characteristics of each scale and gives examples of data for each.

TABLE 10.1. **Scales of Measurement**

Scale	Characteristics	Examples
Nominal	Used for labeling or describing Categories are mutually exclusive No value or order is placed on categories	Gender Ethnicity Educational level Job classification
Ordinal	More precise than nominal scale Used for ranking No assumptions of measurable and equal distance between the categories (ordinal data can measure the order but not the degree of separation between the categories)	Likert scales ranging from *strongly disagree* to *strongly agree* Arranging response options from most preferred to least preferred Arranging response options from most important to least important Arranging response options from high to low
Interval	Can also be used to rank-order Distance between the categories is known (the degree of separation, or distance, between two consecutive points is the same no matter where in the scale, for example, the distance between 2 and 3 is the same as 17 and 18) No absolute 0 point (a value of 0 does not imply the absolute absence of something)	Test scores Temperature in Celsius or Fahrenheit
Ratio	Includes characteristics of the previous level Has an absolute 0 point	Money Distance Weight Temperature in Kelvin

Source: Kaufman, Guerra, and Platt (2006).

DEFINING REQUIRED DATA FROM PERFORMANCE OBJECTIVES

A fundamental source for deriving useful evaluation questions is a list of performance objectives. These objectives should have been the product of a needs assessment process in which each need identified and selected for reduction was clearly stated as a performance objective. Performance objectives should include who or what entity is to be responsible for the accomplishment, the accomplishment to be observed, what measurable criteria would be used to determine whether the result was accomplished satisfactorily, and the conditions under which this result would be acceptable (Mager, 1997). These objectives simply state where you are headed and how to tell when you have arrived.

Some evaluators, such as Mohr (1992), limit the focus of their studies to the impact analysis of just one result per program. In his words, Mohr does not consider the "worthwhileness" of the program in order to concentrate on the logical relationship between the program and the selected outcome. What some perceive as improved precision in describing relationships, others see as avoiding the central issue. The emphasis of this book, for example, argues that the prime criterion for evaluation is whether the program fulfills valid needs (as opposed to "wants"). In Mohr's approach, the desire for precision (and avoidance of political considerations) narrows the methodology and the focus of the evaluation study. Other evaluators, such as Stake (2004), cast a wider net, adopting methodologies that allow the inclusion of controversy, politics, fairness to multiple stakeholders, and side effects.

Programs and their objectives exist in both hierarchies and networks. That is, in an organization, and indeed in society, everything is related to everything else. Thus, when we evaluate to determine whether a given solution or group of solutions has met its intended objectives, we should look not only at the direct objectives but also the ultimate objective (and any and all in between) to which it is supposed to contribute. One useful framework is Kaufman's levels of results (2000, 2006a, 2006b): societal impact, best expressed through an ideal vision; organizational accomplishments, as expressed through organizational missions; and internal deliverables, usually expressed as operational goals or objectives. At this last level, most performance solutions or interventions have more obvious and immediate influence. In addition, this last level can be subdivided into supporting results. For example, an operational objective may be related to a department, and that department in turn may have clusters

TABLE 10.2. Data Collection Plan Flow

Organizational Elements Model Level	Required Results	Evaluation			
		Evaluation Questions	Indicator(s) or Required Data	Data Source	Data Collection Tools and Procedures
External or societal impact					
Organizational accomplishments					
Internal deliverables and products					

of team or individual performance objectives on which it depends to reach that operational objective.

The ultimate value test of these solutions is whether they contributed to the higher-order results: the organizational mission and ideal vision. Thus, in order to make a complete and accurate interpretation of the effectiveness of the solution, relevant data that indicate the results at all three levels must be collected.

Table 10.2 illustrates how these three levels of results can be used to create a data collection plan. The relationship of the columns will be elaborated throughout the rest of this book.

As an example of how the table should be used, let us say that the required result or performance objective is, "By the end of year X, the new employee selection program will decrease undesired employee turnover by at least 15 percent and increase employee performance in its respective functions by at least 12 percent, as indicated by the Annual Report on Organizational and Employee Performance." Thus, the evaluation question should be driven primarily by the objective "Did the new selection and recruitment program increase the performance of affected job functions by at least 12 percent and decrease undesired turnover rate by at least 15 percent, by at least the end of the 20XX fiscal year, as indicated by the annual report on organizational and employee performance?"

It is important that an appropriate amount of time have passed to allow the program to have noticeable impact. To determine that time period and quantify notable impact, the evaluator should consult the initial needs assessment report and refer to the objectives set at that time. Recall that an objective in its most useful format will tell exactly what result is to be achieved, when it will be achieved, under what conditions it will be achieved, and what criteria will be used to determine if it was satisfactorily achieved. Those objectives then become the basis for the core evaluation questions.

DERIVING MEASURABLE INDICATORS

Indicators are observable and measurable occurrences that reveal something about the programs being evaluated and thus form a critical part of data collection. It is imperative that indicators bear a constant relationship to the thing being indicated. For example, a consultancy firm may have data suggesting for every $X spent in advertising, visits to the company Web site increased by Y. These data must be reliable and valid, just as tests must be reliable and valid. Matching the evaluation indicators to ones that were developed by a disciplined needs assessment using a systemic framework is ideal. However, even if this type of needs assessment was not performed, the appropriate indicators can be systematically identified during the evaluation.

Many performance indicator frameworks have been proposed. Examples are Kaplan and Norton's balanced scorecard (1992); Lynch and Cross's performance pyramid (1991); the results and determinants framework proposed by Fitzgerald, Johnston, Brignall, Silvestro, and Voss (1991); and Neely, Adams, and Kennerley's performance prism (2002). These can guide the identification and tracking of key performance indicators in the long term; however, as with most other tools, they have to be customized to fit the requirements of the situation. It is unlikely that any one framework will meet all requirements.

If there is no particular framework that can best identify a collection of key performance indicators, the evaluator can select the specific set of indicators relevant to the evaluand. Maskell (1992) proposes that performance indicators must relate specifically to strategic objectives, must reflect the understanding that these measures will vary from organization to organization, and will change over time.

The list that follows sets out some commonly used financial indicators (Niven, 2002, p. 119). Notice that these indicators do not include value added to or subtracted from our shared society and should be understood in that context:

Total assets	Dividends
Total assets per employee	Market value
Profits as a percentage of assets	Share price
Return on net assets	Shareholder mix
Return on total assets	Shareholder loyalty
Gross margin	Cash flow
Net income	Total costs
Profit as a percentage of sales	Credit rating
Profit per employee	Debt
Revenue	Debt to equity
Revenue from new products	Times interest earned
Revenue per employee	Day's sales in receivables
Return on equity	Accounts receivable turnover
Return on capital employed	Days in payables
Return on investment	Days in inventory

Economic value added

Market value added

Compound growth rate

Inventory turnover ratio

Value added per employee

Although all of these are all financial indicators, specific indicators will be relevant to some financial goals but not others (for example, growth, profit, value, and risk management).

Table 10.3 offers other indicators, grouped according to common general categories.

TABLE 10.3. **Commonly Used Indicators Grouped by General Categories**

Category	Indicator
Time	On-time delivery receipt
	Order cycle time
	Order cycle time variability
	Response time
	Forecasting or planning cycle time
	Planning cycle time variability
Cost	Finished goods inventory turns
	Day's sales outstanding
	Cost to serve
	Cash to cash cycle time
	Total delivered cost
	Cost of goods
	Transportation costs
	Inventory carrying costs
	Material handling costs
	Administrative
	Other

(Continued)

Category	Indicator
	Cost of excess capacity
	Cost of capacity shortfall
	Returns restocked
	Cost of complaint satisfaction
	Costs of lawsuits
	Costs of filed grievances
Quality	Overall customer satisfaction
	Processing accuracy
	Perfect order fulfillment
	In-time delivery
	Complete order
	Accurate product selection
	Damage free
	Accurate invoice
	Forecast accuracy
	Planning accuracy
	Schedule adherence
	Profit and profit over time
	Meeting of corporate social responsibility requirements
	Safety

Source: Adapted from Niven (2002).

Table 10.4 illustrates a broader range of examples and the relationship between expected results and the measurable indicators required to evaluate the results.

As you move toward the column on the right, you can see how the precision with which the organization defines the results to be pursued increases, and thus, the precision or the efforts (including the strategically driven allocation of limited resources) to achieve them increases. Furthermore, the precision with which we can measure whether the results have been achieved increases. This kind of rigor, articulation, and linkages provides strategic alignment.

TABLE 10.4. Example of Linkages Between Results and Required Data

Organizational Elements Model Level	Required Results	Indicator or Required Data
External, societal impact	Increased quality of life of customers	Disabling accidents caused by our product
		Deaths attributed to our product
		Public image
	Contribute to the health of the served communities	Toxic pollution reports (compliance certification or violations)
		Economic contribution to community
Organizational accomplishments	Increased profit[a]	Money collected
		Money paid out
		Total assets
	Increased customer satisfaction[a]	Customer satisfaction scores
		Customer loyalty
		Customer complaints
		Average duration of active accounts
		Number of products sold per account
		Accounts retained
		Accounts closed

(Continued)

Organizational Elements Model Level	Required Results	Indicator or Required Data
	Employee satisfaction[a]	Referrals
		Return rates
		Number of customers
		Employee satisfaction scores
		Filed grievances
		Documented complaints
		Performance levels
		Turnover rates
		Absenteeism
		Promotions
		Employee suggestions
		Average years of service
		Lost time accidents
		Diversity rates
		Employee productivity
Internal deliverables	Increased sales[b]	Items sold (service or product)
		New accounts generated
		Inventory turnover

	Sales volume
	Sales per channel
	Frequency (number of sales transactions)
Increased quality production	Production rate
	Error rate
	Efficiency
	Rework
	Rejects
	Equipment downtime
	Repair time
	Work backlog

[a]When tracked as continuous (for example, continuous profits, continued customer satisfaction, and the like), these can be considered at the mega-, or external impact, level. The rationale is that if good levels of these factors are sustained or continuously improving, then the organization is continuously focusing on external needs and requirements.

[b]Sales figures are another interesting type of result, in that we may view them as either a macro-, or organizational level, result, or a micro-, or internal, result, depending on how the organization classifies its hierarchy of results. Regardless of the level, the key idea here is that of hierarchy: what results support sales, and to what results sales contribute. What is most important is clearly depicting the relationship between the various levels of results. For instance, production contributes to sales, which contributes to profits. When this relationship is correlated over a continuous period, it may indicate that the organization is having a positive external impact.

Since these indicators will become the basis for the data collection plan, making such linkages is at the core of evaluation. The evaluation's view of reality (for example, what is actually going on with the company's programs internally and externally) will be framed by these indicators (which in turn were framed by the initial evaluation questions). Therefore, it is critical that they are in fact fair and complete indicators of the results sought.

The following case study is an example of public sector work that prepares people for survival in our shared society (Guerra, 2005):

Case Study: Vocational Rehabilitation

The Division of Blind Services (DBS) is a state agency dedicated to providing a three main programs: the Vocational Rehabilitation Program, the Independent Living Adult Program, and the Children and Families Program. Linking the results and efforts of all three programs could have potentially strengthened all three programs and better serviced the community; the scope of the project, however, was to be limited to the Vocational Rehabilitation Program.

One of the first challenges of working with this program was moving from providing services as the reason for being to a focus on ultimate results that the clients greatly required and expected. In this case, the results at the external or societal impact level were societal self-sufficiency, self-reliance, and positive quality of life of current and potential clients. Along with the challenge, there was also great fortune: The two Vocational Rehabilitation Program key decision makers and contacts for this project had the vision and integrity to recognize that the old ways of seeing and doing would simply produce more of the same, with no demonstrable value added, and so consensus was established for revising the current mission.

Results

The shift in focus was manifested by abandoning the old mission, which focused on activities and resources: "We will advocate, build, implement, integrate services, and deploy the resources necessary to achieve our vision. Our mission will be achieved through responsiveness, quality in all areas, and attention to our customers in need of independent living and employment outcomes. We will never compromise on quality in anything we do." The new focus was on results at three key levels:

Societal: All DBS clients will be self-sufficient, self-reliant, and enjoy a good quality of life.

Organizational: All DBS clients will be continuously employed.

Internal: All DBS clients will attain their integrated plan of employment objectives (IPE).

Indicators

With the key organizational results defined, the next task was to identify indicators that could be used to measure these results. To get an accurate representation of each result, a content review of various national and state quality reports, DBS and Vocational Rehabilitation internal reports and documents, the procedures manual, policies, and regulations was conducted, in addition to focused discussions with stakeholders. The result was the following measurement framework, which consists of a list of measurable indicators, categorized by their associated results:

RESULTS LEVEL	RESULT	SOME INDICATORS
Societal	Self-sufficiency	Government transfer payments
	Self-reliance	Private disability payment, worker's compensation, insurance com-pensation
	Quality of life (QOL)	Institutionalization where the participants are consumption $\leq$ production (sheltered workshops, mental hospitals, drug abuse treatment centers, and so on)
	Continued employment at consumption less than production level	Income (itemized benefits plus expenses) over time
		Employment catchment area cost of living or higher
		Annual earnings rate greater than that of the general population

(Continued)

RESULTS LEVEL	RESULT	SOME INDICATORS
Organizational	Successful competitive employment	Employed a minimum of ninety days full time or part time (based on integrated plan of employment objectives), integrated work setting
		Benefits (health, vision, dental, life, disability, other) for visually impaired are the same as those for nonvisually impaired
		Job skills, knowledge, attitudes, and abilities (SKAAs) requirement and client SKAAs matched
		Employee satisfaction with employment at 5 or higher on seven-point Likert scale survey
		Employer satisfaction with employee at 5 or higher on seven-point Likert scale survey
	Successful self-employ-ment or integration into homemaker role	Setting certified as fulfilling requirements of IPE by rehabilitation counselor
		Client satisfaction with situation at 5 or higher on seven-point Likert scale survey
Internal	Attainment of IPE objective	SKAAs attained
		Activities of daily living training completed
		Vocational training completed
		Postsecondary education completed
		On-the-job integrated training completed
		Social preparation for integration setting completed

RESULTS LEVEL	RESULT	SOME INDICATORS
		Socialization completed
		Socialization training completed
		Recreational training completed
		Management of medical treatments
		Job placement obtained

A Glance at Evaluation Findings

In a nutshell, the 2,546 client cases tracked yielded the following information:

Societal: Clients' self-sufficiency, inferred by those earning at or above the state average for that year: 106 individuals out of the 2,546 were found to be earning at or above the state average; 2,400 of the clients did not attain this level of outcome.

Organizational: Employment, inferred by reported wages at any level: 1,031 individuals out of the 2,546 included in the study reported wages

Internal: Attainment of IPE objectives, inferred through successful closure of case: 1,565 successfully closed cases

Notice that the narrower our definition of success is, the better the results seem. Conversely, the wider our view is, the more realistically we can see the value of the solutions, programs, activities, and so forth.

Although the list of indicators should be complete, data may not be available for every one of them. This in itself is important information. It is very difficult to determine whether something is being achieved, done, or used if there are no data on which to base such determinations. And without relevant data, how can sound decisions be made about what to keep, what to modify, or what to abandon? Thus, the ideal list of indicators can also help make decisions about what additional data should be tracked from that point forward, and how. Just tracking key data alone can be a powerful tool for improvement by increasing awareness, promoting accountability, increasing motivation, and facilitating just-in-time feedback,

The more specific performance objectives, and thus specific evaluation questions from which they derive, will come directly from indicators.

For example, did we increase the number of program participants whose income is equal to or greater than the general population? Did we decrease the number of program participants requiring government transfer payments? Questions such as these flow directly from the objectives and their rigorous performance criteria.

Of course, there is still work to do between identifying the right indicators and data and actually collecting these. We must identify the data sources. It does little good to identify which data should be collected if we do not also find out where to collect them. (We also need to find out if these data are already being collected, an important finding in and of itself.) The evaluation team members, which include a representative group of stakeholders, should together be able to provide excellent leads as to where these data might be found.

FINDING DATA SOURCES

Another important issue to consider before collecting data is determining where to find them. Data can be gathered from a variety of financial, social, political, and technological sources. Today our access to data is unprecedented. The Internet and advances in telecommunications and other technologies allow us to link to reports, documents, databases, experts, and other sources not previously possible.

For example, social indicators such as those related to quality of life (average income levels, divorce rates, crime levels, and the like) can often be found in chamber of commerce archives, census reports, police records, and community quality-of-life reports, and many of these are available electronically. Others, such as those related to the environment (pollution and corporate toxic waste, to name a couple), can also be obtained from the Environmental Protection Agency, as well as from studies published in scientific journals. A number of other national and international government agencies and research institutions publish a series of official studies and reports that could prove to be valuable sources of data.

In many cases, you can find the data that you are looking for within the organization itself. Existing records about past and current performance may be available, but collected by different parties in the organization and for different reasons. Be sure to search thoroughly for these potential sources, because having them available could save valuable time, money, and other resources. Here are some specific examples and descriptions of useful sources (Niven, 2002):

- *Strategic plan.* This is the guiding source of information for many data collection initiatives. If done correctly, it should have statements of the vision, mission, values, and other key functions and objectives that were derived from a valid needs assessment process. It often provides the rationale for solutions previously selected.

- *Annual reports.* These provide a wealth of information, both financial and nonfinancial. They may also discuss market position, key products, and opportunities for the future.

- *Project plans.* Successful projects should be aligned to the strategic plan. If they are not, this is an important clue about the worth of a given project (and perhaps an indication to review the vision or mission statement).

- *Consulting studies.* Sometimes individual departments contract consulting services without necessarily sharing the fact, or the results of the study, with other departments. Consultants can gather priceless information regarding baselines, background issues, state of the industry, and other important pieces of information. Sometimes this information is left behind with the organization, and sometimes the consultant must be contacted to determine what information is available.

- *Performance reports.* Particularly if there is a performance management system in place, periodic reports of individual, team, department, and organizational performance can be a good place to find initial indicators.

- *Financial analysis reports.* If the organization is publicly traded, these reports provide a good sense of how the market values the organization.

- *Newspapers and journals.* If you are particularly interested in evaluating the impact of an intervention on public opinion, finding out what the press is saying about the organization is a good place to start.

- *Competitor data.* Looking at what a competitor is doing is not a good place to come up with novel ideas, but it certainly can provide good lessons of what not to do. It can also provide preliminary input for original ideas.

Table 10.5 illustrates an excellent list of specific sources according to general data category. People-centered sources also apply and may include clients, executives, employees, managers, participants, students, administrators, instructors, vendors, and experts on a given issue.

TABLE 10.5. Data Sources

Data Category	Specific Sources
Financial	Annual report
	Performance report
	Analyst report
	Trade journals
	Benchmark reports
Customer	Marketing records and department in general
	Trade journals
	Consulting studies
	Project plans
	Strategic plan
	Performance reports
	Benchmark reports
Planning	Strategic plan
	Vision
	Mission
	Organizational history
	Consulting studies
	Project plans
Processes and inputs	Operational reports
	Production reports
	Manufacturing reports
	Competitor data
	Benchmark reports
	Trade journals
	Consulting studies
	Project plans

Employee development	Performance reports
	Human resources data
	Consulting studies
	Training

Source: Niven (2002).

One key consideration in obtaining access to data is confidentiality. If you are denied access altogether, you may be able to get this decision revised because it is not generally important to collect individually identifying data. Most of the time, aggregate data, such as averages and totals, should be sufficient. Because data in this form can present less of a threat to others, they are therefore easier to gather.

FOLLOW-UP QUESTIONS AND DATA

Additional evaluation questions may arise as a result of the preliminary findings of the evaluation. For example, if preliminary findings reveal that a particular result is not being achieved, the obvious related question is, Why not? Thus, specific follow-up questions that get at the causes for not reaching targets will likely have to be derived and answered before the data findings are fully interpreted.

Certainly this and other types of relevant questions could have been asked from the beginning and in fact could be grouped around clusters of questions relating to one particular result. The benefit of doing this is that it would have been included in the initial scope and project plan and thus be already built in tasks and timelines. Here is an example of such a cluster.

Central Question Cluster

Did the new selection and recruitment program increase the performance of affected job functions by at least 12 percent and decrease turnover rate by at least 15 percent by at least the end of the 20XX fiscal year, as indicated by the annual report on organizational and employee performance?

(Continued)

INITIAL FOLLOW-UP

- If the performance did increase, did it contribute positively to the organizational bottom line (financial and societal)?

- If the performance did increase, did it contribute positively to the attainment of the organizational mission and vision?

- How did this selection and recruitment program affect other job functions?

- Have the benefits of the new selection and recruitment outweighed costs? Will this change or continue in the future?

- If turnover decreased, can we confidently attribute it to the new selection and recruitment program?

- What other implemented solutions, events, or any other factors have had an effect on our target results?

- How have the various solutions, events, programs, and other known factors interacted to achieve the observed results?

FOLLOW-UP QUESTIONS IDENTIFIED AFTER INITIAL FINDINGS

- Why did this solution not result in expected results?

- What were or are the obstacles to its success?

- What were or are the factors that have supported the solution?

- What, if anything, could be modified so that this solution is successful from now on?

- Were there other benefits that the solution did bring about?

- What specifically went wrong? Design? Development? Implementation?

- Were people using the solution at all? If not, why not?

- Were people using the solution correctly? If not, why not?

The questions illustrate the range of issues associated with general evaluation questions. Some follow-up questions will be logically identified from the beginning, and others will not be considered until initial findings reveal them.

The process for answering these is virtually the same as the initial questions: identify the relevant, reliable, and valid indicators that will help you answer them. The next chapter discusses how to go about collecting these data.

KEY POINTS

- Data are documented records of something of interest to the evaluation.

- For data to be useful, they must be relevant, reliable, and valid.

- Hard and soft data are different, and both can be useful. The same is true of collecting methods for qualitative and quantitative data.

- Data can be measured on nominal, ordinal, interval, or ratio scales. These scales of measurement have significant impact on how the data are analyzed later and the soundness of the conclusions drawn.

- The data collected are based on true measurable indicators of the results of interest for the evaluation study.

- The quality of collected data and their relevance to the evaluation questions will have an important effect on the quality of the evaluation.

REFLECTION QUESTIONS

1. Why is it important to consider the scale used to measure data? What implications does the scale of measurement have on an evaluation study?

2. What is the relationship of results, indicators, and data?

3. Where do we find data? What are some of the issues that must be considered in finding the appropriate data sources?

DATA COLLECTION

This chapter provides a wide-ranging review of data collection methods. It emphasizes the importance of choosing an appropriate method, analyzes the role of the observer, and surveys a variety of person-centered and instrument-centered approaches. It then reviews the role of classic and variant experimental designs in evaluation and discusses the evaluator's use of existing data and literature searches.

Just as the interpretations and recommendations that the evaluator makes depend on the range of the data collected, so too the data collected are a function of the data collection tools used. Unfortunately evaluators often limit the data they collect by employing a narrow set of observation methods with which they are comfortable, sometimes without even considering other viable alternatives. The methods used for data collection must be selected after the data required to answer the evaluation questions have been identified and the appropriateness of various methods for collecting those data have been considered. It adds no value to spend resources collecting irrelevant or meaningless data simply because you know how to use the method that accomplishes this end. In fact, as

Ackoff (2000) succinctly states, "The overabundance of irrelevant information is a bigger problem than the shortage of relevant information, because it requires more time to filter through the mass of information that's available to find out what's relevant (*Technos: Quarterly for Education and Technology,* 2000). All methods you select should be focused on answering the right question of whether the evaluand accomplished that which you set out to accomplish.

Practically, there is no way to gather all possible data that are generated in the organizational setting, but of course you are not required to do so in order to conduct a rigorous evaluation. Remember that the only data you have to target are those that will provide answers to the evaluation questions. Following the process described in this book will reduce the chance of missing relevant data, as well as the chance of collecting data that will not help make better decisions and improve performance. Well-chosen data collection tools and methods will yield the required data relevant to answering the evaluation question set. It is an error to pick the tools first and then be limited by the data that tool will generate. Yet I often hear novice evaluators, managers, employees charged with collecting information, and others stating that they plan to conduct a survey, focus groups, or other data collection method without considering the questions they want answers to and the data required to answer them. This approach is a wild goose chase.

This chapter provides an overview of the options for data collection and reviews the advantages and disadvantages of each. This information will serve you well as you consider each option in the context of your own evaluation project. However, in addition to these inherent advantages and disadvantages, you should also consider factors such as the characteristics of your sample, time, cost and budget, comprehensiveness, experience with a given instrument, and feasibility, among others.

Here too the success of the data collection stage depends in great part on the support or sponsorship of key stakeholders. Keep them involved, and you will likely avoid unnecessary obstacles.

OBSERVATION METHODOLOGY AND THE PURPOSE OF MEASUREMENT

All methods can include some form of measurement, and measurement should be included as often as possible in data collection. Measurement is not an automatic feature of observation. Let me clear up some common confusions with these rules:

- Every observation can be reduced to measurement.

- Rigorous measurement makes comparison more precise and meaningful.

- Not all measurements are appropriate; what you are measuring (and why) is primary.

- Pay attention to measurement scales.

The first focus of an evaluation is data relating to results. The second focus is data gathered on the process activity—how things are going— even though these data are gathered before results data are available. Process data will support analysis and decision making in the event the results are not what was intended in order for the organization to meet the needs—gaps in results—identified during planning. A third category of data may be gathered on factors and issues that intervene to support or detract from the process activity. Side effects such as bad weather, sudden budget supplements, equipment breakdown, and other disruptions fall into this category. These environmental data will also be used in the analysis of the results and decision making to modify, keep, or discard the program being evaluated: What do you keep, and what do you change?

Person-Centered Direct Observation Methods

Tom Peters popularized a technique called *management by walking around* (Peters & Waterman, 1982): The manager stays on top of the operation by directly observing workers to find out what is taking place, asking questions, listening, and maybe even working alongside them. You may want to include "evaluation by walking around" in your inventory of methods, to be used when the types of events or tasks of interest are directly observable.

Observation as a method for gathering data can be broadly defined. Adler and Adler (1994, p. 378) describe observation as "gathering impressions of the surrounding world through all relevant human faculties." The practical extension of this definition recognizes that in many cases, the evaluator can be an effective data collection vehicle who can take in the total environment and respond to any event contingency with a minimum of prior expectation and no data collection instrument that automatically limits observation potential. The mind-set created by preset expectations can be problematic if it prevents you from detecting other aspects of the performance setting that contribute to or detract from performance.

Scriven (1973) coined the term *goal-free evaluation* to prevent the sometimes narrow objectives-only focus of evaluation. Of course, it is important that evaluators look at the objectives and the results, but at the same time they should not forgo collecting the types of data that can arise unexpectedly, especially where the unplanned data are relevant to the reasons that objectives were or were not obtained. Direct observation provides the evaluator with firsthand knowledge of what is going on and can be flexible and responsive to the situation. Unexpected events can be noted. Subsequent observation opportunities can be focused based on developing trends and issues. However, these advantages are counterbalanced by some limitations.

Direct observation has a few variations. One is to participate in activities and get to know what is going on from the participant's point of view. Social scientists call this approach "participant observation." It has some good points and some drawbacks. Participants tend to identify with the personnel who can lead to insider information, but at the same time, the participant observer may be co-opted by the group, which can bias observations. Nonparticipant observation can also have some risks, because the mere presence of an outsider (especially an evaluator) can change the conditions in the observation setting. A stranger who walks up and down the hall unannounced and stands at the back of the room will no doubt make employees uneasy and suspicious. Remember that most people view evaluation with worry, and if you add to that worry rather than minimize it, conducting the evaluation will be a difficult task and the fear itself will bias the evaluation results.

Direct observation options are valuable and can be nearly free of fear if a little common courtesy is afforded those who are under the looking glass. Start by arranging to make visits ahead of time, and visit often to ease the tension and gain the trust of those involved.

Obtrusive versus Unobtrusive Observations can be obtrusive—individuals being observed are aware they are being observed—or unobtrusive—individuals being observed are not aware they are being observed. The key to obtrusive observation is to have a well-defined purpose for observation. After a while, most people get used to the possibility of being observed, and any potential effects over the behavior become submerged in their routines. If observers take the time to inform all affected parties and then consistently observe often, the intrusive nature of the observation visit is reduced over time. In unobtrusive observation, there is no real concern that the behavior of those individuals being observed will be affected by the observers. The most important consideration is of an ethical nature, particularly where issues of invasion of privacy and informed consent are concerned. If there is not significant benefit to choosing this approach, it is difficult to justify its use, in which case using an obtrusive observation approach is recommended.

Structured versus Nonstructured After several observation visits, you may want to narrow the focus to look for specific behavior. You can use observation rubrics, such as a behavior checklist, which can aid in recording and measuring specific predetermined behaviors. These can be designed to record whether the behaviors occurred at all as a rating scale or as a frequency count, depending on what is appropriate for the behaviors being observed. While observations certainly may be conducted without highly structured observation guides that specify beforehand what indicators to look for, the increase in precision and accuracy that results from a structured approach tends to make up for the structure's imposed limits in range. This of course presupposes that the targeted information is justified by its relevance to an evaluation question. This approach is particularly useful in the presence of multiple observers. Inter-rater reliability can be increased if all raters are using the same criteria for observation.

Controls on Observation Two serious problems can arise from direct unstructured observation: (1) the observations can be tainted by observer bias, and (2) the observer can incorrectly classify instances of behavior that are called out on structured checklists.

The problem of observer bias is controlled by making sure that the observers on the evaluation team have regular discussion about their observations with the purpose of standardizing interpretations of observed behaviors and events. This in turn will lead to reduced observer bias. These types of bias are obstacles to a high-quality evaluation study. However we all have many hidden, perhaps unconscious, biases that will color our observations. That can be controlled by using more than one observer and cross-checking findings. Periodic discussions of observation findings can clarify emerging issues, weed out irrelevant data, and bring issues into clear focus.

Leading such discussions takes skill and patience. Not every evaluation leader can perform this function. We are all cautioned to keep a healthy skepticism alive as we accept observation data into evaluations.

The second problem is controlled by carefully examining the checklist and limiting the categories of behavior to observable behavioral acts rather than more powerful but less classifiable constructs of behavior. For example, when observing a work group attempting to apply creativity and ingenuity tools, observers may differ on what they think is creative behavior and who is unfocused. These labels or classifications are laden with what philosophers call "surplus meaning." Recorded instances using these constructs may prove to be unreliable across observers. Observers can relatively easily use a behavioral frequency count, where they note specific behavior such as frequency of proposing an idea, frequency of the use of different tools or props to arrive at a solution to a problem, and frequency of ideas that have resulted in implemented solutions. Note that the operational definitions used in this manner must be proven over time to add up to the construct in question.

Participant Observation Participant observation is a method of data gathering used in the field of sociology mainly for observation, discovery, and description. Increasingly evaluators are using it to gain insight into groups and organizations in their natural settings. When program evaluators sense that something is going on inside a program that is not immediately apparent to an outsider, they may try this method to find out what is really going on.

In this approach, an observer who can function as a member of a group works alongside other members to perform tasks and engage in normal communication with group members. The observer then reports insights, problems, and event descriptions to the evaluation team. As a strength of this approach, the observer may find out important behind-the-scenes information and uncover practices that are hidden from outsiders. In addition, the observer may gain the trust of other members and learn their points of view. Or the observer may be rejected or co-opted by the group, in either case probably losing a sense of balance and interfering with her or his ability to provide objective reporting. Another potential drawback is that the method takes a considerable investment in time and resources.

As a measurement consideration, the observer may find events and behavior that can be counted and construct tables and matrices comparing productivity, resource use, and other interactions between members and members and outsiders.

When to Use Participant Observation Executives, managers, and employees are all participants in organizational processes. As they engage in functions and tasks aimed at achieving specific goals and objectives, they can be interviewed to obtain information about performance, reactions, methods, procedures, and the work environment in general. Although valuable, this information is volunteered by the persons being interviewed. They are simply responding to questions; the evaluator provides purpose and structure to the questions asked. If the evaluator has a blind spot, he or she may miss something.

A participant observer who is aware of his or her role can obtain data on events as they unfold. This often include surprises and unforeseen circumstances that would not be included in the question set of an outsider. Effective participant observation requires considerable skill. Although the observer remains open to events, some sense of what is important and what is trivial must govern the observation process. Not everyone can maintain that sense of awareness and yet blend convincingly into the group. The use of a participant observer should be reserved for occasions when the evaluation team has a member who can fill the role successfully, meeting the criteria of group membership while maintaining the frame of mind of the disciplined observer.

Acceptance by the Group The participant observer must be able to fit into the group. He or she will not be able to function effectively without acceptance by the coworkers in the group. Age range, general background, skill, and knowledge must be compatible with the other members of the group.

The Effects of Participation Will the participant observer change the behavior of the group? Suppose a group effort was failing to complete a task, and the participant observer joins the group and provides leadership, insight, skill, and knowledge that the group did not have before his or her arrival. What can be said of the observations that will result from such a case? This may depend greatly on the goals and purpose of the group. Organizations and groups, especially in school settings, are created specifically to obtain desired ends. When the organizational solutions are not working, evaluators want to know why and what changes can fix the problem. If the introduction of leadership, new knowledge, and skills does provide a change in status, the evaluator will want to know the particulars and if the change can be maintained. In this example, we want to know whether the personal leadership effects can be separated from the knowledge and skills that brought about change.

The evaluation team leader must tease out the threads of cause and effect. This may often require the addition of more observers and a period of continued observation.

Person-Centered Indirect Observation Techniques

Not all information is directly observable. When that is the case, we rely on others' accounts of such information. This section examines data collection tools that draw primarily on opinions, attitudes, and perceptions. These can be useful in organizations such as service-oriented businesses with quality concerns affected by intrinsic performance inhibitors. For example, in a marketing company whose quality assurance department consistently releases ad copy to clients with grammatical errors, direct observation of quality assurance staff reading ad copy would not illuminate the underlying problem.

Focus Groups Conducting focus groups is a powerful and popular way to collect data. In this process, one or more evaluators interact face-to-face with a group of anywhere from six to twelve people to collect their thoughts on a given topic over a two- to four-hour period. Like questionnaires, focus groups tend to be used to collect qualitative data, and the key questions addressed by the group should be based on previously identified indicators. The purpose here is not necessarily to have everyone agree on a response, but rather to learn from a variety of perspectives on the issue. Focus groups are particularly useful when detailed descriptions and explanations are required.

One advantage that this process has over questionnaires is the ability of the evaluator or facilitator to see the participants' facial expressions and body language. This can be useful information in itself and can help uncover underlying key issues. This observation can also lead to important spontaneous follow-up questions, which is not possible when using a questionnaire. In addition, interaction among the participants can stimulate them to reflect on, clarify, and support their perspectives.

Another advantage of using focus groups is the potential meta-message this approach sends to participants with regard to the importance of the data collection effort and their role. Participating in a focus group feels like a more selective process than being asked to participate in a mailed or online questionnaire, and thus, an individual can perceive that his or her input is valuable. One drawback of focus groups is that anonymity cannot be guaranteed on the same level as it can with questionnaires.

Still, measures can be taken to assure participants that what they say will not be linked to any one individual when findings are reported.

Another relative disadvantage of the focus group as compared to the questionnaire is that the focus group is not as efficient in reaching a wide range of participants in terms of time, effort, and cost. This is particularly true when respondents are dispersed across a wide geographical area. However, if the target population is relatively small or manageable and is geographically centralized, focus groups can be efficient and inexpensive.

Process When planning focus groups, careful attention should be given to making each group homogeneous with regard to characteristics relevant to the types of data being sought. For instance, if the goal is to determine the perceived value added by a given program, this information should be collected from a variety of stakeholders—employees, managers, clients, and vendors, for example. Any given focus group should consist of only one type of stakeholder. That is, it should be homogeneous and representative of that particular type of stakeholder. In this case, the stakeholders' role with regard to the program in question will likely have an impact on their perception.

The Sample The sample of clients selected to participate in the focus groups should be representative of the population of clients in the same way that the sample of employees should be representative of the population of employees. For example, participation in a focus group should not be a reward exclusive to veteran postal carriers if new carriers are shareholders too.

Although focus group sessions can be loosely structured, a protocol should still be developed in advance to give the facilitator some organizing framework for conducting the process and arranging the data gathered. The basic elements of a protocol should include an introduction that thanks the participants for taking the time to be there and provides them with a brief background on and purpose for conducting the focus group. The protocol should also include a basic overview of the agenda and process (for example, participant introductions, dynamics of the discussion, and breaks). Once this basic context is established, the protocol should provide the key questions and other items that will be covered during the focus groups. Finally, it should contain general concluding remarks or points, including thanks for participants' cooperation, with which the facilitator can close the session. This protocol should be used as a general guide for the facilitator rather than a strict agenda to be read aloud to the participants.

When conducting the focus group, the facilitator should demonstrate as little bias as possible for or against any particular point of view, while creating a supportive environment in which participants feel comfortable sharing their ideas. The facilitator should listen carefully and talk mainly when it is required in order to keep the discussion going or when it is important to clarify or summarize an idea. Keeping a discussion going means more than just asking additional questions when the conversation seems to lag; it can also mean, among other things, bringing the participants back to the subject at hand when the conversation derails to irrelevant topics.

Participants' tone of voice, facial expressions, and body posture can be revealing. The facilitator should remain observant and attempt to detect key emotions behind comments. These can reveal underlying issues that can become important data.

It is also important that the facilitator recognize underlying themes. While qualitative data analysis techniques can be used to detect patterns once the data are collected, it is also useful for the facilitator to be cognizant of such themes during the focus group, as it allows him or her to ask important follow-up questions.

Soon after concluding the focus group process, it is critical for the facilitator to review and further record the data collected. The data should be arranged according to the items and sequence included in the protocol. If unplanned but important issues arose, they should be arranged in relation to the items that triggered them. If the official information recorder is someone other than the facilitator, it is important that the two compare notes and reconcile any inconsistencies.

Just as it would usually be inappropriate to generalize the findings of one questionnaire to an entire population, it is generally not justifiable to use the findings of one focus group to explain an entire population. If findings from additional—and comparable—focus groups are consistent, then generalizations may be more credible.

Nominal Group Technique The nominal group technique is a group process only in name, since input is recorded on an individual basis. Unlike focus groups, the nominal group technique is used for consensus building. As such, one of its advantages is that each individual has the opportunity to contribute. It is more structured than a focus group in that its main purpose is to identify and rank-order issues in order of importance for the participants.

The recommended group size is roughly the same as for focus groups, as are sampling issues and the elements of its protocol; however, the actual process differs. Here, the participants are asked to take a few minutes to brainstorm individually or think carefully about a specific question and write down their responses. After the participants have been given sufficient time, perhaps ten minutes, the facilitator asks each participant to share his or her first response. Each response is then recorded on flip chart paper. Once everyone in the group has provided a response, this process is repeated a second or third time until all participant responses have been recorded.

The facilitator of a nominal group once again plays an important role: he or she must make sure that the procedure is properly applied in order to generate reliable data. The facilitator may also ask for clarification of any responses before proceeding to request participants to put their ideas in rank order. During this period, duplications should be omitted. Each idea is then assigned a number or letter to identify it. The facilitator instructs participants to choose up to ten or twelve responses that they consider of most importance, and then rank them according to their relative importance. Rankings are collected from all participants and then aggregated. Table 11.1 provides an illustration of such ranking and record keeping.

Delphi Technique Like the other group techniques, the purpose of the Delphi technique is to elicit information and judgments from participants to facilitate problem solving, planning, and decision making. However, this technique does so without assembling the participants face-to-face. Rather, participant input is exchanged through regular mail, fax, or e-mail.

There are usually forty to sixty participants (or perhaps even more) who are experts or individuals considered to have significant knowledge about the issue at hand. The facilitator must obtain the commitment of the group to participate in a few questionnaires, spread out over some length of time.

The facilitator uses the information gathered from the questionnaires to develop the next iteration of the questionnaires. Respondents have an opportunity to examine the degree to which their responses are similar to or different from those of others in the group, thereby simulating the type of pressure for agreement experienced in other face-to-face groups. Additional questionnaires may be sent out until consensus has

TABLE 11.1. Example of Ranking and Record Keeping in Using a Nominal Group Technique

Response	Participant 1	Participant 2	Participant 3	Importance
A	Ranked first	Ranked second	Ranked second	Ranked first five times
B	Ranked third	Ranked first	Ranked third	Ranked third seven times
C	Ranked second	Ranked third	Ranked first	Ranked second six times
D	Ranked fourth	Ranked fourth	Ranked fourth	Ranked fourth twelve times

Source: Kaufman, Guerra, and Platt (2006).

been reached. The iterative nature of this process sets it apart from the other techniques.

The Delphi technique requires the facilitator to organize requests for information and information received and to be responsible for communicating with the participants. He or she also needs a reliable communication channel to link with each participant. It is common to use regular mail for this purpose; however, faxes and e-mail can decrease the time required. Even with the time other media can save the overall process, the facilitator still will have to do significant work.

Interview Methods Interviews are best suited for soft data. They allow analysts to gather information directly from all categories of clients and stakeholders. Interviewing requires a high degree of competence and commitment on the part of the analyst.

Interviews have some of the same advantages that focus groups have over questionnaires. They have a better participation rate, and they allow the interviewer to read facial expressions and body language, clarify responses, ask follow-up questions, and sense areas for further inquiry. One disadvantage is that neither of these methods reaches a large number of participants as efficiently as questionnaires do. The two kinds of methods can be successfully combined when appropriate. For example, interviews may be used as a follow-up to questionnaires when the latter reveal that further probing is required.

The protocol here also contains similar elements to those of focus groups: appreciation for the participants' willingness to cooperate, a brief overview of the evaluation project and purpose of the interview, key questions and other items to cover based on previously identified indicators, and general concluding remarks, once again thanking the participants.

Critical Incident Technique The critical incident technique, developed by Flanagan (1954) according to many accounts, is a tool used to collect people's reports, recollections, or examples of specific behaviors that were deemed critical to performing a task or reaching an accomplishment.

Borg and Gall (1989, p. 387) define this technique as a qualitative approach that employs the interview method to obtain "an in-depth analytical description of an intact cultural scene." Thus, this tool can be particularly useful in situations where understanding the culture in which performance and behavior occur is critical to the interpretation of data collected. For example, when a foreign-owned and -managed company locates a facility in a new country, the differences in culture will be exhibited through differences in behaviors related to management practices, communication processes, and professional relationships, to name a few dimensions. These will likely have an impact on performance at various levels.

It is worth noting that a critical incident does not consist of people's attitudes or opinions. Rather, it is based on accounts of specific behaviors or events observed by the person providing the account—whether about themselves or others.

The approach typically follows this structure:

1. Deriving plans for collecting factual incidents (for example, determining from whom the information is to be collected, establishing specific procedures for collection, and establishing protocols for collection)

2. Collecting critical incidents from qualified individuals

3. Identifying themes or trends from the data (critical incidents) collected

4. Sorting the incidents into meaningful categories

5. Interpreting and reporting and taking the context for applying this approach as a foundation

As with other data collection approaches involving people (and instruments, for that matter), there is room for varying interpretations and biases. When well implemented, this tool can be quite useful.

Instrument-Centered Methods

Using tests and other data collection instruments like questionnaires and surveys is perhaps the most common approach to collecting data. Using an instrument magnifies the ability to reach more information targets but at the same time limits the response possibilities to some extent. Open-ended items on questionnaires can expose some information that was unforeseen in the design of the data collection instrument, but they cannot do this to the same extent that an observer can in person. Nevertheless, the efficiency of using instruments like tests makes them an attractive option, especially true when the tests are well made. The structure of the test can ensure that all items of importance are covered; observers, in contrast, are subject to forgetfulness and inconsistency. Tests must of course be reliable and valid. Questionnaires must also be well structured and carefully worded to minimize ambiguity of meaning, for those responding to items and for later interpretation of the responses.

Choosing the Right Instrument More than likely, the evaluators will have identified a range of indicators, which may call for different kinds of data collection tools. The first consideration is the type of data each of the indicators represents and what type of data collection method would be appropriate. Answering an evaluation question may call for the collection of several indicators, and each of these indicators may represent a different type of data. For instance, if financial data must be collected, data reviews would certainly be more appropriate than an attitudinal questionnaire. Another indicator may call for program participants' attitudes about their experience, in which case, one or more of the person-centered data collection tools may be appropriate.

In addition, the source of the data or the target population may call for a particular type of tool. For instance, in an educational sector example, evaluators may want to collect attitudinal data from community members, faculty and staff, and institutional leaders. Because the community members are much more numerous and dispersed across a relatively large geographical area, a questionnaire can be used to obtain their thoughts. Because faculty and staff for the most part already work proximally to each other and are substantially fewer in number, they are easier to bring together in one location for interviews or focus group. Moreover, organizational leaders are much fewer in number, but arranging their schedules so that they can all meet at the same time in the same place could be quite a challenge; thus, individual interviews may be the most appropriate way to collect information from them.

Target population characteristics such as culture, language, education, experience, and gender, among others, are also essential to consider. Whether written questionnaires, group techniques, interviews, and tests are used, one must understand the impact of these characteristics when deriving questions and methods to collect data from individuals. One question can mean different things to different people based a multitude of factors. In some instances, those developing the data collection instruments can unconsciously overrely on their own experiences. For example, questions might include colloquialisms that are well known to one group of people and but baffling to other groups. Imagine disseminating a questionnaire that includes items such as "I *pull all-nighters* in preparation for important sales presentations" or "My manager gets *bent out of shape* when I don't *hit* my sales targets" to the sales force of a company with offices around the world. Even if all respondents speak English, some may puzzle over these colloquialisms if they had not been exposed to them before. The results from questions that do not take population characteristics into account are often particularly misleading, because the interpretations of these questions can potentially be as numerous as the respondents. Similarly, one approach can be appropriate in a given culture and perhaps not in others. For instance, in some cultures, it is considered rude to disagree publicly with the position of others. In such cases, a standard group technique may not elicit what a facilitator from a more conflict-accepting culture would consider to be honest responses from a group.

Other important factors to consider when selecting data collection instruments are the relative costs, time, and expertise required to develop or obtain them. Once a range of suitable alternatives has been identified based on the type of data required and their sources, the ultimate selection should be based the relative feasibility of each alternative.

A face-to-face interview might be the best choice in terms of the data the evaluator is after on a given project, but the sheer number of people to be interviewed might put the time and money required beyond the scope of the project.

Questionnaires and Surveys One of the most widely used—and sometimes misused—data collection tools is the questionnaire. Questionnaires are commonly used to collect soft data such as perceptions and attitudes, but they may also be used to collect hard data. Usually questionnaires gather data about respondents' reactions, perceptions, or "personal reality," as in attitude surveys. If this is the evaluator's intent, results should be interpreted and presented in that context. Questionnaires are not adequate tools to measure actual learning or individual performance gains or the performance gains of the organization.

When used in the context of measuring participant reactions to a program or performance solution, these instruments are also referred to as "reactionnaires" (Newby, 1992). These are the very forms that were discussed during Kirkpatrick's level 1 evaluations in Chapter Four; as you might recall, they are also called smile sheets or happy sheets. When designed and implemented well, reactionnaires can provide useful information for improving programs and supporting their perceived quality, utility, and acceptance.

As a general guideline for increasing the utility of questionnaires, the questions posed should be geared toward informed opinions, such as those based on the target group's personal experience, knowledge, background, and vantage point for observation. Questionnaire designers are well advised to stay away from questions that lead the respondent to speculate about the information being requested, and they should never use a questionnaire to confirm or shape a preexisting bias. It is possible, and undesirable, to bias the responses by the way question items are phrased. The goal is for the questions to get as unbiased results as possible.

Perhaps no questionnaire can be regarded as perfect or ideal for soliciting all the information required. Nevertheless, most have inherent advantages, as well as flaws (Rea & Parker, 1997). However, factors such as professional experience and judgment may help ensure any advantages and reduce the effects of inherent flaws of questionnaires.

For just about every questionnaire advantage, one could perhaps find a disadvantage. In the context of a survey method, questionnaires can be used to solicit information from a large number of people across a large geographical region, and relatively inexpensively. However, there is no opportunity for instant clarification or follow-up questions as there are in focus groups or interviews, for instance.

Another advantage of questionnaires is that they can be completed by respondents at their own convenience and pace. Although a deadline for completion should be given to respondents, they will have sufficient time to reflect, elaborate, and, if appropriate, verify their responses. Of course, the drawback here is that mailed or online questionnaires can require significantly more time to administer than other methods. The sooner you can get a response, the more likely it will be done.

Perhaps one of the most important advantages is the possibility of anonymity. Questionnaires can be administered in such a way that responses cannot be traced back to individual respondents. Explicitly communicating this to potential respondents tends to increase the chances for their cooperation on at least two levels: completing the survey and being more forthcoming and honest in their responses. However, even if guaranteed anonymity may increase response rate, the overall response rate for questionnaires is usually still lower than for other methods.

When responses are low, follow-ups, oversampling, respondent replacements, and nonrespondent studies can contribute to a more representative, random sample, which is critical for generalization of findings. Still, there will usually be some bias in the sample due to self-selection; some people, for their own reasons, might not respond to a questionnaire. But a representative sample is vital.

There are number of characteristics across which respondents and nonrespondents may differ, and these can be important to the findings. You want to know where people agree and where they do not. This is another important issue to acknowledge with interpreting and presenting data collected through questionnaires.

So exactly what data are collected with questionnaires? How can you determine what questions to ask? The fundamental source of information for the items that will be included in your questionnaire instrument is the set of results, indicators, and related questions you want answered as a result of the evaluation (or a needs assessment process, if that is the context of the data collection).

Basic Types of Questionnaire Items Whereas some question crafters speak of the simplicity, intelligibility, and clarity of questionnaire items, experimental researchers speak of task difficulty and respondent burden. Either way, many questionnaires are difficult to understand and answer (Converse & Presser, 1986). Keep in mind who the authors of questionnaires usually are: educated people with an in-depth understanding of the topic at hand. Thus, the questions or items are often (and sometimes inappropriately) directed at individuals with similar characteristics. The importance of simplicity in language and tasks of a questionnaire cannot be overstated, but at the same time, it is counterproductive to oversimplify to the point that the important variables and nuances are eliminated.

Open- and Closed-Ended Questions Open-ended questions require the respondents to provide a response in their own words in approximately a few sentences—for example, "How has your performance on the job improved as a result of your completion of the Leadership Series training program?"

Closed-ended questions provide the respondents with a list of answers to choose from. Examples are multiple-choice and category scales. Here is an example of a multiple-choice item:

1. How has your performance as a leader improved as a result of your completion of the Leadership Series training program?

    a. My team consistently meets or exceeds objectives.

    b. We have increased active participation in strategic planning activities.

    c. We have increased the number of new accounts.

    d. My team has had decreased turnover.

    e. None of these

Category scales may focus on frequency (for example, from "always" to "never"), amount (from "most" to "least"), and agreement ("completely agree" to "completely disagree"). To force a decision toward one side of the range or another, even-number scales (with four or six points, for example) can be used.

The most frequent type of item in questionnaires is the closed-ended response option. Closed-ended questions tend to increase the likelihood of getting a response, since they require the least time or work on the part of the respondent. It certainly seems easier to choose an appropriate answer that is already provided than create a response. Another distinct advantage to this format is the relative simplicity with which the evaluator can make comparisons among responses, thereby facilitating the data analysis phase. Having predetermined categories of responses helps the respondents focus exclusively on responses that are of particular interest to the evaluation team. By the same token, however, these categories may also exclude or limit other important responses not thought of by the questionnaire creators and therefore may force respondents to choose responses that do not apply to them.

Other Question Formats There are various other types of closed-ended questions. For instance, rankings are used to rank items in order of importance or priority. In a ranked question, respondents are provided with a predetermined number of responses and asked to prioritize them based on some specified criteria.

Sometimes the evaluator may be looking for more than one response on a given question. In this case, checklist items can capture all responses that apply.

Advantages of Open-Ended Questions Open-ended questions are one way to avoid these potential drawbacks. However, they bring their own set of challenges. For one, they may result in a lot of extraneous, and perhaps unintelligible, information, which will require extra attention and work in the analysis phase. Also, the range of responses may be significantly wide. One way to alleviate—not eliminate—these issues is to make the questions as specific as possible and design them so that they relate to ends and not just means. Not only does this help respondents focus on the issue of interest, but it also helps them recall information.

Before comparisons can be made in the analysis phase, a coding system will have to be put into place for the standardization of responses to open-ended questions. However, there are instances in which these additional challenges are worth facing.

Finally, it is possible to combine both formats into one item. These items usually consist of predetermined response options, as well as an additional option for "Other, please specify." If a pilot test revealed that this option was used frequently, that would indicate that keeping the option is a good idea. But if a pilot test revealed that the option was rarely used, it might not have to be included in the final version.

Questionnaire Structure Respondents are sensitive not only to the language used in each question but also to the order in which the questions are asked. Keep in mind that each question can become the context for the next. Thus, poorly structured questionnaires can confuse respondents and cause them to provide inaccurate responses, and they may also lead respondents to abandon the questionnaire altogether.

A well-structured questionnaire should begin with straightforward yet interesting questions so as to motivate the respondent to continue. It takes time for an individual to feel comfortable with sharing sensitive information, so save sensitive items for later in the questionnaire.

Questions that focus on the same specific issue should be presented together so as to maximize the respondent's reflection and recall. One way that can work for both the questionnaire designer and the respondent is to cluster specific items around different categories. This, however, should not be confused with placing similar questions consecutively. The latter, instead of maximizing the respondents' reflections, could instead elicit an automatic response. One way to decrease the likelihood of this problem is to vary the type (for example, open- or closed-ended and checklist) of questions within a category.

When information beyond what a closed-ended question can reveal is required, an open-ended question should follow. Usually these types of items should be placed later in the survey, within the constraints of following a logical sequence. Finally, more general, open-ended closing questions such as those that request respondents to add anything else that may be important but was not asked should be used to conclude the series of questions.

Questionnaire Length Simplicity is key. Nobody wants to complete a long and complicated questionnaire. The questionnaire should include exactly what is required—nothing more, nothing less. Recall that the previous chapter went over the process of identifying relevant indicators, which should be the central focus of the information collected. Although there may be plenty of interesting information that could be collected through the questionnaire, if it is not central to the indicators being investigated, it will be a distraction—for both the evaluators and the respondent.

The questionnaire crafter should think not only about the actual length of the questionnaire but also about the length of time the respondent will invest in completing it. As a general rule, most questionnaires should take no more than thirty minutes to complete; ideally, most should take about half that long.

Traditional Knowledge Testing

Perhaps the most widely used method of determining what someone has learned is the use of a knowledge test (traditionally referred to as a paper-based test, though computer-based testing is used to meet the same purpose). An enormous amount of information is available to guide the construction and use of such tests. Provided the tests are well made (valid and reliable), they are a good way to measure knowledge, as well as being efficient and economical to administer. When tests are standardized, they yield information about the relative ranking of test takers in a general target population. When they are valid predictors, they can be used in screening and selection. However, most instructor-made paper-based tests are not validated as predictive or standardized instruments and so have much less interpretive value; their value is related only to the direct content in the test. Knowledge tests can play only a limited role in performance measurement of skills that involve physical action integrated with knowledge. They cannot replace performance testing that involves actions and interactions of the test takers with physical tools or operator controls.

Instructor-Made Tests for Training Situations Instructor-made tests are the most popular form of data collection used in education and training. They vary in quality due to their informal development, and they include a mixed bag of methods and types. In general, instructors want to measure how much the participants learned from the content of the lessons and learning objectives that were used in the instructional phase of the training. Rarely do instructors make testing exhaustive. Although exhaustive testing would be a good way to find out what the students know or do not recall from the instruction, it is not very efficient. Instead, most instructors sample from the content and make the test content a subset of the delivered content.

Instructor-made tests can fall prey to some typical errors: (1) The sample content is not representative, (2) the test contains new content not featured in the instruction, or (3) the test requires a level of integration of content and behavior to synthesize answers that was not part of the instructional sequence. Even before addressing these errors, the instructor must first ensure that the tests are not compromised to result in no ability to assume a relation between the test results (based on the sample) and the learning that took place. Then the instructor must avoid the three errors noted. In some situations, errors 2 and 3 are actually good tactics for advanced students in that correctly responding requires higher-order thinking skills such as analysis, synthesis, and evaluation (Bloom, 1956). Unless the instructor is including them intentionally and appropriately, tests with these errors are generally regarded by the testing community, and especially by the students, as unfair.

Criterion-Referenced Tests A popular form of testing that has gained use in recent years is criterion-referenced testing in which the test items are scored relative to a fixed standard. These tests tend to include more performance objectives, although knowledge-based tests can also be based on fixed standards. The key idea is that students are expected to obtain a desired level of performance. If students must know the safety procedure for using a tool in shop class, for example, the instructor wants them to use the entire procedure. Relative class ranking has no bearing if being the best in the group still results in cutting off a finger in the band saw.

The reliability and validity of criterion testing has been discussed by Berk (1980). In general, testing and reuse of the test over time can establish the reliability of the test. Validity of criterion testing rests in the relationship between skill and knowledge required to perform in some designated situation and the fidelity of the test situation to duplicate that skill and knowledge in a testing mode. In issuing drivers' licenses, states want to see a demonstration of minimum skills and knowledge related to safe operation of the vehicle on the public highways. Criterion-referenced tests are good for areas of performance that involve minimum performance for safety or demonstrated skill at some tasks (especially when human well-being is involved).

The validity of a criterion-referenced test lies in the accomplishment of the testing aim. Two important issues relate to the aims of testing: domain coverage and inferences made from results. Consider two questions when approaching a testing situation: How comprehensive or inclusive should the content of the test be? and What do the test results mean? The first question is often considered to be an issue of domain, and the second deals with using the results in a practical way.

Suppose you are training novice shop workers to change the saw blade in a band saw. If there are seven steps and all are essential to doing the task correctly, you could make a test that has each participant perform each step. In a criterion-referenced test, the standard could be that every step has to be completed correctly. Participants who get all of the steps pass, and students who miss even a single step fail. In this example, the test items and the test objective have what Berk (1980) refers to as "item–objective congruence." Here the domain is small (just seven items: one for each step), and the test is a virtual reproduction of the desired objective: to correctly change a band saw blade. The instructor can have high confidence that trainees who pass the test can now change the blade.

But what about different model band saws, or blades of other tools like arbor saws, jigsaws, and planers? This is where the issues of domain and transfer enter the picture. If the shop teacher wants to be sure that students can change all of the blades, the domain of test items can be enlarged. Now the test would include all the procedures and take longer to administer. The validation of tests that include all items in the domain hinges on the clarity of instructions, availability of required resources and tools, and inclusiveness of required test items (issues that can also affect reliability of the test). A shop class may have a large but manageable total domain of items over the course of a class period.

What if the instructional objective implies a really large, perhaps infinite, domain—for example, the mathematics professor wants advanced calculus students to be able to solve every conceivable problem that will ever arise within the limits of analytical calculus? How could a test be constructed to meet this objective? What criterion standard could ever be used to declare that a student was competent in calculus?

The answer lies in the nature of the subject matter. Whereas the shop procedures were specific to the limited domain, the application of calculus involves a different level on Bloom's (1956) taxonomy of objectives. At the most basic level, Bloom's taxonomy begins with knowledge, then understanding and application, and proceeds to more complex levels such as analysis, synthesis, and evaluation, in that order. In calculus, the abstractions and generalizations of problem procedure enable students to cope with each new problem. The large but finite domain of rules, models, principles, language, notation, complex procedures, and generalizations has to be mastered. The domain of potential problems is infinite, but the learning domain of rules, models, principles, language, notation, and procedures is not. True, it is much larger than the shop class example, but still manageable in the sense that a significant number of people manage to learn it. Test construction here could include breaking the subject into small sections, and the accumulation of all of the subtests would eventually measure the entire domain. The instructor can still require a set standard and specify a fixed criterion related to the set of tests (a criterion-referenced approach) or use test scores to compare students to each other (a normative-referenced approach, as described below). It is useful to consider the role of domain in this decision.

Norm-Referenced Tests Norm-referenced tests have a strong traditional history in education, which tends to make them seem acceptable to teachers even when they are being used unwisely.

The essence of norm-referenced testing is that the standards or criteria involve a raw score and then a relative score, which is based on the curve of performance. Usually a normal curve (also known as a bell-shaped curve) is assumed. When the objective of the testing is to sort out stronger from weaker performers (as measured by the test items), a normative test is a good choice. Some organizations use these tests in their hiring process as part of an effort to filter out individuals who will likely not perform as well as others. However, some cautions are due here. Norm-referenced tests may sort out individuals who are very good at taking the test and are not necessarily good in performing the tasks associated with it.

Reliability and Validity of Tests

Validity is an essential concept to consider. When interpreting test results, no matter how positive or negative the results may seem, you should rely on them only if you have established confidence in these results. This confidence can be established if the test measures what it is supposed to measure—that is, it is valid; and it must consistently yield the same results for a given individual—that is, it is reliable.

There is no simple way of determining validity, since a test can be valid for one purpose and audience but not for others. Nevertheless, a variety of ways can be used to determine whether a test is sufficiently valid to be useful. One of the simplest is content validity. Content-related validity, which should begin with instrument construction and is based on the judgment of experts, involves careful examination of the test content to determine whether it is representative of the behavior domain in question. Content validity requires both item validity (the test items measure the intended content area) and sampling validity (how well the test samples the total content area). Still, while a test may seem to be valid, it can still measure something different from its intended domain, such as test-taking ability and guessing. Thus, content validity does not guarantee a good test.

Face validity has been used to describe tests. Although this is not a rigorous approach, it can be useful in initially screening test selection.

It basically refers to the degree to which a test appears to measure what it claims to measure. On its face, does the test seem to provide what it is supposed to deliver? Face validity is the sort of thing test constructors attempt to establish when they conduct pilot tests of questionnaires in order to improve the questionnaire before fully implementing it.

A more rigorous approach to determining validity is comparing the instrument with a predetermined criterion of validity. One type of criterion-related validity is concurrent. Concurrent criterion-related validity deals with measures that can be administered at the same time as the measure to be validated. For example, in order to establish this type of validity, a test designer may want to correlate the results of a new personality inventory test with the results of an established one, such as the Myers-Briggs, the Minnesota Multiphasic Personality Inventory, or other validated tests. A correlation will yield a numeric value known as a *validity coefficient,* which indicates the degree of validity of that new test.

The other type of criterion-referenced validity is predictive validity, which seeks to determine the degree to which a new test predicts a future behavior or, in other words, how well a test taker will do in the future. This type of validity is critical for tests that will be used to classify or select individuals, and is commonly—though not exclusively—seen in the educational sector, with tests such as the Scholastic Assessment Test and the Graduate Record Examination. Predictive validity is determined by administering the test and later correlating the scores of the test to some other measure of success. This correlation yields a predictive validity coefficient.

Construct validity is the degree to which a test measures a hypothetical construct. A construct is a nonobservable trait that is derived to explain behavior. For instance, intelligence is a construct that was created to explain why some people learn better than others. Although we cannot observe intelligence directly, we can infer it based on the observable indicators. Establishing this type of validity involves testing hypotheses deduced from theory. A number of independent studies are usually required to establish the validity of a construct measure. For example, market research conducted by or for the advertising industry relies heavily on validating consumer types based on purchasing behaviors.

Reliability refers to the degree to which a test gives consistent results each time it is administered, provided it is done under the same circumstances. An unreliable test is useless, since no one can have confidence in the results. In order for a test to be valid, it must be reliable, though reliability is not sufficient to establish validity.

There are various ways to establish reliability. The "test-retest" method, as the name implies, requires that the same test be given twice and that the correlation between the first and second set of scores be determined. One of the problems with this approach is that memory can sometimes play a role in the test results. Although extending the period of time between test administrations can reduce this problem, the test takers may have changed on the trait being measured if the interval is too long.

The "equivalent of alternate forms" method is another approach to establishing reliability. This approach eliminates the memory problem associated with the test-retest approach. Here, two tests are identical in every way except for the actual items. That is, both include valid indicators or items of what they are measuring but different sets of such indicators or items. Both tests are administered to a group, again under the same circumstances, and the test scores for each are then correlated.

If a test is derived to measure one specific concept, it is safe to assume that the items of that test are highly correlated with each other. Split-half reliability is an approach used to determine internal consistency. A test is split into two equivalent halves, each part is administered to one group, and the correlation between the two sets of scores is established. If the correlation is high, the test has a good split-half reliability.

Yet another approach to establishing internal consistency is the Kuder-Richardson formula, which examines the extent to which items in one form of the test have as much in common with one another as they do to those of the other form. Thus, these procedures are sometimes referred to as "item-total correlations." Perhaps one of the most commonly known internal consistency coefficients is alpha. It is similar to the Kuder-Richardson but can be used on multiple-choice tests instead of simple yes-no or right-wrong formats (for example, attitudinal surveys that use Likert scales).

Internal consistency measures are appropriate only if a test contains similar items that measure only one concept. For instance, they would be appropriate if a test measures cost accounting ability; they would not be appropriate for a test including one section for cost accounting ability and another for macroeconomics.

Treatment-Centered Methods

Often the kind of information required to answer evaluation questions is the by-product of activities that must take place in order for results to be obtained. This is true of many organizational activities, projects, and programs, but sometimes evaluators impose additional controls on the situation that are not unlike the classic scientific experiment. The controls that can be imposed in the performance setting are not usually as precise as in a laboratory setting, but the social sciences can on occasion use the experimental method with some degree of success. In recent years, an innovative treatment-centered method of obtaining evaluation data is the use of simulation to monitor behavior under controlled conditions that model the conditions of a special performance situation. Treatment-based methods of gathering evaluation data are often used when there is a need to sort out several possible causal factors. Although this method is rarely used due to the resources and level of intrusive control that it requires, it nevertheless has a place in evaluation, especially when performance stakes are high.

Experimental Research and Evaluation: The Relationship

There has been much debate about the utility of using experimental designs in evaluation (Guba, 1969). On the one extreme, some contend that there is absolutely no utility in experimental design, and on the other extreme, some contend that this is the only valid means for conducting evaluations. Stufflebeam's position (1971) is that educational evaluation includes much more than experimental design methodology and that the utility of experimental design can be increased by incorporating procedures that do not require common criterion instruments and uniform decision rules for all participants in an experiment.

Classic experiments usually involve the comparison of two or more groups, although single-group methods do exist. The main aim of an experiment is to see what happens under specific conditions. If the design is carefully done and controls are used, an inference about cause and effect can be made. This aspect of classic research design has made the approach attractive to evaluators when they are not sure if the observed results of a program are in fact due to the program treatment or some other cause. Numerous factors—both internal and external to the organization—affect the success (or lack thereof) of a performance solution.

It is important to point out that establishing causality is not the same as establishing the value of the program or results. Value is assigned to obtained results when they meet the valid needs of the organization and the clients and community it serves. A program has instrumental value to the degree it is able to deliver consistent desired results.

Much discussion has taken place in the evaluation and research communities to draw distinctions between the disciplines of research and evaluation. Classic experiments are generally regarded as falling in the domain of research, whereas evaluation is in part concerned with the determination of worth or merit. Although widely accepted, this distinction should not prevent an evaluator from using experimental methodology when issues of causality are in question. Nor should research attempt to be value free. Ethical norms and procedural norms should be part of any research regimen. Attempts to be value free are confusions with the general aim to control bias. The results obtained by an evaluator (or any investigator) should never be altered because the experimenter holds a bias.

DESIGNING THE EXPERIMENT

Sometimes you might be able to conduct an experiment to get answers that are important and useful to the organization. For example, you might want to determine empirically if one incentive program is better than another. When this is an option, here are some basic considerations.

Experimental design is built on the idea that when something happens, you can observe the result directly. If you treat something in a new way and find that you have a new result (the dependent variable), you assume that the change is due to the new solution (the independent variable). For example, you implement a new incentive program (the independent variable), and you observe an increase in the performance of the affected employees (the dependent variable). The problem with this arrangement is that it is not always so simple. To make sure that the observed change was in fact due to the treatment and not some other unobserved cause, investigators might enlarge the scope of the design in two ways. First, they might insist on repeating an experiment several times to ensure that results are consistent; second, they could add controls to rule out alternative explanations. A control is a measure that can be understood as having two general types. First, controls over conditions operate to ensure consistency. Second, additional features of an experimental design can address the most typical alternative explanations.

Experimentalists have identified several potential causative factors and developed ways to rule them out as major contributing forces in the experiment. Some of the most common are the effects of prior learning, age and sex, training during the procedure, and maturation based on normal growth. An example of a control might be the use of a second group of performers who get the same conditions as the experimental treatment group except the key treatment in question, for example, the implementation of the treatment in pilot sites or branches of an organization before implementing it throughout the entire organization. This control is designed to rule out the possibility that performers may learn the new behaviors on their own. If the experimental group that gets the new treatment shows an improvement in performance over the control group and statistical analysis finds it is not due to chance, we are more certain that the treatment caused the change than we would be if we had just observed the experimental group alone. We can then use the new incentive program again and track the performance of employees in two different but comparable branches before and after the program, except we implement the program in only one of those branches. If there is a change in performance in the branch where we implemented the program but not the others, we may conclude that the change was due to the program.

Note that this kind of comparison is not the same as comparing two different treatments to see which one works better. In the strictest sense of experimental design, comparing two treatments is less desirable than doing an experiment with one treatment and several controls. Although you may have one treatment with outcomes that appear to be more desirable than the other treatment, the overall ambiguity of confidence in the results is no greater than when you are using the simple one-treatment design with no controls. The object of design in experimentation is to produce data on cause and effect between a treatment and the result. Those data should include a statement of the confidence that can be attributed to the findings. In a typical experimental design for a single treatment, the sample is randomly assigned to each group (either the treatment or the control group), and the rest looks like Table 11.2. Notice that the only difference between the two groups is the treatment; the remaining conditions are exactly the same. It must be noted that the two samples should

TABLE 11.2. **Typical Experimental Design for a Single Treatment**

Group	Testing/ Data Collection (baseline)	Treatment or Solution Is Implemented	Testing/Data Collection
Treatment	X	X	X
Control	X		X

not have overlapping members but will come from the same target population. The strength of the design will increase with sample size. Statisticians have generally accepted the arbitrary number of thirty subjects as representative enough to overcome small sample measurement error.

PROBLEMS WITH CLASSIC EXPERIMENTAL STUDIES IN APPLIED SETTINGS

Although the classic experiment is useful to increase confidence in findings about treatments and results, the use of classic experimentation is rare in most evaluation studies. First, the method does not address the value of the outcome. Second, the classic experiment requires resources and time that are usually not available to the evaluator. Third, organizations are not always willing to commit the time and resources to conduct experiments. For instance, if the organizational leaders make a decision to implement the new incentive program based on needs assessment data, they may want to move ahead and implement it across all relevant branches in the hope that overall performance improves as quickly as possible. From their perspective, time is money, and the sooner they get improved performance from all branches, the better.

Finally, classic experimental designs do not capture the breadth and depth of what a program or solution has produced and contributed or the unintended consequences of such means. In part, this limitation is because they ignore the interdependencies between the evaluand and other programs, solutions, and events that interact to cause the observed effect. Even if multiple regression analyses were conducted, one would have to assume that all the contributing variables are known.

Understanding the issues that surround the design of a classic experiment can, however, help evaluators as they observe events and consider the results. Evaluators must attempt to avoid the error of assuming that all observed results are directly traceable to the programs and nothing else. They must remain alert to the possibility that other causes may be operating. Some of these may be one-time events, and some may be built into the performance setting.

TIME-SERIES STUDIES

While traditional experimental research has been quite successfully applied in the natural sciences, time-series designs are considered more useful for many social scientists, including economists and applied behavior analysts (Brethower, 2006). By some accounts, a well-executed time-series design could be even more powerful than a classic experimental design (Brethower, 2006; Campbell, Stanley, & Gage, 1966).

A simple time series consists of the collection of quantitative observations at regular intervals through repeated measurements. Brethower (2006) summarizes four variations of this design:

- The AB design: Measure what is happening now (A), do something (B), and measure what happens as a result.

- Repeated AB design: Do several AB designs with the same intervention (B) in different locations at different times—say, the Milwaukee plant in June, the Albany plant in July, and the Miami plant in August.

- Reversal/ABA designs: Do an AB design; then reverse and go back to what you were doing in A.

- The ABC . . . D . . . design: Do an AB, then try something else (C), and maybe do something else (D), and then something else (E), and so on. Measure what happens each time.

One way to look at this design is that it begins with needs assessment (something was measured: a result, specifically, let us say, a gap between the desired and the current level of a result); then continues with the implementation of a solution (something was done); and then we evaluate the impact that something had on those results (measure that result again). For a more rigorous assurance of the impact the solution had on the results, you could apply any of the variations of this approach described by Brethower.

SIMULATIONS AND GAMES

The use of simulation and game theory to create performance improvement treatments is on the increase following successful applications in business and military settings. The objective of a simulation is to enable participants to experience the problematic factors of events but under controlled and safer conditions than occur in the real setting. Simulations have been used to teach the operation of the court system, the U.S. political system, flight training, electrical systems, and parenting and child care, among many other examples. In all cases, the participants experience some, but not all, of the aspects of the actual situation being modeled.

Determining What to Model in a Game or Simulation

The game or simulation should contain a reasonable approximation of the setting in which the behavior is to occur, although the setting elements may model only some aspects of the real setting. Only the cues and behavioral responses are important. Therefore, a simulation of an electrical panel need not be energized with high voltage so long as the cues and student interactions can be performed using low voltage. A cardboard cutout of a traffic light may be sufficient as long as the red, yellow, and green lights are sufficient cues for learners to make decisions leading to the desired learning. When modeling a game or simulation, make a flowchart of the desired behavior in the actual setting, and list all of the cue response patterns that lead to correct behavior. Next, look for ways that the same cue or signal can be duplicated in the simulated environment of the game or exercise. Test the substituted elements using real participants to see if sufficient fidelity exists to obtain the level of cue response required to complete the task being modeled. After some experimentation, build the simulation model around the task flow using the substituted elements. Safety and control are key. Many simulations are made more effective when the simulation has provision for instructor control to stop and instead have the instructor provide coaching only as students require assistance. A pilot study is normally required to arrive at a final design of a simulation.

Using Simulation and Gaming for Evaluation

Evaluation is easily accommodated if the simulation is designed for easy observation of the participants. Since the simulation or game will have been designed using a work flow or task model, the correct behavior is specified ahead of time, and evaluator observers will be able to compare participant behavior with the standard for correct performance. For example, using the vehicle navigation system simulation, participants can be given a task or scenario using the simulation to determine the efficacy of the simulation in achieving its learning goals, for example, that sales consultants can demonstrate the navigation system's functionality to customers. In addition, most simulations are designed to allow control over prompts and cues so that participants can be prompted to perform the correct sequence or act at the appropriate time. If the real setting does not include a rich set of prompts, the simulation can be designed to gradually reduce the prompts as the performer builds internal cues and memory patterns.

DOCUMENT-CENTERED METHODS

Extant Data Review

Extant data are data that already exist in some form of organizational record. The wisest place to start is by considering whether these sources contain relevant and useful data. Some examples of extant data sources might be current strategic plans, industry reports, current budget records, census data, previous needs assessment reports, previous evaluation reports, performance evaluations, or other sources you might uncover (and there are many). Other examples are records collected by bodies such as public and private agencies, institutions, and corporations.

In this approach, relevant organizational records are identified and reviewed for information on key elements of the intervention or program, including past evaluations, meeting notes, and organizational mission statements. One strong point is the ability to take advantage of data that already exist, which can be time efficient, particularly if this information can be searched and analyzed electronically. However, the data are not always sorted into the categories the evaluator may be looking for, and thus determining what is relevant and what is not may be time-consuming. Here too it may be possible to use the frequency with which ideas appear as some indication of the importance or time spent on an issue.

While questionnaires, group processes, and interviews are traditionally associated with the collection of qualitative—soft—data, extant data tend to be associated with quantitative—hard—data. For instance, if you wanted to know the itemized financial investment for a given program or what the rate of successful completion was, asking for someone's opinion about it would not likely produce the type of valid and reliable data that examining documented organizational records might render (assuming, of course, that the data entered were accurate).

With extant data, the preliminary task is the same as in the previous methods. That is, before selecting this as a viable data collection method, you start with the evaluation questions and the associated indicators previously identified. If relevant data can be obtained from existing records, then there is little utility in creating new data collection tools to get those same data. In this case, it is most feasible to review the existing data. Even in this circumstance, you should still consider extant data in the context of other data collected during this evaluation process.

Literature Review

It is hard to underestimate the value of a well-planned review of literature. The existing literature on evaluation, school administration, program effectiveness, strategies of instruction, and decision making, for example, can assist the evaluation team in planning and implementing an evaluation. Citations from the literature may add credibility to evaluation reports.

In a review, you make a list of keywords and topics and use it to conduct database searches to identify books, articles, reports, and other periodicals and sources. It will be helpful to list topics and relate them to keywords that are used in the various search programs available in libraries. Several special databases are now updated on a regular basis. A search librarian can help in structuring this search and guiding you to the appropriate database. Most libraries use databases that are designed for electronic search and location of titles, authors, and topics, which makes the process quite efficient. Of course, once a list of items is drawn up, someone has to read or scan them to glean the valuable part, and that can take considerable time. As a bonus, this type of search may identify other measurement-based studies that have been conducted in similar settings.

Artifacts and Work Products

Another source of evaluation is the product produced. If, for example, you want to check out the gaps in a supervisor's performance, you might want to check the performance of the team she leads. If the evaluation reveals that 45 percent of the team members are not meeting the performance standards, this is one indication of the supervisor's competence. If you want to judge her competence with more certainty, you would look at other performance products or indicators of supervisor performance (in efforts to triangulate the current data), as well as look further into the gaps of her team's performance, so that other contributing factors are clear and comprehensive recommendations for improving performance can be made.

CONCLUSION

This chapter has covered a wide (though not completely exhaustive) range of data collection approaches and methods available to evaluators and other investigators. The data collected have to be representative of reality, and thus what you do and how you go about collecting data is central to good evaluation. If inappropriate or invalid methods for a situation are used, the data collected—and, in turn, the interpretations and recommendations—will be considered invalid. Rigor, of course, is not the same thing as inefficient use of time or overly complex data analysis. Instead, rigor refers to the care and attention paid to all decisions related to the selection, use, and analysis of data collection tools and the resulting data. The credibility and validity of findings and recommendations are directly related to the rigor of the data collection.

KEY POINTS

- Selecting appropriate data collection methods depends in great part on the types of data sought.

- Committing to use data collection methods that are familiar before knowing what data must be collected, and from where or whom, could lead to incomplete or irrelevant data sets. It is an error to pick the tools first and then be limited by the data that tool will generate.

- All observations can be reduced to measurement.

- Person-centered, indirect methods such as focus groups and interviews may be best for collecting open-ended data from a comparatively small number of participants. These methods require significant facilitator training, time, and effort.

- Instruments such as tests and questionnaires may be best for collecting specific hard or soft data from a large range of participants. These methods require, among other things, an understanding of the cultural characteristics of the respondents. Questionnaires are not adequate tools to measure actual learning or individual performance gains or the performance gains of the organization.

- Evaluators must attempt to avoid the error of assuming that all observed results are directly traceable to the programs and nothing else.

- If inappropriate or invalid methods for a situation are used, the data collected—and in turn the interpretations and recommendations—will be invalid.

REFLECTION QUESTIONS

1. What are the most important issues to consider when selecting the appropriate data collection instruments?

2. How does the selection of the appropriate data collection instruments have an impact on the data and, in turn, the entire evaluation study?

3. When might you use an experimental design in an evaluation? How often would you expect this to occur?

4. You have been asked to develop a questionnaire to evaluate the success of the new leadership mentoring program. How will you go about designing the questionnaire? What information must you seek before proceeding with the design?

ANALYSIS OF EVALUATION DATA

This chapter provides a review of methods for analyzing collected data. It begins with advice on analyzing soft data in a structured discussion format. For hard or numerical data, the chapter focuses on descriptive statistics. It also provides some brief guidelines on the use of inferential statistics. Finally, it discusses the relationship between data analysis and inter-pretation and stresses the importance of interpretation to an evaluator and the stakeholders the evaluator represents.

Data analysis is more than number crunching. Recall from Chapter Ten that evaluators deal with both hard and soft data. The analysis of evalua-tion data is the means by which the evaluators organize information to discover patterns and fortify arguments used to support conclusions or evaluative claims that result from the evaluation study. In a nutshell, we are merely summarizing large volumes of data into a manageable and meaningful format that can quickly communicate its meaning. In fact, one might say that analysis of the data begins even before their collection, by virtue of analyzing the characteristics of the required data, as we do before selecting the methods for data collection.

If you have quantitative data, various statistical operations can help you organize them as you sort through your findings. Qualitative data are also subject to different analytical routines. Qualitative observations can be ordered by source and by impact or sorted according to general themes and specific findings. Checking the frequency of qualitative observations will begin to merge qualitative into quantitative data. Remember that qualitative and quantitative data sets must be obtained from relevant information targets.

Not all data collected will come neatly measured on a scale. Recall that a variety of methods for collecting qualitative data may have been used (for example, observation, interviews, and focus groups). Methods for analyzing qualitative data range from narrative descriptions to quantitative analysis of such descriptions.

ANALYSIS OF MODELS AND PATTERNS

Continually reflecting on and searching for patterns within the data even while the data collection process is still going on can help evaluators adjust and refocus their data collection to render useful information.

These general steps should guide the analysis of qualitative data:

▪ Review notes, and carefully reflect on the impressions they make.

▪ Recognize recurrent themes, and code them accordingly.

▪ Organize data according to identified themes.

▪ Look for potential relationships among the themes.

▪ Identify explanations, causal factors, potential impact, and so forth for each theme.

▪ Validate preliminary interpretations by triangulating data (using three or more sources) to support or disprove hypotheses. (This is a good time to entertain alternative explanations.)

▪ Draw conclusions.

For excellent resources on analyzing qualitative data, see Miles and Huberman (1994), Richards and Richards (1994), and Weitzman and Miles (1995).

ANALYSIS USING STRUCTURED DISCUSSION

From time to time during the course of an evaluation, the evaluation team leader may gather observers to discuss observations made at that point in the study and later to discuss results in relation to observed events. The purpose of structured discussion is to clarify issues that have emerged in the study and identify possible cause-and-effect relationships regarding events and results. Each issue is identified and sorted according to relevance to the study and possible influence on programs and results.

One benefit is that all issues can be entertained even if they are not anticipated in the planning stage of a study. Other advantages include the fact that issues can be modified as additional data become available, hypotheses can be formulated for continued review and confirmation between events and results, and data can be organized with this method of analysis using both emerging and initial data collection categories.

The reactions of observers, however, are not a method of strong proof. In addition, observers cannot vote that something is true or false; they can only identify issues that must be investigated and subjected to further testing or inquiry. Finally, if these discussions are not conducted with discipline and leadership, they can generate abundant red herrings; at the same time, strong leadership can introduce strong bias.

Imposing Structure on Emerging Issues

The structure of this type of analytical discussion comes from the standards of conduct imposed by the evaluation team leader. A structured discussion should not be a free-for-all with each observer bringing up any odd tidbit that happened during observation. The team leader should begin each discussion with a question designed to focus on a specific part of the study, for example, "Does anyone have an observation that is relevant to the use of the mentoring program as part the support of leadership development?" At this point each member of the group has a chance to offer observations that bear on the question. The first standard of conduct could be "Stick to the topic." A second good standard would be "No observations will be discarded or discredited in the first round of questioning." A third rule might be that all comments are written down.

The team leader then opens the forum to general discussion, and the group rates all observations as potential explanations of causes and effects and as useful for further investigation or for relegation to the "not sure what this means" category. At this point, the leader moves on to the next question, and the process is repeated. After all of the questions on the leader's list are explored, each participant in the discussion should have the opportunity to add a question if he or she feels something was left out of the initial discussion. The product of structured discussion is a list of observed events or issues that may bear on the study, a set of possible cause-and-effect relationships, and a list of areas that require further investigation. These are organized by the question structure and general relevance.

Relevance

Relevance is decided on the basis of the issue's potential or demonstrated bearing on the main focus of the evaluation study: Is it important, and will it make a difference? The shorthand logic of this approach to evaluation is that organizational solutions should flow from valid needs—gaps in results—of the organization's clients and that the primary focus of evaluation is to ensure that solution results meet those needs. The secondary focus of evaluation is to identify program factors that contribute to or interfere with the desired results. Therefore, all information that supports this chain of logic is relevant.

When evaluators note that managers have deviated from required objectives, that observation is bound to be relevant to later discussions of the results and what caused them. If an evaluator decides to jot down the location of the parking place that employees use each day, that information is more than likely not going to be relevant to the main focus of the evaluation (unless tardiness is a problem and the physical structure of the organization is far removed from the employee parking lot). To be considered relevant, data must bear on the study and have some plausible tie to performance. Both performance-disruptive and performance-enhancing events count as relevant.

Controls on Structured Discussion

Structured discussion works best when it is guided by a strong leader who is knowledgeable as an evaluator and respected by the group. The main tools to keep discussion focused and productive are a set of standards of conduct and the respect of the group for the discussion leader—for example:

- Always prepare an agenda with topical questions to focus discussion.

- Keep discussion to the questions at hand until the end, when the forum is open to new questions.

- Each participant has a turn at presenting issues and observations.

- No issues that could bear on the question are ruled out.

- Each issue is checked for relevance.

- Issues are ranked according to relevance and potential causality.

- Hypotheses are formulated only after all issues are presented.

- Written records are kept for each discussion.

- Further observations are assigned to specific members of the group as action items for the next discussion.

METHODS OF QUANTITATIVE ANALYSIS

Selecting the appropriate quantitative analysis technique depends not only on the scale used to measure the data but also on the specific purpose of the analysis. Here are some examples of such purposes and the types of appropriate quantitative analysis techniques for each:

- To show the relative position of an individual in a group (measures of central tendency). Example: Is there a salesperson who stands apart from the rest of the team?

- To describe the shape of a data set (measures of variability). Example: Are the sales figures consistent for this branch, or do individual salespeople's figures vary significantly from one another?

- To show relative ranking (measures of central tendency). Example: How do Jane's performance scores stack up against her group's scores?

- To compare two sets of data (measures of variability). Example: Does the team in this branch perform comparably to the team in the southeast branch?

▪ To discover relationships (measures of relationship). Example: Is there a relationship between the number of training courses taken and sales?

▪ To show cause and effect (statistical testing). Example: Did the new incentive program cause an increase in sales?

▪ To make statements of likelihood or make a prediction (statistical testing). Example: Does performance as a sales agent predict performance as manager?

Having raw data is one thing; answering questions with those data is another. In order for data to reveal the answers to evaluation questions, they must be represented in a way that is meaningful to those viewing them, using them, and making decisions based on them. Over the years, various types of statistical methods have evolved to refine raw data. Here is a short overview of some useful statistical options.

STATISTICS

While the mere mention of the word *statistics* may be intimidating for some, every one of us is truly more familiar with them than we think. We hear them in advertisements all the time (for example, "95 percent of dentists surveyed recommend . . ."). You may have heard someone ask how many miles a vehicle averages per gallon. Understanding statistics is useful far beyond formal data analysis and evaluation. It truly helps us be more aware consumers of knowledge, products, services—everything in everyday life—so that we can make good decisions and evaluate with knowledge.

There are two main types of statistics: descriptive and inferential. The first step in making sense of data is to summarize or describe them. As the name implies, *descriptive statistics* are used to this end. They allow you to summarize an almost endless list of individual scores into one, or various, indexes. In some instances, obtaining descriptive statistics is the sole data analysis procedure necessary to answer an evaluation question, for example, "What did the sales team average (sales figures) last quarter?"

You may also want to find out how well a particular individual did in relation to that average (for example, "How do Steven Hill's figures compare to his team average?") or how spread out the scores are from that average ("Are the sales figures across team members relatively consistent, or do they vary significantly from person to person?").

Inferential statistics are used to make generalizations from a sample to a population. As the name implies, we are inferring that the findings derived from a given sample are representative of the findings we would see from an entire population. Thus, one prerequisite for using inferential statistics in a meaningful way is to be sure the data come from a representative random sample. For instance, before investing in an implementation of a program across all sales associates of a global pharmaceutical company, a manager may want to randomly select a representative group of sales associates and determine the impact of the program on that group. If the study is well conducted, the findings should provide confidence that the organization can expect the same impact across all sales associates. Thus, stakeholders can make a decision about implementing the program across all associates in all branches. The biggest challenge is isolating other variables that may also be affecting the findings, such as environmental differences, cultural differences, or differences in managerial styles.

While the main focus here is on descriptive statistics, some inferential statistical tools are briefly described later in this chapter.

Measures of Central Tendency

The most commonly used descriptive statistics are measures of central tendency, measures of variability, visual representations, and measures of relationships. Measures of central tendency are probably the best way to describe data when there is a need to rely on a single number to represent an entire set of scores. There are three measures of central tendency: the mean, the median, and the mode.

The Mean The mean, perhaps the most frequently used measure of central tendency, is technically the mathematical average of a set of scores. It is calculated by adding up all the individual scores in a data set and dividing that total by the number of scores.

One characteristic that makes it so commonly used is its stability. Because all the scores are included in its calculation, it is more stable than those measures of central tendency that use only a couple of individual scores. However, the flip side of using all the scores is that the mean is also susceptible to the effects of extreme scores. For example, take a look at the following set of scores:

18; 19; 17; 18; 18; 18; 16; 59

The mean for this set of eight scores is approximately 23, yet all but one of the scores range from 16 to 19. Does this mean truly represent the average score? Were it not for that one single outlier, or extreme score, of 59, the mean would be approximately 18. Since the mean is affected by extreme scores, it is usually not the best choice when dealing with a set of scores that contains one or two (or even a few in some instances) extreme scores. (Note that the reasons it is skewed may be important.)

Using the mean is appropriate when the data are measured on an interval or a ratio scale. (See Table 10.1 for examples of things measured at each scale.) Unfortunately, the mean is often inappropriately used without regard to the type of data measurement. One example of inappropriate use is mean scores of questionnaire items, which tend to be measured on a nominal or ordinal scale, even if a numerical value is attributed to the items (for example, Likert scales ranging from strongly disagree to strongly agree). It is of little significance to add up a variety of responses, such as strongly disagree, agree, and neutral and then say that the average response was "agree and two-tenths" (or 4.2). For ordinal data, the median or the modes (described below) are more appropriate measures of central tendency. Specifically, for data measured with a Likert scale, even the percentages of each response as compared to all responses may be a more accurate and useful way to summarize results.

The Median The median is the midpoint of a distribution. Since half the scores are above it and half the scores are below it, it is also referred to as the fiftieth percentile. When there is an odd number of scores, the median is the middle score. When there is an even number of scores, the median is the average of the two middle scores. The best way to recognize the middle score is by arranging the set of scores in numerical order (either ascending or descending). For example, take the following set of scores: 18, 17, 16, 19, 20. These are first arranged in numerical order:

16

17

18

19

20

In this list, the middle score, 18, becomes obvious.

Now consider what happens if there is an even number of scores:

15

16

17

18

19

20

In this case, the two middle scores, 17 and 18, would be averaged as such: $17 + 18 \div 2 = 17.5$.

As you can see, the median does not necessarily have to represent an exact score from the data set.

The median is the most appropriate measure of central tendency for data measured at an ordinal scale (for example, the Likert scale responses from an attitude questionnaire). Because it is the midpoint of a set of scores, the median is not necessarily affected by every score. Compared to the mean, it is not sensitive to outliers and thus is a better measure of central tendency when the distribution of scores is skewed by an extreme score. Thus, it could potentially be used for data measured at an interval and ratio scale, particularly when the distribution of scores is significantly skewed and the mean thus misrepresents the typical score.

The Mode The mode, the least used measure of central tendency, is the most frequent score. No calculation is required to identify the mode. Instead, it is established by looking at a data set or a graphical representation to see which score occurs with the most frequency. The mode has one significant limitation: a distribution of scores can easily have more than one mode. If two scores are tied for the highest frequency, then the data are said to have a bimodal distribution, and if they have three or more scores tied for the highest frequency, they are said to have a multimodal distribution. Finally, if each score occurs with the same frequency, there is no mode, and the data set has a rectangular distribution.

The mode is the most appropriate measure of central tendency when using data measured at a nominal scale. For instance, if you are conducting an evaluation for the Department of Transportation and one of the indicators you look at is the most commonly used method of transportation to a busy section of the downtown business district, the median response of the answers given to this item on a questionnaire would not be useful. However, if you use the mode, you can easily determine the most common method used (that is, the most frequent response) and communicate this result to stakeholders. One way to support the presentation of the mode is to accompany it by percentages (X percent of people indicated Y) or proportions (80 out of 100 people indicated Y).

A common misconception about the infallible nature of numbers is often phrased as "The numbers cannot lie." Keep in mind that just as other things can be manipulated to tell a story that is not exactly accurate, numbers can too. When taken out of context, calculated with flawed figures, or analyzed with inappropriate statistical methods, numbers bring you no closer to making good decisions than you were at the beginning of the evaluation. In fact, if you are clinging to data that are completely unfounded, invalid, or unreliable, you might be even further from the truth. For example, a measure of central tendency can be misused to render the most favorable index rather than the most accurate. Thus, it is important to consider the characteristics, limitations, and appropriate uses of each measure of central tendency (and, in fact, all methods of analyzing data) because each will inevitably have an impact on representations of a given data set and, in turn, the conclusions drawn from them.

Measures of Dispersion (Variability)

Measures of central tendency are essential for describing a data set, but they do not tell the full story. Before you can make sense of those descriptions, you also must have an estimate of the spread and variability of that data set within a given distribution and between distributions. The indexes used to make these estimations are called *measures of variability*. The most commonly used measures of variability are the range, the quartile deviation, and the standard deviation.

The Range The range (also called the *spread*) is probably the easiest and quickest of the measures of variability to estimate. It is defined as the difference between the highest and lowest score (R = H − L) or the difference plus one (R = H − L + 1), which is more specifically referred to as the *inclusive range*. For example, the ranges for the following two sets of data are determined as such:

90

94

93

96

95

Range = 95 − 90 = 5

40

55

60

80

95

Range = 95 − 40 = 55

Thus, a small range represents a set of scores clustered close to-gether, and a large range represents a more spread out set of scores. A potential drawback is that since it takes into account only the highest and lowest scores, an extreme score (either at the high or low end) can result in a misleading range—for example:

90

93

95

97

99

Range = 99 − 90 = 9

38

93

95

97

99

Range = 99 − 38 = 61

Only one score distinguishes each of these data sets from the other one, yet the change from a score much like the others to an extreme score (90 to 38) has an astonishing effect on the range.

Although the range is easy to calculate and gives a quick snapshot of how widely or how narrowly a data set is distributed, the reality is that it tells only about the two extreme scores and practically nothing about the scores in between. Moreover, what is in between is often more representative of the data set than the extremes. For example, if customer service representatives resolve a range of twenty-six calls within a one-hour period, then we know that the most productive representative (if we define production by the number of calls or issues resolved) answered twenty-six more calls than the least productive. But it does not tell much about how call productivity for the rest of the customer service reps is distributed.

The Semi-Interquartile Range The SIQR, also known as the *quartile deviation,* is estimated by the middle 50 percent of the scores. As such, it is not as sensitive to extreme scores as is the range. It essentially tells how wide and distributed are the performances we measured. The formula is as follows: $SIQR = Q_3 - Q_1/2$.

Here, Q_3 represents the third quartile, the point below which 75 percent of the scores fall, and Q_1 represents the point below which 25 percent of the scores fall. Recall that the median is the midpoint of scores, and as such, it corresponds to Q_2, or the second quartile. In fact, the median is usually used along with the SIQR. For example, if a data set has 40 scores, Q_3 is the score below which there are 30 scores (75 percent of $40 = 30$), and Q_1 is the point below which there are 10 scores (25 percent of $40 = 10$). If you arrange the scores in numerical order, you can quickly identify each quartile. In the case of even distributions, each quartile can be estimated as we did with the median (Q_2).

The same characteristic that makes the SIQR less sensitive to extreme scores (estimated by the middle 50 percent of scores) can also be considered a drawback. After all, 50 percent of the scores are being excluded from its calculation. So while the semi-interquartile range is a better estimate of variability than the range, it is not the most stable.

The Standard Deviation Perhaps the most stable measure of central tendency, and perhaps the most commonly used measure of variability, is the standard deviation (SD). It is most appropriate when the data are measured at an interval or ratio scale. Recall that the mean is the most appropriate measure of central tendency with these scales, and thus the mean and standard deviation are usually reported together. Like the mean, the standard deviation is estimated using all scores in a given data set, which is what provides it with stability. If you have both the mean and standard deviation of a data set, you have a good idea of how the scores are distributed.

Many software packages allow users to estimate the standard deviation (and basically any statistic) with a mouse click. For your own curiosity and understanding, here is the formula for calculating the standard deviation:

$$SD = \frac{\sqrt{\sigma(X-\overline{x})}}{N} \text{ or (because } X - \overline{X} = x) \quad SD = \frac{\sqrt{\sigma x^2}}{N}$$

The uppercase X stands for score; the $\overline{X}$ (pronounced "X bar") stands for the mean; and the lowercase x stands for the deviation of a score from the mean of its distribution. Thus, one must first calculate the mean and then subtract the mean from each score. Then, each deviation is squared and then added (as indicated by σ). The value of this formula is then divided by the number of scores (N), and the square root is calculated. For example:

X	$X - \overline{X} = x$	x^2	
14	$14 - 17 = -3$	9	$SD = \frac{\sqrt{13}}{5}$
16	$16 - 17 = -1$	1	
18	$18 - 17 = 1$	1	$= \sqrt{2.6}$
18	$18 - 17 = 1$	1	$= 1.6$
19	$19 - 17 = 2$	4	
$\overline{x} = 17$		$\Sigma x^2 = 13$	

As with other measures of variability, a small standard deviation value represents small variability; that is, scores are clustered close together. The bigger the value of the standard deviation, the bigger the variability is. A high variability could indicate that the solution we are evaluating is not the only factor that has an impact on performance. There may be other factors (for example, previous education or experience, or a different managerial environment) that, coupled with the solution we are examining, create one level of impact among some performers, whereas performers not exposed to those other factors demonstrate a different level of performance.

Here is how to use the standard deviation to make inferences about an individual's performance. Let us say that for a given distribution (a set of scores) of items sold per day for retail sales clerks, the mean (average number of items sold per day) is 18 and the standard deviation from this mean is 4. If we are evaluating the performance of a sales clerk, Mary, and see that on average she sells 26 items per day, we can infer that Mary is an exemplary performer because her performance score is 2 standard deviations above the average performer. The operation below explains this inference:

$$\overline{X} = 18 \text{ items sold per day}$$

$$SD = 4 \text{ items}$$

$$X = 26$$

If we add 1 SD to the average score, we would get 22; if we add 2 SD to the average score, we get Mary's score, 26 ($\overline{X} + 2(4) = 26$). The following discussion about the normal distribution will clarify this rationale.

The Normal Curve The results from the evaluation must make sense to stakeholders, especially at the point where they must make important decisions about improving performance. The following discussion covers some clear ways of thinking about and communicating the evaluation data.

The normal curve (also known as the *bell-shaped curve*) is a hypothetical concept that allows us to make comparisons among scores based on mathematical principles. Although no actual distribution probably fits this model perfectly, distributions can come close enough to make the model useful in making decisions. In fact, this distribution shape is often found in our environment. For example, most people's height clusters around an average. Comparatively few people are either taller or shorter than that average range, and even fewer people are considerably taller or considerably shorter. The further away we get from the average, the fewer people we will find. Some people may be 4 foot 9 inches or 6 foot 11 inches, but not very many will be. Take a look at Figure 12.1 for an illustration.

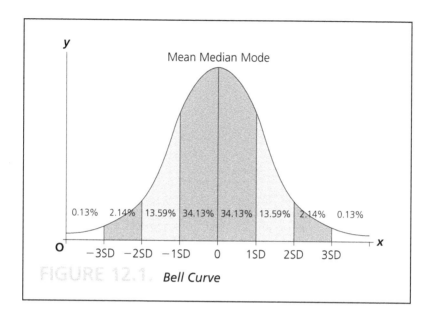

FIGURE 12.1. *Bell Curve*

The curve in Figure 12.1 represents the normal distribution. In such a distribution, the mean, median, and mode all coincide. Note that 99.9 percent of cases fall within plus or minus three standard deviations (add up the percentages of each interval to get this figure). To accommodate the potential for extreme scores, the sections of the model intentionally do not add up to 100 percent. For example, if we used the normal curve to illustrate a distribution with a mean of 50 and a standard deviation of 5, we could assume that 34.13 percent of scores fall between 50 and 55. Because the same percentage of scores could be found between 45 and 50, we could also claim that 68 percent of scores fall between 45 and 55. Again, refer to Figure 12.1 to view how these percentages are related.

The normal curve is often assumed to be useful because people believe that it represents reality, that it shows what happens when nature has its way. The idea, of course, is that we are looking for performance solutions that do not resemble the bell curve too much. Ideally, we are looking for solutions that cause all performers to perform at an exemplary level, or at least have the mean on the high end of mastery (reflecting a negative skew, as illustrated in Figure 12.2). In this ideal situation, the distribution will be quite small. The more effective the performance solutions are, the more that the performers will perform above "average." For example, in a negatively skewed distribution, the number of

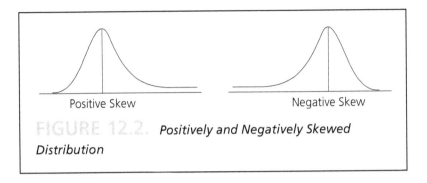

FIGURE 12.2. *Positively and Negatively Skewed Distribution*

items sold per day per performer would look something like this: 10, 11, 22, 24, 26, 26, 25, 24, 27, 27, 28. Notice that most of the scores are on the high end, and only two outliers pull the distribution down. Conversely, a positively skewed distribution would have the majority of the scores toward the low end and very few scores at the high end of performance.

Although it is well established in the minds of many, the normal curve is not useful in many operational settings. In operations, we want to have some impact, and thus are seeking something other than a normal distribution. For example, if we are training people to process credit applications, what we want at the end of the training is not a normal curve but a negatively skewed one that shows that we moved toward more people demonstrating competence than if we had done nothing.

GRAPHICAL REPRESENTATIONS OF DATA

The power of visual representations cannot be overstated. This is especially true with calculations and statistical data. Graphs help us quickly interpret information without the use of many words, and in fact, many people find them easier to understand than statistical test results.

Frequencies, for example, can be graphically represented by bar graphs. In Figure 12.3, categories are organized vertically and values horizontally.

Line charts, also commonly used, show trends in data at equal intervals. They display trends over time or categories and can be created with markers displayed at each data value. Figure 12.4 shows a stacked line chart with multiple categories (Europe, United States, and Japan).

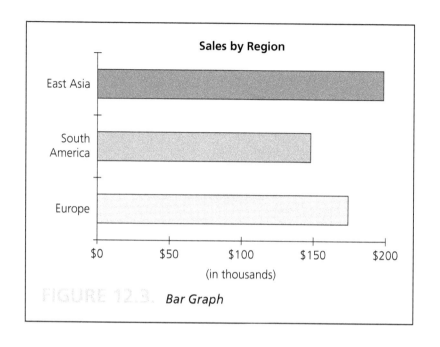

Sales by Region

East Asia

South America

Europe

$0 $50 $100 $150 $200

(in thousands)

FIGURE 12.3. *Bar Graph*

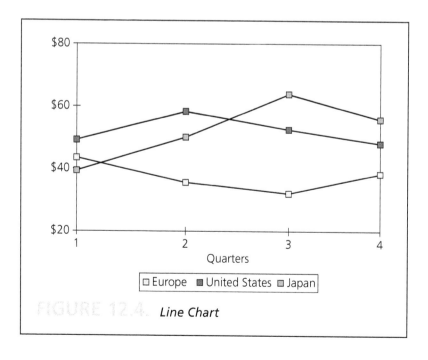

$80

$60

$40

$20

1 2 3 4

Quarters

☐ Europe ■ United States ■ Japan

FIGURE 12.4. *Line Chart*

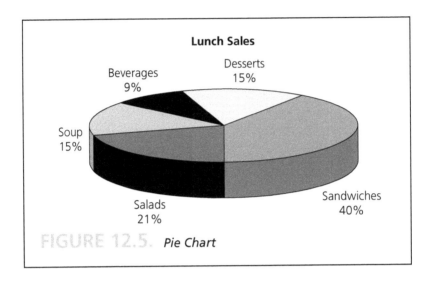

FIGURE 12.5. Pie Chart

Another useful way to represent distributions is the pie chart. A pie chart shows the size of categories that make up a data set. It is particularly useful in communicating relative effect. Figure 12.5 provides an example.

MEASURES OF RELATIONSHIP

In some instances, evaluation questions focus on the relationship between two scores or factors. For instance, you might want to know if high performance in one area is related to high (or low) performance in another area, or if one participant characteristic is related to another characteristic. These might affect decisions about admission of potential participants into a particular program. You want to know whether performance in these two different areas is correlated. To answer this question, you compare the two sets of data by using a correlation coefficient, or r.

The correlation coefficient is a number ranging from .00 to 1. It indicates the degree of relationship between two sets of scores. The closer the coefficient is to 1, the stronger the relationship is, and the closer to .00, the weaker the relationship is. It is important to note, however, that this is not a causal relationship (you may remember from Chapter Seven and other resources that correlation does not imply causation). The fact that two factors may be related does not imply that one is affecting or causing the other. It is entirely possible that a third, unidentified, factor may be causing the relationship. Yet it is a common interpretation mistake to assume that if two variables are correlated, one must be causing the other. (Many superstitious beliefs and behaviors are based on this fallacy.)

Although there is no universally accepted rule as to what precise coefficient constitutes a strong correlation versus a weak one, here are some general guidelines (though these will likely vary across different fields or areas of study):

.00 to .20	Weak
.30 to .40	Moderate
.50 to .60	Moderate to strong
.70 and above	Strong

Relationships can be positive or negative. In a positive relationship, both factors vary in the same direction. For instance, performance across two different programs may both be high or may both be low. In a negative relationship, the two factors vary in opposite directions: high performance in one area may be correlated with low performance in another area. A negative correlation is expressed with a coefficient ranging from .00 to -1.

Here are some sample interpretations:

$r = .25$: Low positive. Although the two factors vary in the same direction, they do not appear to have a strong relationship. For instance, both production and absenteeism figures could be up this month, but the relationship between those two variables, as indicated by this coefficient, would seem to be low. Thus the two figures are likely not related to each other.

$r = -.40$: Moderate negative. The two factors appear to be inversely related to one another, with this relationship being neither very weak nor very strong. For instance, although warranty returns continue to go up in a given quarter, we could observe the profit levels going down. With a coefficient of $-.40$, we might infer that the two have a fairly good chance of being related.

$r = -.05$: Very weak negative. There probably is not much of a relationship between the two factors despite traces of a potential inverse relationship. For instance, the performance evaluation scores for a given population might be decreasing as the number of training courses they take increases. However, with a coefficient of $-.05$, it is doubtful that the two are related.

$r = .76$: Strong positive. This suggests that the two factors are strongly related and vary in the same direction. For instance, we might observe that as quality (as illustrated by relevant measurable indicators) goes up, sales also go up. With a coefficient of $.76$, we can be confident that these two factors are closely related.

Although there are numerous ways to estimate a correlation coefficient (and the appropriate one, once again, depends on the scale of measurement), two of the most commonly used methods are Pearson r (also referred to as *product-moment correlation coefficient*), which is most appropriate when data to be correlated are measured in an interval or ratio scale, and Spearman's rho, which is appropriate if at least one of the factors being correlated is measured on a ordinal scale.

INFERENTIAL STATISTICS: PARAMETRIC AND NONPARAMETRIC

There are two main types of inferential statistics: parametric and nonparametric. Parametric statistics are mathematical procedures for hypothesis testing, which assume that the distributions (set of scores) of the variables being evaluated have certain characteristics. For instance, analysis of variance (ANOVA) assumes that the underlying distributions are normally distributed and that the variances of the distributions being compared are similar. While parametric techniques are generally robust—that is, they have substantial power to detect differences or similarities even when the assumptions are violated—some distributions violate these assumptions so strikingly that nonparametric techniques are warranted in order to detect differences or similarities.

Nonparametric statistics are another type of mathematical procedure for hypothesis testing that make no assumptions about the frequency distributions of the variables being assessed. Some commonly used methods include chi-square, Mann–Whitney U, and Kruskal–Wallis. When the assumptions underlying the use of parametric testing are not satisfied, nonparametric tests can have more statistical power.

Selecting the right inferential statistic tool depends on a number of things:

- The scale used to measure these variables (nonparametric tests tend to be appropriate for nominal and ordinal data, and parametric tests are used for interval and ratio data)

- The number of groups being compared

- Whether groups are related (for example, pretest and posttest for one group) or independent (for example, a control group—receiving no treatment such as participating in a program—and an experimental group—receiving the treatment)

While an extensive list of statistical tests is not covered here, Table 12.1 should be helpful in selecting the right tool. For instance, if you

TABLE 12.1. **Comparisons and Ways to Assess the Results**

Number of Groups Being Compared	Measured on Interval or Ratio	Measured on Ordinal[a]	Measured on Nominal (Binomial)[b]
One group to a hypothetical value	One-sample t test	Wilcoxon test	Chi-square or binomial test
Two independent groups	Unpaired t test	Mann–Whitney test	Fisher's test (chi-square for large samples)
Two related groups	Paired t test	Wilcoxon test	McNemar's test
Three or more independent groups	One-way ANOVA	Kruskal–Wallis test	Chi-square test
Three or more related groups	Repeated-measures ANOVA	Friedman test	Cochran Q

[a]An example is questionnaire items with attitudinal scales.
[b]Two possible responses, for example, male/female, Democrat/Republican, or Coke/Pepsi.

want to compare the differences between males and females in terms of their preferred method of transportation to work in a downtown metropolitan area (for example, public versus private transportation), you would be dealing with data measured on a nominal scale. Thus, you would not be able to test those differences with parametric statistics (a *t* test, for example) because your data are not measured on an internal or ratio scale. In this case, a chi-square test would help you determine if there is a significant difference in the preferences of these two groups.

Even after determining whether the results are significant (that is, they were not due to chance, resulting in a rejection of the null and consideration of the alternate) or not (fail to reject the null, which basically means there is no evidence to claim that the treatment had an effect), we are still not ready to draw conclusions. As we shall see in the next section, statistical significance is one piece of information, and practical significance is a separate piece. Figure 12.6 illustrates the progression between analyzed data and the final recommendation. Final evaluation

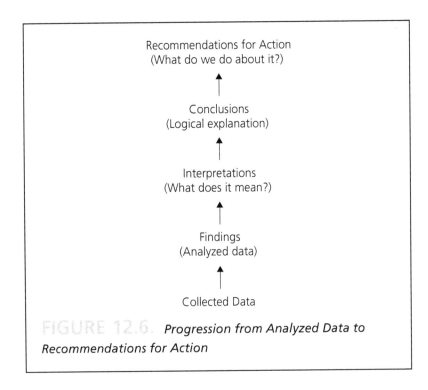

FIGURE 12.6. *Progression from Analyzed Data to Recommendations for Action*

reports should contain, and align, all of these elements. In order for an evaluator's recommendations and conclusions to be credible, the evaluator must establish this order of logic throughout the communication of the evaluation results in a written report or an oral briefing.

INTERPRETATION

Data analysis focuses on organizing and summarizing information. In your findings, you begin to highlight the most important elements, thereby engaging in the process of turning data into information. Your findings begin to give meaning to the numbers and patterns that the analysis rendered.

Interpretation attaches meaning to such organized information in order to draw plausible and supportable conclusions. In this sense, data analysis deals with the facts, while interpretation calls for value judgments. Because this is an innately subjective process, careful attention and effort should be spent on ensuring fairness, openness, and as much objectivity as is realistic under the circumstances. Even the fairest and most well-meaning evaluators will be biased to some extent. Our perceptions are formed by our experiences, preferences, values, and habits. Thus, it is helpful to clearly articulate our rationale for our interpretations by linking each one back to the findings, which are of course based on the data analyzed. This alignment is critical throughout the evaluation process. The data collected are relevant and valid indicators of the results we want to achieve, which we previously related to important evaluating questions and want to answer so that stakeholders can make sound decisions about how to improve performance.

Another helpful tactic is to involve others in the interpretation. Including stakeholders in the interpretation of data provides the opportunity to consider the data in a variety of different perspectives. Reviewing results from other relevant projects is also helpful in incorporating other perspectives. These can provide helpful insights that may have been missed in the evaluation being reported.

Even perfectly quantifiable data require interpretation. Suppose that your results are statistically significant. Now what do you do? One basic question that you have to ask is whether the results observed were of practical importance. For instance, suppose the data for an evaluation question dealing with relationships between two variables, sales figures and number of training courses taken, yielded a correlation coefficient of .22, which was found to be statistically significant (too strong to have occurred by chance). Is it of practical significance? You and your stakeholders will have to make that call. Is the actual relationship strong enough for you to base important decisions on it? Perhaps not; thus, one data-driven decision in this case would be to look for other data on which to base your decisions. Remember that the whole point of evaluation is to make valid and useful decisions for continual improvement.

In interpreting results, it is also important to keep the purpose of the evaluation in mind, as well as the evaluation questions that were to be answered. These should be linked to needs—gaps in results—identified during the initial needs assessment. These pieces of information will be instrumental in making relevant interpretations and conclusions. Based on these inferences, a detailed list of applicable recommendations should be derived. Such recommendations for action provide the central basis for decision making and thus are the drivers for the evaluation in the first place. You can see why this might be the section of the evaluation report that draws the immediate attention of decision makers.

In sum, there are numerous considerations and approaches to making sound interpretations—for example:

- Involve stakeholders in the process.

- Consult various perspectives, such as people, other evaluation reports, and different related studies.

- Review the purpose of the evaluation: What questions have we asked and answered?

- Determine whether the evaluation questions have been satisfactorily answered by the data collected. Remember that these should be linked to the needs identified in the needs assessment process. In other words, determine if needs—gaps in results—have in fact been reduced or eliminated.

- Determine the value and implications of findings.

- Look for consensus where appropriate, but do not force it if none exists.

- Distinguish between statistical significance and practical significance.

- Be forthcoming and explicit about limitations of the data and their interpretation.

- Be conservative where linkages between the intervention being evaluated and the impact observed is concerned.

KEY POINTS

- Data analysis helps evaluators identify patterns and fortify arguments used to support conclusions and recommendations.

- When you are dealing with soft data, carefully structured discussion plays an important role in analysis.

- The scale at which a given data set is measured plays a central role in selecting appropriate data analysis techniques.

- There are two types of statistics: descriptive and inferential. Descriptive statistics analyze a given data set, and inferential statistics help draw connections between a sample and the group from which the sample was drawn.

- While data analysis begins to reveal emergent themes and patterns, interpretation is necessary to attach meaning to such findings that will later lead to plausible conclusions and recommendations.

REFLECTION QUESTIONS

1. How could the use of appropriate (or inappropriate) data analysis techniques affect the evaluator's credibility?

2. How does the scale at which a given data set is measured influence the analysis of the data set?

3. What is the distinction between analyzing data and interpreting them?

4. Once a statistically significant correlation has been established, what is left to decide about the relationship between two data sets?

COMMUNICATING THE FINDINGS

This chapter addresses the recommendations that flow from the evaluation data and interpretations, providing advice on how to define and describe these recommendations, as well as how to present them to stakeholders. It discusses how to write an evaluation report, addresses how to present both final and various forms of interim reports to stakeholders, and finally examines possible roles for an evaluator after the evaluation is "finished" and the final report is delivered.

Communicating the findings is one of the most important aspects of the evaluation. After all, the whole point of doing the evaluation is to help stakeholders make decisions about how to improve performance. Hence, how we communicate those findings will determine what actions stakeholders will take, if they take action at all.

It is imperative to note that communication of the findings is not something that occurs only at the end of the evaluation process. Recall from our early discussion about the relationship with stakeholders that keeping them active in the evaluation process is a requirement for useful evaluation. One useful, and formalized, mechanism for maintaining open communication is to integrate it into the evaluation project management plan as a stage for stakeholder review, feedback, and revision at the end of each major project function. Continual verbal and electronic communication should supplement this mechanism. A colleague of mine has had great success with the "Monday morning update," a weekly e-mail that in one page gives a current snapshot of a project: status (green, yellow, red—in terms of on-time completion), tasks completed the previous week, tasks to do this week (including stakeholders responsible), and tasks coming next week.

Open communication and transparency give everyone a sense of influence over the process and the future, as well as providing multiple points of view that can be used to minimize bias, which promotes more accurate findings.

RECOMMENDATIONS

While open communication about the process and the discoveries is desirable, the evaluator should avoid making premature, unsubstantiated judgments about what these discoveries mean or how to fix apparent problems. Recommendations are precisely about how to get to the ends you want and require. You can certainly offer a preliminary set of recommendations based on your expertise, research, and experience; however, recommendations are a perfectly appropriate topic to develop in conjunction with stakeholders. In fact, the likelihood that solutions that stakeholders come up with will be implemented is significantly higher than the likelihood that solutions you come up with will be implemented. Although people sometimes have a difficult time articulating what ends they are really after, there is usually no shortage of ideas about how to get there, primarily because most people's work is focused on those ends. Nonetheless, one important evaluator function is to provide a data-driven framework from which appropriate recommendations can be identified: the requirements that define a successful solution to the identified problems.

Look at it this way: You would never hire the first person who walked off the street just because he or she popped into your office. You would first determine what the functions a new person in the position would have to fulfill in order to contribute to the objectives of the team, department, organization, and so on. Similarly, a recommended solution has to meet certain qualifications; only if it meets them all, or at least the most important ones (sometimes this is the most practical way to go and still get the job done), does it get the position. To reiterate, if you are going to provide a data-driven framework that communicates to the stakeholder the requirements for an effective solution, you should not open the door to pet solutions that you know will not benefit the organization.

Table 13.1 provides a list of steps that can help provide a solid framework for identifying effective solutions. Although it is systematic, the process does not have to be slow and long if it is facilitated well. Keep everyone focused on the desired impact.

TABLE 13.1. Framework for Identification of Solution Recommendations

Step	Considerations/Tasks
1. Define the issue to be resolved.	To what result is it related? What factors does it involve? Performers? Management? Programs? External value added? Funding or budget issues? Other resources? This may seem obvious, but being clear about the central issue will make life much easier for all involved. What are the costs and consequences for fixing it versus stalling or avoiding it?
2. Identify the requirements for resolving the issue.	What critical things have to happen in order for the issue to be resolved? What characteristics does the solution to this issue have to possess in order to make those critical things happen? Within what time frame should those things take place? What overall value should it add?
3. Identify the possible alternatives.	The stakeholders and evaluators jointly identify alternatives, and the more that people feel they were involved in creating solutions, the higher their personal investment in the success of that solution will be. The key driver in the generation of viable ideas is whether they meet the requirements for solving the issue, as identified in step 2.

(Continued)

Step	Considerations/Tasks
4. Identify pros and cons (including estimated costs).	For each identified alternative, consider the strengths as well as the weaknesses. Do the strengths outweigh the weaknesses? This question is not only about the number of strengths versus weaknesses but also about their importance. There may be only one apparent strength against five apparent weaknesses, but if that one strength is, for instance, "it saves lives," it will likely outweigh the weaknesses and costs. In the next step, ranking them, you can compare the alternatives to determine whether you can get the same strength in an alternative at a lower cost. What overall value will each alternative add?
5. Rank alternatives.	With this information at hand, you are in the position to rank the alternatives in order of appropriateness and feasibility. What is appropriate and feasible will vary from organization to organization. Stakeholders must come up with a list of pertinent criteria that makes sense for their organization and purposes. Criteria might include effectiveness of the alternative, cost, previous experience with it, if any, and political considerations, to name a few.
6. Make a decision.	After ranking, you will ultimately have to decide which alternatives make the most sense. The previous step may have facilitated this stage quite well or may have left decision makers with more questions than before. Even considering taking no action at that time with regard to a particular decision may be wise. All alternatives and their potential impact should be carefully considered.

CONSIDERATIONS FOR IMPLEMENTING RECOMMENDATIONS

Implementation is perhaps the most neglected step in performance improvement. Typically performance improvement professionals, including evaluators, needs assessors, and performance analysts in general, engage in an investigative process, come up with data-based recommendations for actions, and then bid farewell, expecting stakeholders to take the baton and run with it. Unfortunately, many stakeholders are unfamiliar with how to implement solutions—whether they designed or developed the solutions themselves or not.

Implemented solutions fail for two main reasons: Stakeholders implemented the wrong solution, or the right solution was poorly implemented. In the general scheme of performance improvement, the needs assessment and causal analysis are meant to ensure that the solutions and programs selected are clearly based on documented needs and causal factors. These front-end products should include a thoughtful implementation plan that will support the success of the solution or solution sets in closing the performance gaps. Regrettably, this is not nearly as commonplace as it should be. In addition, evaluation deliverables should include useful guidelines for stakeholders to base their implementation plans on.

Any recommended action should be considered in the context of the entire performance system; otherwise, the risk is fixing one thing but damaging five others. Here are some general guidelines:

- Confirm that these recommendations are right for identified problems in this organization and at this time.

- Be clear with everyone about what has to be done, by whom, by when, and why.

- Attempt to ensure that leadership will actively communicate and support the expected changes.

- Ensure that those who will manage the implementation understand how those affected perceive the change. People will not go along with changes they feel will harm them in the end. Sabotage becomes the name of the game.

- If there are misperceptions about the expected change, eliminate them by clarifying the facts. If people really could be hurt by the expected changes, then decision makers should rethink what they are asking of organizational members.

- Ensure commitment from the top leadership to all organizational members.

- Be clear about what conflicts may hinder in implementing each recommendation (for example, who will be affected and what the effect is).

- If anyone's responsibilities will change, document the changes, and make sure that all of those involved know about them.

- Ensure that appropriate consequences are aligned with all expectations. Telling someone to do something is not enough incentive.

- Identify all potential barriers to successful implementation, and develop a plan for how to neutralize them.

- Make sure that the appropriate project management plans are developed, approved, revised as required, and completed. Then ensure that the appropriate consequences are aligned with completing (or not) the tasks.

- Ensure that the appropriate resources have been secured to complete the implementation process. Running out of resources midway through the implementation process breeds cynicism and lack of trust among organizational members. People will later hear, "We tried that, and it didn't work," and a potentially good recommendation will be forever rejected.

- If feasible and appropriate, pilot recommendations on a smaller scale before implementing them throughout the organization.

- Ensure a tracking system is in place to monitor the appropriate implementation, and take immediate corrective action if the implementation is off track. (Chapter Fifteen presents more information on self-evaluation frameworks and continual improvement.)

The key during the implementation phase, as in all other phases of performance improvement, is to maintain open and continuous communication, document and track progress toward stated objectives, and use feedback from tracking mechanisms to improve just in time.

DEVELOPING THE REPORT

Before moving on to preparing the report, keep this in mind: One useful habit to develop with your evaluation clients is to provide them with preliminary drafts (clearly marked as such). When a report draft is provided, the evaluator may simultaneously provide one or more questions for the stakeholder reviewers to answer about the report. The questions may ask the reviewers to paraphrase the meaning of key marked parts of an excerpt or of the whole. Or the evaluator may ask the reviewers to answer specific questions on meaning, tone, or emphasis. The stakeholders charged with reviewing the report should also be asked to provide any comments they believe to be appropriate. This approach is similar to usability testing and cued-response protocol testing, used by a wide variety of government and corporate agencies to improve documents of all types (Dumas & Redish, 1999).

There are some important considerations for developing a useful and effective evaluation report. You should consider these at the beginning of your evaluation project, not just when you are ready to prepare the report.

Know the Audience

Language Language is critical to effective communication, yet too often it is taken for granted. The final report is supposed to provide clear and concise information to decision makers about which decisions the study supports. One risk is that a decision maker could make an inaccurate decision based on misinterpretation or overreaction to report language. It is imperative that you know to whom you are directing the report. Will the audience include financial people, technical people, politicians, others, or a mix of any or all of these? Make sure that you and your audience are clear about the audience for the report. You should also consider the audience's education, background, experience, and other relevant factors to ensure that your communication is effective.

One term can have different meanings to different people, so be on the lookout for language that could be interpreted in different ways by the different groups represented. Although language in general is open to some degree of interpretation, take steps to ensure you minimize the variability of interpretations as much as possible. One way to do this is to provide operational definitions, or elaborate the terms in question by providing concise explanations and examples while simultaneously avoiding long justifications.

It is important that statements be descriptive rather than judgmental. The better you can describe your findings, as supported by data analysis, the less basis there will be for disagreement and resistance. And the less evaluative that your statements are, the less likely it is that people will resist them. Substitute behavioral descriptions for words like *excellent, poor, good, bad, controlling, strong,* and *weak.* For instance, saying, "Tom is an excellent supervisor," is different from saying, "The Group A supervisor and his team have consistently met or surpassed the operational objectives over the previous fiscal year."

The Center for Instructional Research and Curriculum Evaluation at the University of Illinois is one of several professional evaluation organizations that checks the impact of results and language of presentations by using reviews by a professional evaluator outside the immediate investigative team. This review, a form of meta-evaluation, can be used to spot words that trigger hot issues and tender feelings that could lead to unwarranted programmatic actions. But how can evaluators determine if the report communicates well? That is, how can evaluators assess the likelihood that decision makers who read an evaluation report will interpret it as the authors intended? One variation on the meta-evaluation is to use a surrogate (substitute) decision maker to review findings and courses of action that follow from the findings. The aim here is to reduce the risk of communication error. A surrogate decision maker should consider these questions in reviewing the report:

- Do the findings appear to be stated in the correct order of importance? What is the rationale for this order?

- Are the format and organization appropriate for this client?

- Is phraseology overly emotive, that is, does it contain loaded words?

- Is wording ambiguous (phrases easily taken two ways) or imprecise (vague terms or phrases)?

Format An effective way to find the best format for a particular audience is asking. You can ask your liaison, the project sponsor, or anyone from the client organization who has been supporting your efforts or is in a position to provide helpful feedback. The basic question is, What kind of report does the client expect? Written or verbal? Formal PowerPoint or informal discussion? Short or long? General format or a special internal format?

The key is to adapt the report to the expectations and preferences of the client. A wide-ranging evaluation study will require a larger report than a tight, small study designed to answer just a few evaluation questions. The following four types of written reports and three types of oral reports cover most situations.

Written Reports The type of report must support the type of evaluation. The main emphasis is on confirming that the results obtained are the ones that were initially intended and expected when the solution or program was implemented.

The function of evaluation can be emphasized at different stages of a program. It is not uncommon for administrators to request progress reports—formative evaluations—that evaluate milestones that lead to ultimate overarching results. This is especially true when the stakes are high. All managers should know the costs and penalties for failing to hit the targets and that timely program adjustments can make the difference between success and failure. Evaluators may be called on to assist in making these ongoing adjustments, as well as to report final findings.

The following typology of reports is based on the requirement to report findings at differing points in the life cycle of a program. The term *program* is used here in the most general sense as course of action or solution strategy that has a beginning and an end as can be managed. In the course of real events in time, many programs coexist, start, and stop in a complex context of social, economic, and physical forces. Evaluators who can tease out the important facts from background noise and confusion by writing and presenting a clear and well-founded report can contribute a great deal to the organization.

▪ *Report of findings based on program evaluation results.* This report is used at the end of a program or evaluation contract to present findings relating to the various levels of results of the solution or program under study. This report should include a comparison of the obtained results to the expected results and explanations about the differences based on observations, which occurred during the evaluation study. The report will include recommendations as to a future course of action regarding the program.

▪ *Report of findings based on evaluation of alternative courses of action.* This report is used following needs assessment, when goals and objectives (the ends) have been derived and are linked to an organizational vision based on societal needs. At this point, alternative solutions to reach the goals and objectives (the means to be employed to reach desired results) are evaluated based on cost benefit ratio and other criteria related to the specific stakeholders. This report can also be used to report findings and recommendations related to midcourse adjustments. When milestones are missed, some adjustment may be required. Unpredicted events can cause disruption to the tactics. Changes can be required due to a cut in resources, a change in the populations, a change in the political situation, and a host of other factors.

■ *Report of findings based on evaluation of goals and objectives.* This report is used when the evaluation team has reason to question the legitimacy of goal and objectives. Perhaps a needs assessment was never done. The team may want to recommend that one be carried out and provide guidance.

■ *Report of findings based on evaluation of performance records.* This report is used to present findings of an evaluation study directed at a perceived deficiency in performance. The report will contain the evidence and arguments stemming from each candidate causal or contributing factor. The factors are rank-ordered. Sometimes recommendations are made concerning how the deficiency might be reduced or eliminated.

Most written reports include the same general components, albeit some elements may be organized differently. This following outline for a written report is appropriate for a formal and technically elaborate report:

I. Executive Summary

II. Body of Report

 A. Introduction

  1. Statement of Purpose

  2. Background and/or Antecedents

  3. Description of the Evaluation's Scope of Inquiry

  4. General and Specific Evaluation Questions

 B. Description of Methodology

  1. Specific Results and Indicators to Observe

  2. Data Sources and Instruments/Methods of Data Collection

  3. Observation Chronology

  4. Discussion of Relevant Factors

  5. Data Analysis Results

 C. Findings and Interpretation (that answer each evaluation question)

    D.   Recommendations and Conclusions (that are directly linked
to findings and relevant data)

III.   Key Appendixes/Exhibits

The next way to organize a final report might be more appropriate
for an audience interested in a comparatively "quick-and-dirty" account
of what is going on and what to do about it. It is worth noting that
although the first two sections are organized in the same fashion as they
are for the formal report, in this example, they should likely be much
more concise. In the first scenario, they would usually be more elaborate and detailed.

    I.   Executive Summary

   II.   Body of Report

        A.   Introduction

            1. Statement of Purpose

            2. Background and/or Antecedents

            3. Description of the Evaluation's Scope of Inquiry

            4. General and Specific Evaluation Questions

        B.   Description of Methodology

            1. Specific Results and Indicators to Observe

            2. General Data Sources and Instruments/Methods of
Data Collection

        C.   Evaluation Findings

            1. Theme 1

               Finding 1

               Supporting Data

               Recommendations

            2. Theme 1

               Finding 2

               Supporting Data

               Recommendations

3. Theme 2

Finding 1

Supporting Data

Recommendations

4. Theme 2

Finding 2

Supporting Data

Recommendations

5. Theme 2

Finding 3

Supporting Data

Recommendations

6. Theme 3 [and so on]

III.   Key Appendixes/Exhibits

Here, the findings are clustered around themes (maybe three to five in total), with each theme containing between two and five specific findings. The themes might be around one general problem such as lack of linkages among various levels of strategic, tactical, and operational results, with specific findings providing more specific instances of each, supported by the data.

Oral Reports Evaluators are often called on to make oral presentations. Here are three situations that are highly likely to be requested in any evaluation study:

▪   *Executive briefing.* The executive briefing should be short and to the point. Pay particular attention to avoid repetition, and know the content of previous briefings so as not to address material that has already been covered. It is all right to begin with a brief recap of previously provided information, but even then, the points should be limited to those that are relevant to the rest of the presentation. In general, the list of report guidelines below will provide a structure for your presentation.

Remember that as an evaluator, you take your lead from the agreed-on goals and objectives derived from needs assessment and linked to the organization's vision and mission. As such, you are there to brief the facts of the findings, not make a sales pitch. Many public-speaking advice books are aimed at making convincing arguments and closing the deal. There is no deal to close in an evaluation. You report the findings relative to the goals of the program and the guidelines of professional ethics. When you jump over to advocacy or spin doctoring, you have moved away from evaluation into a new role.

Public forum. Speaking in public can be daunting for some people. Toastmasters (www.toastmasters.org) is a good place for practicing. The presentation of evaluation findings has an added requirement to inform more than entertain. The use of a logical structure in the presentation, clear visual aids that are simple and direct, and notes to keep you on track will help you serve the audience. In a public forum, you must be prepared to answer questions. Although it is your duty to be impartial in presenting the findings, your audience will often contain passionate advocates who hold varying views. The evaluation findings presentation is not the proper forum to argue or defend these points of view. If your program was initiated using a disciplined approach to needs assessment, you will be in a position to answer questions because the societal benefit and the linkage to program goals are made explicit in that process.

Demonstration. Demonstrations are often more effective than words in presenting evaluation findings. Video and audio recordings can convey the results in cases where the performance goals involve psychomotor skills. Medicine, sports, and manufacturing are areas of performance where seeing results in action can provide a valuable supplement to other measures of performance.

Identify the Key Message: Take Action!

This consideration goes along with the first. The format and language that are appropriate for the client should be linked to the action the client should take in order to improve the organization and its ability to meet clients' (and clients' clients) needs. Thus, you have to determine almost simultaneously the who and the what.

Along with identifying who must do what, part of this guideline will be fed by this chapter's discussion on recommendations. Communicating to a client what should be done may seem completely clear to the evaluator or other consultants, but for most clients, this is seldom enough. It is also important to articulate how this recommendation should be carried out—in loose terms, how it will be implemented.

Taking these considerations into account, the evaluator can begin to articulate the content of a final report, whether oral or written. Remember that conducting an evaluation is merely a vehicle for making sound decisions about how to improve performance. This report is where you recommend, based on the data, how to achieve that goal.

The guiding question here should be, So what? What did the data consistently point to, and what is the most likely way to deal effectively and efficiently with those findings?

Make Clear Distinctions and Linkages

The overarching message you should get from this book is alignment—alignment between

- Value added to or subtracted from external and societal partners, organizational internal partners, and associates within the organization

- The evaluation purpose and the subsequent evaluation questions

- The questions and the results that matter

- The results and the key performance indicators

- The indicators and the sources and methods used to collect the relevant data

- The types of data and the techniques used to analyze them

- The results of the data analysis and the likely interpretations

- The interpretations and the recommendations for action

Think of it as a building: if any of these elements are not well aligned, you do not have a solid structure. If you are not demonstrating a solid structure, people will have little or no confidence on the ground you claim to hold.

You must not confuse your interpretation of what the data suggest with the data themselves. You have to be clear about this in communicating the results. If you are not clear, someone will surely point that out. It's better to lean toward a more conservative stand than to stick your neck out without sufficient evidence and have a stakeholder point out that what you are saying is unsupported by the evidence. If this occurs, a cloud of doubt will hang over your other conclusions and recommendations, even if they are perfectly supported.

Make sure that the evaluation findings you worked hard to obtain do not cause the audience to make decisions unsupported by the data. Make clear linkages, not only throughout the communication of the results, but also throughout your entire evaluation process.

Be Clear About the Stakeholders' Responsibilities

As you are clarifying what actions should be taken, be specific about the roles and responsibilities of the stakeholders in implementing the recommendations. It is important that they understand that they are not helpless in improving their situation, regardless of how much work and effort the process will demand of them.

Be sure to link and align results and consequences for each organizational element, even though your original charge might have been just a single program, project, or activity. Note the value added to or subtracted from your shared society, the organization, and your associates.

At all costs, avoid nurturing an external locus of control, where stakeholders convince themselves that they have little or no power to change things for the better. Although authority and decision-making power are not equally distributed throughout the organization, everyone at every level has some control over their unique and collective contributions to the organization. Be clear and specific, where possible, about how different groups and individuals can be active participants in the performance improvement recommendations.

One way to communicate stakeholder responsibilities, as an additional deliverable or as part of the evaluation report if negotiated in this way, is to provide a general project management plan for implementing recommendations that the stakeholders selected and approved. In this situation, the evaluator, in consultation with experts of a particular recommendation and the stakeholder group, can define major functions, key tasks, timelines, and groups or individuals responsible for a given task or function. Flowcharts can often help the client visualize the implementation process.

THE EVALUATOR'S ROLE AFTER THE REPORT

Although evaluators are usually not involved in the implementation of recommendations, giving stakeholders as vivid an image as possible of what the ensuring process will be can provide the required momentum for implementing the recommendations. If the evaluation project is ongoing, they may also be responsible for creating the evaluation framework for whatever alternatives were selected for implementation. In addition, they could be involved in the design, development, implementation, and formal evaluation after implementation. The evaluator's involvement at every stage encourages everyone to stay focused on the measurable results and improvement that the recommendations are meant to deliver.

KEY POINTS

- Communication with stakeholders should occur throughout the evaluation process in order to promote their sense of ownership over the process, findings, and steps recommended to improve performance.

- Evaluation recommendations should fit a clear set of criteria and should not reflect evaluator bias.

- Stakeholders can play an important role in identifying potential solutions, provided the solution criteria are clearly communicated to all.

- In preparing a powerful final report, the evaluator must consider the audience, the action to be taken, alignment between recommended actions and analyzed data and interpretations, and the stakeholder responsibilities for implementing recommendations.

- The evaluation report is not always the last step in the evaluator's role.

REFLECTION QUESTIONS

1. What specific steps could you take to ensure ongoing communication with the evaluation stakeholders?

2. What are the pros and cons you foresee in involving stakeholders in the identification of potential solutions?

3. What, in your opinion, should be the role of the evaluator after the evaluation report has been delivered? When is the evaluation work done?

PART

4

CONTINUAL IMPROVEMENT

COMMON ERRORS IN EVALUATION

This chapter lists nineteen errors, some common and some less frequently seen, that can show up in evaluations. The errors are divided into three groups: errors of system mapping, errors of logic, and errors of procedure. Attention to avoiding these errors is key to completing a successful and productive evaluation.

This book is intended to help evaluators and those who use evaluation data to conduct and understand meaningful, timely evaluations that are effective in guiding and adjusting programs and solutions. It provides models and advice on doing an evaluation.

Another way to keep you on track is to show you what to avoid doing. This chapter has been framed as a discussion of errors in evaluation. Some of these are distressingly common and others less often troublesome. A complete picture of the domain of common evaluation errors is presented because understanding the scope of possible errors helps illuminate the fundamentals of how to make evaluation useful.

Much of what social science has learned about organizational behavior can be applied to evaluation. At the same time, much of the current thinking in the field of evaluation must be carefully examined to separate the "-isms" from realism. Some models and approaches can be used for practical evaluation, while others are best left to academic discourse.

The working definition of *evaluation* here focuses on the concept of results: asking the right questions and identifying what worked and what did not, so that we know what areas of performance to improve and how. Since performance results have been emphasized, the discussion begins with a question that might also be posed by social scientists: How do you know that the results you have observed (and measured) are in fact caused by your program or solution and not by some other force or forces acting in the background? Social scientists often use control groups here: comparing the results for a group given the intervention with the results for a group that got nothing. But evaluation settings often preclude the use of controls, both because of time and because there might be an ethical problem with not working with some groups while working with others. Evaluators must rely on understanding the system and the ethos of the environment in which they are operating. We must take care to properly conceptualize the overarching system and the component subsystems that are important to any program or solution. Therefore, the first set of errors is grouped under the heading "Errors of System Mapping."

ERRORS OF SYSTEM MAPPING

Errors of system mapping occur when evaluators make inaccurate relationships between phenomena.

Error of Causal Path

Most of the time, evaluators teach. They observe the effects of teaching directly and are correct in assuming the direct link between the teaching (or other instructional tactics) and the results. In one-on-one coaching and mentoring, this is usually a safe assumption. But what happens when they try to apply this direct causal linkage to whole programs, many students, and averaged scores on tests? The larger and more complex the program and the longer the time frame, the more they have to consider a wide range of variables that may or may not influence the outcomes of programs. What if a one-time disruption contributed to low test scores in an otherwise sound program? What if extra effort on the part of one teacher influenced the results of a weak program? Educational administrators could make a bad decision by assuming a direct link between teaching and results. Scrapping a good program and supporting a weak program are two errors of causal path—the roadway to results (you may see a parallel here in the famous type 1 and type 2 errors talked about in statistical hypothesis testing).

Error of Misattribution

In today's workplace, managers tend to think in terms of problems and solutions. Most of the time, that is a helpful way of approaching a situation, but occasionally a complex problem is addressed by a simplistic solution that does more harm than good. This is usually accompanied by a misattribution of causes and effects or problems and solutions.

For example, the Chicago school board once set out to improve academic performance in one of its schools. They perceived that a lack of progress in that school was the result of the lack of will or ability on the part of the school's principal, and thus their solution was to replace the principal. It took a wise evaluator (Stake, 1970) to point out that the school was in a neighborhood where a lot of drug dealing took place, most of the students were from single-parent homes, the one good meal that the children got each day came from the school, and the local principal had been encouraging mentoring of troubled youth. The principal had created a safe harbor each day for the students. Academic progress was not at the standard set by the board, but in the light of the other accomplishments relating to the fundamental survival of these children, the principal had done a remarkable job. Replacing her would not have improved academic performance and could have made things worse.

Error of the Missing Player

Sometimes we look for a cause to explain a result; in the case of undesirable consequences, we want someone to blame, that is, a scapegoat. However, whenever we are not sure of the cause or causes acting to bring about the result and, in the absence of any data, we attribute the success or failure of a program to a given person or group of persons, we commit the error of the missing player.

Error of Local Value

Evaluation is all about making an unambiguous statement about what is good and what is bad, what is useful and what is not, what to save and what to throw out. It is important, however, to remember that what we take as good at one level of a system is derived from the next level up, and sooner or later we arrive at the societal level of good. Morality and ethics cannot be divorced from the everyday workings of education. However, sometimes we get so wrapped up in local issues that we define what is good based on a closed system that in the extreme can be devoid of ethics and acceptable morality. For example, cults and gangs try to "educate" members in part by shielding them from the larger societal view. That is the error of local value. If we are not adding value to our shared society, we might be subtracting it.

ERRORS OF LOGIC

These errors occur when interpretations and conclusions are not well supported by the data.

Error of False Conclusion

When we claim to reach a conclusion regarding a program, even though that "conclusion" is unsupported by the facts of the case or is influenced by undue bias, we commit the error of false conclusion. Remember that conclusions must be based on solid interpretations that justifiably flow from the analyzed data. If this alignment is not obvious, the conclusions are on shaky ground. It is far better to spot the error of false conclusion than for stakeholders to identify it while going over your evaluation report or listening to your oral briefing.

Error of the Expert

When we rely on the advice of an expert who operates outside his or her area of expertise, or when we treat expert advice as infallible even when the expert opinions fly in the face of the facts, that is the error of the expert. Expertise is both context and content dependent. Many so-called experts are identified as such because of an advanced degree or position, which others then infer are indicators of competence. But we all at one point or another have run into incompetent people in all sorts of positions in spite of their advanced degrees or other qualifications. The point here is that an expert may know a lot about one thing, but it does not mean that person knows everything or has seen it all, even in his or her area of expertise. In fact, the more an expert specializes in one small area, the more myopic that person can become.

Error of Wishful Thinking

A conclusion based not on the facts of the case but on the expectations and desired objectives of the stakeholders is the error of wishful thinking. This is a surprisingly powerful error. Some individuals can look at the facts and not see them for what they are, but instead for what they had already made up their mind they would see even before the evaluation study.

Error of Association

A conclusion that flies in the face of the facts because a noted personality took part, or because of the past reputation of the participants, or because of advertising is the error of association. (In fact, most advertising depends on its audience making the error of association.) Take a close look at the attributions you make about apparent associations, and be sure the attributions are based on sound evidence.

Error of the Quick Fix

Actions and conclusions based on the desire to look effective and decisive but in fact putting in place half-baked programs in order to say "we did something" is committing the error of the quick fix. The overwhelming majority of the time, quick fixes make things worse; they consume more time and resources, for example, and lose others' trust. Real solutions are usually more efficient and cheaper than quick fixes.

Error of Explanation Creep

When observing behavior, we have a tendency to explain it in terms of motivation and other constructs, or social forces like striving for success. All of these motivational explanations are in fact just hypotheses, which must be verified, grounded with other observations, and tested against alternative explanations. That is acceptable if it is open and done in the proper context. Occasionally, however, we invent, or construct, attractive explanations that are so convenient that they can become detached from the original behavior. These explanations are then used to support planning and decisions as if the explanations, rather than data and interpretations, were the bedrock of cause and effect. When we overextend explanations to the point where we reason directly from them to plan and execute actions, we run the risk of creating a self-contained rationale that is detached from the real world. The consequences of this error can range from mildly embarrassing events to horrific social calamity.

ERRORS OF PROCEDURE

These errors occur when evaluation methods have been tainted by inaccuracies, miscalculations, or faulty assumptions.

Error of the Instrument

Evaluators often use instruments—electronic and mechanical, as well as paper- or computer-delivered tests and exercises. Keep in mind that all instruments are subject to failure, loss of calibration, or incorrect use. Some electronic instruments require setup procedures that are complicated and must include warm-up time. Hooking up attachments may require particular care and correct placement. Written instructions may be confusing. Tests may be unreliable or invalid. Language use may differ by group, so that a test using complex medical language will work differently if it is given to medical professionals or to persons with no medical background. All of these potential problems should increase the care devoted to the use of instruments. Failure in this area will compound errors of measurement.

Error of Measurement

Evaluators measure things in order to make generalizations about phenomena in the programs under evaluation. Always consider what is being measured. Are you measuring the right things ("validity"); what can you claim based on what you measure; and what do these measurements stand for in the complete system of events and mix of intention and results? Ask why each measurement is important to your conclusions. Consider how often to measure, what to measure, and what scale to use in measurement. Measurement can add precision to a study, but incorrect measurement (done with flawed procedures) can lead to a false sense of precision where none is warranted. For example, the use of the wrong scale, compounded by subsequent mathematical treatments of the data, can lead to enormous distortion.

Error of the Model

Models can be powerful and useful for planning and executing evaluations, but all models are approximations or representations that may or may not fit the events and situations being modeled. If the model is a good fit, it may be useful in predicting results. However, always keep in mind that the model is not the real thing; thus, when conclusions and plans are based solely on a model, without confirming the prediction with corroborating information from other sources, the error of the model is committed.

Error of the Artifact

Occasionally something in an evaluation study happens only one time and cannot be repeated by any direct manipulation of the program under study. Sometimes the single event (artifact) is good and sometimes bad. It is important that the one-time occurrence stimulate additional study. However, it is equally important that conclusions about the program not be based on a single result. To do so would be to commit the error of the artifact.

Error of the Blind Spot

The importance of using the results of a program as the key focus of evaluation has been stated, but this is not intended to imply that evaluators should not pay attention to the entire execution of the program. For example, in the event that program results were not what was intended or were in some way detrimental to the larger societal well-being, the evaluator would want to discard what did not work. But does that mean the entire program must be scrapped and a totally new program put in place? This might be the case if no observation took place during the program. It is the total penetration of the program in as many observational modalities as possible that provides clues as to what parts of the program could be changed or modified.

Error of Displacement Shift

When observing events in a program evaluation, we tend to look where we can look easily, which is not always were we should look. If we limit observations to the easy parts, we may miss critical aspects of the program. There is an old joke about a man who loses his car key in a dark parking lot and begins to search for the key out in the street. When asked why he is looking in the street and not in the parking lot, he replies that the streetlight makes it easier to see there. Another type of displacement occurs in writing educational objectives that cover only the parts of the performance that lend themselves to easy objective writing. The classic example is trying to evaluate a complex skill by asking questions about the names of the steps in the performance. If you limit your evaluation to that aspect, you have committed the error of displacement shift.

Error of the Forked Path

When procedures that lead to two different end products start with the same steps in common, it is possible to start with procedure A and end up doing procedure B. This is particularly true if you are behind schedule or under pressure, or have just completed procedure B on a prior task. This error can affect evaluators in collecting data, giving examinations, designing instructions, and documenting results. This error can be reduced by creating a "pause and consider restraints" decision just ahead of the branch point.

Error of Population Masking

If data from a subgroup of a general population indicate a problem with a supervisor, you may want to look further. However, if data on employee dissatisfaction were lumped with the data from the general population to get an average level of employee dissatisfaction, the particular subgroup problem would be submerged in the general data pool. If you base conclusions about the existence of problems on only the average data without further analysis, you run the risk of committing the error of population masking.

Error of the Average Person

We often talk about the average performer. However, the limits posed by the class of measurement used and the characteristics measured must be made explicit. The study of ergonomics has profited from the use of data on populations; nonetheless, in most cases, the extremes are used to capture most of the population. (Usually 90 percent of the population falls within the two extremes.) Averaged data should be used to guide general thinking about populations, while at the same time, each individual must be considered by all of his or her multiple dimensions, traits, and states. To reason about a given individual using population norms alone is to commit the error of the average person.

CONCLUSION

Evaluation is far too important to weaken its contributions by failing to avoid defects in thinking and methods. Organizations are complex and include many variables in the context of still another set of interacting variables in their environment. It is nearly impossible to account for every variable in an evaluation. The central challenge is to ask and answer the right questions without distorting the process with errors that can be avoided.

KEY POINTS

▪ Becoming aware of common evaluation errors can help you avoid making them.

▪ Although there can be many variables outside the control of the evaluator, we have the responsibility to ask and answer the right questions without distorting the process by adding thinking errors that can be avoided.

▪ Errors can be errors of system mapping, errors of logic, or errors of procedure.

▪ Attention to avoiding these errors is necessary to producing a successful evaluation.

REFLECTION QUESTIONS

1. Which of the errors examined in this chapter do you think could have the most damaging impact on an evaluation?

2. What are some evaluation errors that you may have observed and were left out of this discussion? What were the implications of such errors?

CONTINUAL IMPROVEMENT

This chapter explains continual improvement and divides it into two phases: monitoring and adjusting. It establishes the value of continual improvement to an organization and the role of the evaluator in implementing processes to encourage continual improvement. Finally, it analyzes the role of leadership in making continual improvement possible.

In the world of business, government, and education, continual improvement is an accepted concept; unfortunately, there is quite a way to go from concept to practice. Terms like *continual improvement, quality control,* and *value added* sound impressive, so much so that people regularly throw them around. I suspect that the frequency with which we hear these terms is not a good indicator of how frequently, or how well, organizations are implementing and sustaining true continual improvement mechanisms in the context of a continual improvement culture.

The benefit of continual improvement can have great payoffs in any endeavor. The ideal process can be controlled to define and then maintain quality and can be adjusted at the earliest sign that something is outside the acceptable range. While quality control measures keep things on track, all parts of the organization are encouraged to look, in a coordinated fashion, for ways to improve the enterprise by adjusting design specifications, altering the various processes to include any improved features, or changing that which will not deliver measurable success. The continual improvement of the organization depends on individual responsibility, supported by the required authority to make indicated changes.

WHAT IS CONTINUAL IMPROVEMENT?

Continual improvement depends on knowing where the organization is headed and continually monitoring that course to get it from where it is to where it should be. This is accomplished by asking the right questions, collecting useful data on an ongoing basis, and then applying those data to make sound decisions about required changes or which current initiatives to sustain. The goal of a continual improvement culture is thus to support the ongoing journey toward reaching the organizational vision through the use of performance feedback.

Continual improvement is much talked about but is done only rarely in practice. One likely reason is that there is much confusion about exactly what continual improvement is. In fact, there are two major components to continual improvement: monitoring and adjusting. Monitoring is about measurement and tracking: we measure what matters and track its progress. Adjusting is about change: We use the feedback obtained from the monitoring stage to promote and facilitate desirable change. This chapter focuses on these two central functions.

MONITORING PERFORMANCE

Building Continual Improvement in Organizations

The benefits that evaluation can provide are not something that happens once, stopping after the final report recommendations are implemented or discarded. Evaluation, conducted properly, can give an organization ongoing useful feedback about how much closer it is to (or farther from) its ultimate goal. In the context of continual improvement, evaluation helps organizations do this by establishing an evaluation framework that allows things that matter to be consistently and reliably measured. You might say that this evaluation framework is the backbone of a performance management system. Performance cannot be managed, at least not effectively, without the required performance data.

Once the evaluation framework is developed, which includes performance objectives at the various organizational levels, measurable indicators, and respective initiatives that target each of these, the data collected will almost naturally fall into meaningful categories. In this sense, it is a lot like facilitating an ongoing self-evaluation that provides just-in-time feedback for opportune adjustments. Feedback is a central concept here and depends on effective communication systems. If feedback is developed appropriately, it will allow leaders and employees to track, manage, and sometimes forecast performance at opportune times. In this sense, it is very much like monitoring the vital signs of the organization.

The evaluation framework can also facilitate collaboration among the organization's various departments. When the individual, yet complementing, contributions of the various departments are published broadly, people more readily understand their interdependent roles and are more likely to see that the key to organizational (and their own) success is not to compete for limited resources but rather to collaborate so that resources can be maximized. This leads to the recognition and elimination of redundant processes or internal products. Again, open, accurate, and consistent information is critical.

Characteristics of the Self-Evaluation Framework

The list of characteristics that follows can guide the development of a personalized evaluation framework. Every organization is different and has its own set of goals, values, strengths, and weaknesses. Thus, although all evaluation frameworks should possess the following five characteristics, their specific implementations will likely be different depending on the details of the organization's culture, history, expectations, and other factors:

- *Align all key results at various organizational levels (systemic).* Recall that the value of any intervention is whether it ultimately helps the organization get closer to achieving its vision. Thus, track more than immediate results at the immediate level; be sure to hypothesize and test the linkages all the way up to the vision-level goals.

- *Provide linkages between interventions or initiatives and the indicators they are to impact.* One task of evaluation is to provide evidence of the effectiveness of implemented solutions. Thus, it is important to articulate for everyone the linkages among these solutions and between the solutions and the organizational indicators they are intended to affect. The clearer the linkages are, the better able others will be to understand and use the data.

- *Stay responsive and dynamic.* The evaluation framework is more of a template than a confining structure. Although the framework might remain relatively constant, the actual indicators, or the results themselves, may change as objectives are met and new ones are derived. Recall that while solutions might address old problems, they may also bring with them a new set of challenges. Modifying this framework in order to keep its indicators current should not be done at the expense of the constancy of the organization's purpose. Changing the mission every year does not make you current but rather gives you a moving target your organization will not likely reach.

- *Be accessible to all decision makers.* Although all of these characteristics are critical, this one is probably the most difficult for leaders to grasp. The idea that the organization's report card will be open for all to see can be daunting. It is important to remember that the purpose of evaluating is to collect and interpret data for improving performance, not for finger-pointing and blaming. All decision makers must have ready access so that they can make timely decisions about how to improve performance—both individual and organizational. These efforts should be coordinated and integrated.

- *Provide feedback and regular communication.* No one can talk about continual improvement without considering the feedback loop on which it rests. The feedback loop represents the reiterative nature of tracking and adjusting. Performance data should not only be accessible by all, but should be clearly understood by all. Thus, providing consistent feedback about performance is part of bigger communication systems. Progress, milestones reached (or not reached), and action plans for reaching desired goals should be consistently and accurately communicated throughout the organization.

All this has to take place in the context of a supportive environment, in which using relevant, reliable, and valid data before making decisions is part of the organizational culture. This can be accomplished only by modeling this from the top of the organization on down and aligning the proper consequences with the desired accomplishments and behaviors related to continually improving.

The monitoring framework, or performance dashboard (Eckerson, 2006), is a potent agent of organizational change. It fulfills this function by helping the organization clearly define, communicate, and focus on important results. It also provides consistent and timely feedback that informs decisions about what changes are required for the benefit of the organization, its clients, and its employees.

ADJUSTING PERFORMANCE

Everyone—individuals, teams, and interdepartmental groups—goes through three critical change processes (Coghlan, 2000):

- *Perception.* This refers to the meaning the change has for them, the degree to which they have control over the change, and the degree of trust individuals have in those mandating or promoting the change.

- *Assessment of the impact of change.* Will the change be for the better? Uncertain but probably positive? Uncertain? Uncertain though probably negative? Threatening? Destructive?

- *Response.* The individual can deny, dodge, oppose, resist, tolerate, accept, support, or embrace the change.

A number of factors bear on these processes. One factor with a significant impact is the availability of information about the change and the process of communication between those mandating the change and those affected by it. Recall that stakeholders are both those who can affect the evaluation process and those who will be potentially affected by its results. Open communication regarding the evaluation process, findings, and recommendations is important to the change process. Lack of information promotes a sense of anxiety and resistance, particularly when individuals begin to make up their own stories about what is going on and what will happen in the future.

Any change initiative, whether it is the evaluation process itself or the recommendations that stem from it, must address these three processes. A change plan that takes into account how these changes will be perceived and evaluated by employees must be derived so that the desired responses are elicited.

While it is critical to the usefulness of the change to take steps to manage the change appropriately, it is also important to consider the other side of the coin: change creation (Kaufman & Lick, 2004). Change creation is essentially what we are doing when we set the direction for a change. An organization should do this through an authentic strategic planning and needs assessment process, where it is identifying where it would like to be years from now and what it has to accomplish in the meantime in order to get there. The hope is that it was through these processes that the solution you are now faced with evaluating was selected. Change management is thus what the organization does to make sure that things go as smoothly as possible on its way to its ultimate destination. Evaluation is one of the tools that facilitate this smooth sailing by providing decision makers with important information required for navigation.

THE ROLE OF LEADERSHIP

One fundamental prerequisite to organizational improvement is the active participation of senior executives and managers, traditionally the individuals accountable for the organization's strategic direction and operation. They, along with other key stakeholders, decide what change will take place, when, and at what pace. Because the executives may not possess the experience, time, and capability to undertake many of the key tasks in organizational transformation, others (either outside or internal consultants) are often charged with this very important function. Cummings and Worley (2005) have done site research that indicates external consultants or externally recruited executives are three times more likely to initiate transformational change than are existing executive teams.

According to Cummings and Worley (2005), the leadership team should take on three key functions in facilitating the continual improvement and change of the organization:

- *Envisioning.* Leaders should articulate clear and credible objectives, including the overarching vision, as well as the performance standards.

- *Energizing.* Leaders should model the personal excitement and commitment behaviors they expect of others, as well as communicate early examples of success.

■ *Enabling.* Leaders should provide the resources required for undertaking significant change and align consequences with desirable behaviors.

The evaluator's recommendations are fundamental to the envisioning process of the leaders and other stakeholders. Change initiatives stem from this ultimate vision and its supporting objectives. The evaluation report also plays a critical role in motivating stakeholders and energizing them into action. Recall from previous chapters that one key consideration in developing the evaluation report is to be clear about stakeholder responsibilities. Here is a good place to begin to clarify expectations and behaviors for the change process.

The importance of enabling organizational members to improve cannot be overstated. This requires creating an environment where change is encouraged and rewarded. Empowering others to change goes beyond telling them they should feel empowered or giving them more responsibility. It requires balancing accountability with authority and the required resources to meet expectations. Further efforts toward creating the right environment include setting up appropriate antecedents or cues for desired performance and behaviors and following them with appropriate consequences. Simply stated, if you want to sustain or improve desired behaviors, follow them with pleasant consequences (pleasant in the eyes of the performer); if you want to eliminate or decrease unwanted behaviors, acknowledge them and remove any rewards associated with them.

One of the common, and fatal, errors leaders make is punishing the good performers by giving them more to do simply because they can, while rewarding incompetence by not providing the appropriate consequences to those who do not perform to standards. Ignoring the problem is reinforcing the problem. Setting up the ideal environment calls for a continual learning process where behaviors are tried, their consequences are assessed, and the required modifications, if any, are implemented.

To make all of this happen, leaders must rely on a reliable and valid information system that helps them clearly and concisely communicate strategies, goals, and specific objectives to all employees on a consistent basis. Evaluators can play a significant role in creating this system. This system should allow leaders and employees alike to track organizational, team, and individual performance, so that all have readily accessible performance feedback.

KEY POINTS

▪ Continual improvement depends on monitoring performance and adjusting accordingly.

▪ The success of a self-evaluation framework for continual performance improvement depends on open, accurate, and consistent information.

▪ Leadership plays a central role in the creation and management of change that supports continual improvement.

REFLECTION QUESTIONS

1. What are the key ingredients for an organization's continual improvement?

2. If you were going to design a self-evaluation framework for your organization, what would it look like? How would you implement the characteristics provided in this chapter? Be specific.

3. If you were going to help an organizational leader create and promote ongoing change in his or her organization, what would the coaching sessions consist of?

CONTRACTING FOR EVALUATION SERVICES

This chapter provides guidance to organizations when hiring an outside evaluation consultant. Some of the information applies to assigning an organizational staff member to an evaluation task, and some is also useful to the consultant being hired. The chapter sets out types of fee structures, discusses the evaluation contract, and provides a detailed sample statement of work that those hiring evaluators or being hired can modify to suit a specific situation.

A challenge in any evaluation is completing the study as planned without letting extraneous but necessary issues such as contract and payment consume too much of the time and other resources. The material in this chapter is based on Kaufman, Guerra, and Platt (2006). The checklists and statement of work provided can be used as guides for planning your own evaluation.

Once again, the set of evaluation questions plays center stage at the contract stage. You can use the question set to make sure that a contractor addresses each question and delivers on those evaluation questions. Likewise, the evaluation questions are the anchor for an in-house evaluation process and all associated activities.

What you cannot control is what the contractor will provide in the way of answers. The credibility of the findings of an evaluation, internal or external, rests on granting the evaluator objectivity and independence and respecting the results. There are ways to guide evaluation teams to stay on track in terms of answering the evaluation questions, but answers cannot be dictated as part of the package.

THE CONTRACT

A contract is an agreement between two parties to provide something in exchange for a consideration—usually payment in money in exchange for goods and services. In principle, a handshake can seal a deal, but prudent people have recognized the value of written contracts that are clear and executed in front of a witness. This proves valuable if the parties are in disagreement about something and one claim or another ends up having to be settled in a courtroom. In fact, a written contract may prevent differences from ending up in legal confrontations at all, or at the least may provide a clearer basis for settling disputes that do arise.

Contract law is a complex field and will not be covered here. Instead, this chapter concentrates on helping you develop a clear description and specifications of the tasks and deliverables you want accomplished in the evaluation, so that you can come to mutual understandings about what will and will not be delivered. This is the part that a contracting officer or procurement official cannot do for you. Included here are controls to guide the contractor, writing proposals, a sample statement of work, and suggestions for types of contract mechanisms for payment—for example, fixed price, cost plus fixed fee, time and materials, and consulting retainer.

Fixed Price

A fixed-price contract means that all of the work is done for an amount of money that is set at the time of the contract award (usually based on a contractor proposal). This type of contract payment works best when proposals are accepted from a set of contractors who are in competition and the work is clear and rigorously specified in the contract. Contractors who know the field can plan work efficiently and figure an adequate price, taking into account their technical approach to the work. Note, however, that if the party contracting for the work starts to make additions to the list of contractor tasks after the award, the contractor has every right to ask for renegotiation of the contract to add more money. After the award, the contractor is not faced with any competition, so there is less pressure to keep costs down in the change proposal. If no technical innovation or discovery is required and both parties know their fields, the risk of a fixed-price contract is about equal to both parties.

A tightly constructed evaluation study could use this form of contract. Keep in mind, however, that some evaluation studies are more in the nature of problem identification studies than they are confirmation of results in an experimental setting. A study that has some latitude can include additional work tasks in the statement of work, which are separately priced options. This requires some anticipation of the nature of the optional tasks, so in this setting, a different form of contract may be more suitable.

Cost Plus Fixed Fee

A cost-plus-fixed-fee contract means that the contractor must keep track of all expenses and bill for the actual cost of doing the work (subject to audit). At the end of the contract, the contractor is paid a fixed fee, which can be a flat, preagreed amount or derived by a formula acceptable to both parties. In this arrangement, the contractor is able to accept some work variations or take time to investigate emerging issues as long as cost records are maintained and the work variation is acceptable to both parties. Note that change orders must be accepted before work variations are initiated. A contractor who goes out of scope without permission can be forced to absorb the excess cost. However, by the same rule, any overly exuberant guidance from anyone on the staff could mean that the contractor will get paid for resulting work that the decision makers or budget watchdogs did not anticipate. It is a good idea to set up a clear paper trail for any change orders and to make sure that both parties know who can authorize a change. This contract type allows risk associated with unknown discovery to be shared as long as good control is maintained.

Time and Materials

With a time-and-materials contract, the contractor gets paid for the hourly rates for each of the workers engaged in providing direct or indirect support to the contract. The contractor also gets paid for expenses such as travel and materials used. A time-and-materials contract is used when the scope of work and the statement of tasks include analysis, discovery, or experimentation that may have to be repeated many times before getting the desired results. Redirection of work activity simply results in more time and material consumption. It is still wise to maintain control over work change orders, but the flexibility offered is greater than in other kinds of contracts. However, the risk to the organization is that work could be expended and funds exhausted before the contractor produced any desired product. Upper dollar limits can be placed on a time-and-materials contract. Reaching that limit without a final resolution of the work is a risk, but can be minimized by attentive management oversight using periodic program reviews.

Consulting Retainer

The most flexible type of contract is an agreement with a consultant or consulting firm to provide evaluation services. Consultants can do entire evaluations or provide guidance as you plan and implement your own study. Each consultant will have his or her own way of arranging for payment. This can range from an honorarium to flat daily fees. Consultants can be extremely beneficial, or they can be provocative and drain resources. It is best to consider the use of a consultant only after checking all internal resources and then doing a thorough background search of candidates.

CONTRACTING CONTROLS

Contracting for evaluation service (and results) is more than a simple matter of hiring a contractor and then turning that person loose while you go on to other work. You can magnify what you can get done with the proper use of a contract, but it will require an investment in time and attention to detail. Some of the management burden can be eased if you start with a clear contract that provides a framework for you and the contractor to advance through the stages of the work and complete the tasks you wanted done, with a desired set of results.

Here are some contract features that will assist you and the contractor by clearly stating what you want done and the limits of the work.

Scope of Work

The scope of work is a statement in the contract that clearly defines what work is to be done and what the limits of the work effort will be.

This is particularly important, because issues of payment may hinge on the determination of whether a given bit of work was in scope.

Statement of Work

The statement of work is a type of specification that requires commonality of understanding on the part of contractors and organizational representatives regarding tasks and deliverables. For example, the simple phrase "conduct an evaluation" does not include enough detail. But the phrase "conduct analysis of variance" may be too specific, especially if another statistical method could better serve the study. In evaluation studies, the contract can be based on the evaluation question set, which should be firm and mutually understood. The two main provisions of any statement of work are a list of tasks to be performed and the deliverable associated with each task.

Other Contract Clauses

It is often useful to include clauses in the contract to cover expectations in the area of rights to any data-based products produced in the evaluation. The publication of findings in reports may include restrictions on distribution or specify distribution requirements. Specifications on the printing of reports, number of copies, shipping costs, and format may be included. In the case of developed instruments, any copyright and future use of instruments developed under contract can be specified at this time.

Management Plan

You can require a contractor to submit a management plan that describes how he or she will proceed with the work and what in-process deliverables will be available for review and feedback. In cases when some negotiation is required to adjust the statement of work, this is one way to include details not possible in the statement (often you have to start work to find out what you are dealing with). The management plan should include provision for progress review, reports, evaluation schedule, and mechanisms for change, quality control, and personnel replacement approval.

Program Review

It is recommended that formal monthly reviews take place in which the contractor is required to show progress on all tasks, show financial accountability for all funds expended, and discuss all possible changes or redirection in the light of any problems or unusual events that affect the evaluation study.

Schedule and Work Breakdown Structure

Each task in the statement of work becomes an item that must have a start and end date on a program schedule. Many excellent project management tools now make creating and using a project schedule a relatively easy task.

Delivery and Acceptance

Each deliverable should have a due date and the conditions of acceptance spelled out in the contract. Many contractors use a cover letter with a place for the decision maker's signature confirming acceptance of each delivered item. Make sure that the contract specifies who will sign for each deliverable. In most organizations, the contracting officer or the contracting officer's technical representative is designated as the official with signature authority.

Often vital is a provision for timeliness for acceptance of what has been submitted. One way to ensure the contractor that the process of acceptance (or rejection) of a deliverable will not hold up the progress of the evaluation is including a clause that notes what happens when response is not made in a timely basis: "If there is no response from the organization within X business days, the submission will become accepted and approved."

ETHICS AND PROFESSIONALISM

Do not sell yourself short and become a "liar for hire." Tell the truth about what you did, how you did it, why you did it, and what you found. Be forthright about all assumptions and limitations. Do not add or omit anything that is not justified, and do not change anything simply because the client wants it.

SAMPLE STATEMENT OF WORK

Now let us look at a representative sample of an evaluation contract statement of work. Although references are made to a corporation, it is based on William Platt's work with the military and government (Kaufman, Guerra, & Platt, 2006). You can use this as a guide and replace the example items as appropriate for your organization and evaluation.

EXAMPLE

Q

General Information

1. Title of Project:

Evaluation of New Sales Incentive Program at Sellalot Corporation

2. Scope of Work:

The contractor shall provide all material and personnel to accomplish the deliverables described in this statement of work (SOW), except as may otherwise be specified. The scope of this task order and associated deliverables include (a) performing a type = "Select a feature type . . ." literature review using university-based search tools, (b) analysis of conceptual/theoretical basis of sales and incentives tactics, methods, and activities, (c) evaluation of alternative approaches to sales incentives, (d) preparation of agreed-on evaluation questions that will drive and guide the evaluation, (e) creation and administration of a database for data collected in this evaluation, (f) data collection using valid and reliable methods and techniques of data collection ensuring valid and reliable data that relate directly with the agreed-on evaluation question, (g) preparation of reports and briefing documents and revising as required, and (h) travel to specified organizational locations for briefings and meetings.

The contractor shall be competent in all phases of the evaluation with a proven ability in evaluation of educational systems and education programs. References are required to confirm this.

Work Steps

Work steps shall include the following: (a) analyze sales and incentive programs and policies at Sellalot and other similar corporations, (b) conduct a literary database search relative to the type of program being evaluated and tools and techniques used elsewhere in similar projects, (c) develop and obtain approval of evaluation questions that will drive data collection and findings,

(Continued)

(d) prepare an evaluation work flow and schedule, (e) identify evaluation methods, means, processes, and techniques and relate each with evaluation questions, (f) identify and document data collection methods selected, (g) define data collection sites, sample, and resources required, (h) collect data, (i) reduce and analyze data using valid and reliable analysis statistics and tools, (j) provide initial findings and recommendations for action to sponsors and revise as required, (k) prepare and submit draft final reports, and (l) revise as required.

Field Visits
All fieldwork and on-site observations shall be coordinated with the office of the sales department director and/or the evaluation project director.

Project Management
Throughout the performance period of the delivery order executed by this SOW, the contractor shall keep the office of sales director and evaluation stakeholder team fully informed as to issues and progress.

3. Background:

This contract is a follow-on to a quick-response, short-term effort to investigate trends and concepts in sales incentives and compensation that impact or will potentially impact sales, sales policies, and sales training at Sellalot Corporation.

4. Performance Period:

The work shall begin within 10 calendar days of award, unless otherwise specified. Work at the site shall not take place on holidays or weekends unless directed by the contracting officer. Report delivery items and schedule to be set at kickoff meeting.

5. Type of Contract:

Time and materials. With fixed price limit.

Contract Award Meeting

The contractor shall not commence performance on the tasks in this SOW until the contracting officer has conducted a kickoff meeting or has advised the contractor that a kickoff meeting is waived.

General Requirements

1. The contractor shall confirm work assignments by telephone with the evaluation project manager. A brief outline of work approach shall be reflected in the technical proposal.

2. All written deliverables shall be phrased in acceptable terminology of the field. Words shall be defined in layperson language. Statistical and other technical terminology shall be defined in a glossary of terms and referenced for validity and usefulness.

3. Unless otherwise specified, where a written deliverable is required in draft form, the school district office will complete its review of the draft deliverable within 10 calendar days from date of receipt. If there is no response from Sellalot Corporation within 10 calendar days, it will be automatically deemed "approved." The contractor shall have 10 calendar days to deliver the final deliverable from date of receipt of comments.

4. This contract will not require access to individual performance records.

5. All deliverables, except where specified otherwise, shall be provided in one electronic copy via e-mail to the project manager. All deliverables shall be delivered via software compatible with the Sellalot Corporation.

6. Sellalot Corporation reserves the right to review résumés of personnel the contractor proposes to assign to each task or subtask and to approve or disapprove personnel assignments based on the résumés provided.

7. The contractor shall provide via e-mail minutes of all meetings, within 3 calendar days after completion of the meeting.

(Continued)

Mandatory Tasks and Associated Deliverables

Description of Tasks and Associated Deliverables:

The contractor shall provide the specific deliverables described below.

Task 1: The contractor shall conduct evaluation studies and data in accordance with the evaluation management plan and the agreed-on evaluation questions. Sellalot Corporation shall review the draft review and provide written comments to the contractor no later than 10 calendar days after receipt of the draft review. The contractor shall then submit the revised review no later than 20 calendar days after receipt of comments. If there is no response from the district within 10 calendar days it will be automatically deemed "approved." The contractor shall update the review as required by guidance from the Sellalot Corporation. The deliverable shall be in electronic form transmitted via e-mail, using software compatible with software available at the school district office.

Deliverable 1: Evaluation Report

Task 2: The contractor shall provide detailed analysis of selected topics and issues identified in the evaluation report number, and the type of topics shall be in accordance with guidance from the project manager. Work shall proceed on a time and material basis not to exceed specific financial limitations of the purchase order. The contractor shall present significant and timely findings to the project management team using an appropriate contractor-developed format in paper and electronic form.

Deliverable 2: Draft and Final Evaluation Report

Schedule for Deliverables

1. The contractor shall provide all deliverables to the project manager as stated in the schedule established at the kickoff meeting.

Unless otherwise specified, the number of draft copies and the number of final copies shall be the same (one electronic copy delivered via e-mail).

If for any reason, any deliverable cannot be delivered within the scheduled time frame, the contractor is required to explain why in writing to the contracting officer, including a firm commitment of when the work shall be completed. This notice to the contracting officer shall cite the reasons for the delay and the impact on the overall project. The contracting officer will then review the facts and issue a response in accordance with applicable regulations within 10 days.

Changes to Statement of Work

Any changes to this statement of work shall be authorized and approved only through written correspondence from the project manager. A copy of each change will be kept in a project folder along with all other products of the project. Costs incurred by the contractor through the actions of parties other than the project manager shall be borne by the contractor.

Reporting Requirements

1. The contractor is required to provide the project manager with weekly telephone or e-mail progress reports.

The progress reports shall cover all work completed during the preceding week and shall present the work to be accomplished during the subsequent week. This report shall also identify any problems that arose and a statement explaining how the problem was resolved. This report shall also identify any problems that have arisen but have not been completely resolved with an explanation. The progress reports shall also provide cost data, schedule data, cost variance data, and schedule variance data, as required by each task order.

Travel and Site Visits

Travel and on-site visits shall be authorized by the project manager; limited travel is envisioned.

(Continued)

Sellalot Corporation Responsibilities

Sellalot Corporation will provide access to technical and procedural information. Sellalot Corporation will provide a copy of the required confidentiality statement at contract award or on request by the contractor.

Contractor Experience Requirements

The contractor shall have experience with educational evaluation research and analysis. Additional relevant knowledge is desirable in research, theoretical literature, and practical application of the following areas: needs assessment, learning development and implementation, criterion-referenced testing development and validity and reliability assessment, formative evaluation, summative evaluation, data collection, data analysis, data and results summary, and evaluation results reporting.

Confidentiality and Nondisclosure

It is agreed that:

1. The preliminary and final deliverables and all associated working papers and other material deemed relevant by Sellalot Corporation that have been generated by the contractor in the performance of this task order are the exclusive property Sellalot Corporation and shall be submitted to the project manager at the conclusion of the evaluation initiative.

The project manager shall be the sole authorized official to release verbally or in writing, any data, the draft deliverables, the final deliverables, or any other written or printed materials pertaining to this task order. No information shall be released by the contractor. Any request for information relating to this task order presented to the contractor shall be submitted to the project manager for response.

Press releases, marketing material, or any other printed or electronic documentation related to this project shall not be publicized without the written approval of the project manager.

- The evaluation questions will be a key driver that the evaluator vendor can use to define deliverables.

- A contract should clearly state what is expected of each party.

REFLECTION QUESTIONS

1. What role do evaluation questions have in the contracting process?

2. What basic components should you look for in a statement of work?

3. What are some potential fee structures for or approaches to evaluation work compensation?

INTELLIGENCE GATHERING FOR DECISION MAKING

Good decision making is guided by intelligence gathering. However, the majority of decisions made are not based on gathered intelligence; rather, they are based on the preconceptions, opinions, or expectations of the decision makers. This chapter discusses how automated performance management systems work and how they can be used to help lead decision makers toward sound, constructive decisions.

Performance measurement and monitoring are central to performance improvement. The serious and responsible practice of performance improvement requires the use of evidence in diagnosing performance gaps and making appropriate recommendations for performance improvement. This is illustrated in part in Gilbert's behavioral engineering model (1978), where various categories of factors important to human performance are presented: clear performance expectations, feedback, incentives, instruments, knowledge, capabilities, and internal motives, for example. All of these have to be considered in measuring performance gaps, their root causes, and their interrelationships. Harless's *An Ounce of Analysis Is Worth a Pound of Objectives* (1970) is also consistent with this notion and illustrates performance measurement as a core process in the identification and resolution of performance gaps.

The use of performance monitoring and management tools can play an important role in the continued success of organizations that operate in an increasingly complex and interdependent world. The use of these integrated tools can provide a means for exploring the dynamic complexity of organizations by tracking and linking performance measures and how these are affected by organizational initiatives that are meant to improve performance at the various levels of the organization: strategic, tactical, and operational).

Berrah, Mauris, and Montmain (2008) hold that even simply accepting the hypothesis that overall performance is merely the sum of independent elementary performances simplifies decision making. However, the authors warn, "In the current context of transverse interactions between criteria, it has become more difficult for decision-makers to identify the performance criteria causing a poor overall performance, or presenting a high-priority need of improvement" (p. 341).

Performance monitoring systems are instrumental in supporting decision making by serving as an overarching framework for timely intelligence gathering. The most neglected aspect of decision making in the literature is intelligence gathering (Eisenhardt, 1998; Nutt, 2007), even though it is a fundamental part of the process. Decision making begins when stakeholders see a triggering trend, such as declining revenues or sales, or event, such as a threat to unionize, as significant, prompting steps to obtain intelligence (Nutt, 2007). Decision makers are often inundated with signals from customers, employees, shareholders, attorneys, competitors, regulators, and suppliers. Identifying the trends or events that are worthy of priority attention can be a challenging task.

Some researchers suggest that signals should be decoded as performance gaps (Pounds, 1969), Nutt, 1979; Cowan, 1986) and that such a gap will be considered significant when an important performance indicator, such as market share or revenue, falls below a preset criterion. Conversely, the signal could be ignored if performance equals or exceeds the expected performance criteria. When a performance gap is detected, it also reveals the magnitude of the concern to be overcome (Cowan, 1990).

This magnitude can be one major consideration in prioritizing performance problems for resolution. Decision making is then employed to choose ways to deal with closing the performance gap and reducing or eliminating the concern.

Nutt (2007) points to a more perilous view of decision making, proposed by social motivation researchers. He notes that in the social motivation view, decision makers' actions are prompted by dissonance, equity, or related consistency theories, where their beliefs, motivations, and drives entice them to look for information that attends to these personal attitudes. In this model, decision makers look for information that reinforces their initial position. Perhaps unconsciously at times, they form the impression that their conclusions are well founded and unbiased by making their interpretations seem fair to all concerned. Nutt goes on to point out that these decision makers likely look for information about a diversion to avoid having to make sense of signals that could render their preferred interpretation invalid. In consequence, they recognize only some kinds of performance gaps and ignore others, leaving these gaps to worsen over time.

PERFORMANCE MEASUREMENT SYSTEMS

Performance measurement systems (PMSs) are instruments that can support objective decision making for improving performance. It is worth noting, however, that where people are involved, absolute objectivity is highly unlikely. For example, some evaluators, assessors, and researchers alike are prone—consciously or not—to use inappropriate data collection and analysis tools, rendering figures and conclusions that are not actually accurate. Those who are not well versed in such tools can be easily misguided.

From a global perspective, a PMS is a multicriteria instrument for informing decision makers about a variety of things. For example, it can track current level of performance, the set of factors for poor or good performance, and the criteria for which improvement is required in an efficient and timely manner. A responsive PMS can also track the resources consumed for an observed performance in order to determine the net value of the performance (Berrah et al., 2008). Here is an approach that follows Gilbert's definition of worthy performance (1978):

$$\text{Worthy Performance} = \frac{\text{Accomplishments}}{\text{Cost of behavior}}$$

In fact, many of the ADDIE steps in performance improvement (analysis, design, development, implementation, and evaluation of program) can form the basis for sets of objectives and criteria tracked by a PMS. A PMS can be made of a network of performance objectives to be consistently aligned with respect to the vision and mission of the organization. For instance, the objectives of the new human resource development (HRD) initiatives contribute to objectives of the manufacturing plants, which in turn contribute to the objectives of the organization. Then, in order to support the decisions (for example, continue to fund the HRD initiative or remove barriers to HRD initiative before deciding to continue or suspend funding), the set of performances has to be reviewed so as to compare any gaps and compare a series of scenarios.

Performance dashboards are perhaps the most prominent example of a performance measurement and monitoring system. They are capable, if well designed, of providing the right information at the right time about key performance indicators and processes. They can be Web based or Intranet based; in either case, individuals who require the information to make decisions can conveniently access the data in real time or near real time. One key benefit is the enhancement of accountability and empowerment of decision makers.

Performance dashboards can provide multiple views customized for multiple levels of users, so that each group has access to information that is intricately related to its responsibilities; for example, executives may have views that focus specifically on strategic indicators, while managers may have a more focused view of operational indicators. What they are able to see are usually graphical representations of quantitative data that enable them to detect gaps between optimal and current levels of performance. Depending on the system design, root causes can often be linked to such indicators, although the complexity of organizations represents a challenge in tracking all possible factors that can affect the indicators. Performance dashboard views can also provide aggregate information, summaries, reports, context, and highlighted exceptions. Some dashboards provide strata for various levels of concerns (high risk, moderate risk, or low risk, for example) that can be defined with specific criteria by stakeholders. This also enables users to detect trends much more easily, without the need for more sophisticated analysis techniques. Some performance dashboards are configured to offer plausible courses of action, in part related to potential causes, and the level of risk of such courses.

The literature supports the benefits of using performance measurement to deploy business objectives and pinpoint and monitor performance improvements (Beer, 1979; Blenkinsop, 1993). Other researchers have also noted the links between performance measures and strategic plans or critical success factors of the business. The research by Neely (1999), Grady (1991), and Eccles and Pyburn (1992) supports the same conclusions.

While systems theory might call for understanding how the overall organization works, the literature on how to view and understand overall organizational performance is scarce. Systemic, and systematic, performance improvement is not the default conceptual framework of decision makers. Instead, at least as social theorists would argue, they tend to make decisions based on their own intuition, interests, and beliefs, and perhaps the same characteristics of others around them. In a recent study, Nutt (2007) found that impressionistic gaps had a negative effect on success, whether in the form of a need or opportunity, with an even greater negative impact on performance needs. He found performance gapping and premising to be crucial activities and explored how each is carried out. After uncovering a variety of premising and gapping tactics, he found some to have better success than others.

These tactics were found to influence the search approach selected to uncover alternatives and the success of the resulting decision. The best results were noted when search efforts were guided by needs documented with a quantitative performance gap and when formal search or negotiation was used to identify alternatives. These findings hold for decisions that have high and low difficulty and for those with high and low resource support.

ISSUES IN PERFORMANCE MEASUREMENT SYSTEMS

As efforts to develop theoretical frameworks for strategically driven and integrated performance measures have increased over recent years, performance measurement as a field has attracted considerable attention. However, if measurement systems are to facilitate the continual improvement process through monitoring and sound decision making, some issues must be addressed. Santos, Belton, and Howick (2002) point to two key issues that inhibit performance measurement systems from reaching their full potential: problems in the design and implementation of PMSs and problems with the analysis and use of the information produced by the measurements.

Poorly designed measurement systems can gravely compromise their implementation, and thus their impact. One important factor for organizations to consider is the selection of an appropriate measurement framework. In Chapter Ten, various performance measurement frameworks were listed. Some strides have been made to articulate procedures to identify and group performance measures in a way that makes interpretation more straightforward. However, authors do recognize that much still has to be done in the way of identifying relationships between measures (Neely, 1999; Bititci, Turner, & Begemann, 2000). While some may recognize the importance of understanding relationships among the various performance measures tracked, organizations continue to design performance measurement systems without formally accounting for the interdependencies in the measures, which could ultimately undermine the validity and utility of the information produced by the system.

To address the identification of relationships, Suwignjo, Bititci, and Carrie (2000) developed quantitative models for performance measurement systems using cognitive maps, cause-and-effect diagrams, tree diagrams, and the analytic hierarchy process. In this work, they described a technique used to identify factors important to performance and relationships and how to structure the factors hierarchically, quantify the effect of the factors on performance, and express them quantitatively. Meanwhile, Kaplan and Norton recommend the use of strategy maps (2001). Although both of these approaches are useful in beginning to address the importance of establishing interdependencies, further research and application is warranted. Santos et al. (2002) recommend the use of qualitative and quantitative modeling to enrich analysis and produce a more insightful design of performance measurement systems.

In addition to design considerations, organizations that are interested in using performance measurement systems must also consider thoughtful implementation. Implementation issues are a usual culprit for why most solutions or initiatives in organizations go wrong. Effective implementation is about creating and managing positive change, and in the case of PMS implementations, it is no different. The potential barriers seen in a general evaluation or needs assessment are present here as well (for example, fear that the information will be used to place blame or shame). Leadership must play an active role in establishing expectations, modeling desired behaviors, and motivating those affected. The PMS must be seen as one helpful component within an entire performance management system.

The other set of challenges facing PMSs is related to the proper analysis of the data and the use of the information to improve performance. A rigorous analysis must take into account the context of the performance data observed. This includes the countless other factors that are affecting performance, and with the obvious limitations of the human brain and PMSs in accounting for every performance factor, the task is not straightforward. For instance, we may have to account for the fact that the gains in one performance indicator came at the expense of another performance indicator. If we study the latter independent of the former, we might draw inaccurate conclusions, which will lead to poor decisions. Performance improvement professionals often face this situation in conducting needs assessment and analyses, where they limit their search to symptoms and stop before they identify actual performance gaps and root causes.

Santos et al. (2000) point out that many authors (Skinner, 1974, and da Silveira & Slack, 2001, among others) have argued that organizations cannot succeed in every performance indicator and that explicit decisions about trade-offs must be defined. Once again, much work in this area of PMSs has yet to be explored.

CONCLUSION

The development of better-integrated, balanced, and strategically driven performance measurement frameworks has been accompanied by an increase in the practice of performance measurement. PMSs can be a formidable tool in monitoring and continually improving organizational performance. However, in spite of the significant advances made, some issues require further study if measurement systems are to be fully effective in the process of management through monitoring and decision making (Santos et al., 2002). Among the issues to keep in mind when considering the design and use of PMS are these:

- Be clear on what must be measured and why.

- Use the right metrics.

- Consider the limited perspective of performance measurement systems.

- Beware of inconsistent data, analysis, and interpretation; limited scope and view; and an overabundance of information.

- Visualizations can be deceiving.

- Performance measurement systems must be used if they are going to be helpful. Thus, integrate use as part of a broader performance management system by, for example, clarifying expectations and consequences for use and nonuse.

KEY POINTS

- Performance measurement and tracking are central to improving performance.

- Performance measurement systems can be instrumental to timely and objective decision making.

- The utility of performance measurement systems can be jeopardized by problems in their design and implementation, as well as by problems with the analysis and use of the information produced by the measurements.

REFLECTION QUESTIONS

1. What role do performance measurement and tracking play in performance improvement?

2. What are performance measurement systems? What are the benefits this type of system could bring to an organization?

3. What factors keep decision makers from choosing the decisions that a performance management system will indicate are the best decisions? What other factors in decision makers' lives affect the decisions they make?

4. What are some potential barriers to successfully implementing a performance management system in your own organization? Would the benefits outweigh the trouble and cost?

THE FUTURE
OF EVALUATION
IN PERFORMANCE
IMPROVEMENT

This chapter discusses the role of evaluation in performance improvement, where it has not yet been embraced as a key factor. Acceptance of evaluation as an essential component of performance improvement is both necessary and inevitable. Technology already plays a key role in integrating evaluation into performance improvement initiatives. Finally, the chapter examines the role of improvement in performance, in evaluation, and as an overarching theme for this book.

The International Society for Performance Improvement (ISPI) defines *performance improvement* as the systematic approach to improving productivity and competence using a set of methods and procedures for realizing opportunities related to people's performance. Pershing (2006) states that the central processes by which this is accomplished are the selection, analysis, design, development, implementation, and evaluation of programs to most cost-effectively influence human behavior and accomplishment. In Chapter One, the roots of performance improvement were traced back to programmed instruction, instructional systems design, and most fundamentally the work of B. F. Skinner and his colleagues with behavior and its environment. This is perhaps why performance improvement has been so closely linked to training and instructional solutions. Thus, many evaluation models that have been popularized in the field have focused on evaluating training programs and other instructional solutions.

Yet performance improvement has evolved from an instructional focus to a performance focus, where instructional solutions are but a subset of the range of solutions required to solve performance gaps. Moreover, beyond providing solutions, performance improvement professionals have an ultimate goal to improve performance through whatever means are appropriate and ethical. General recognition that evaluation is a critical and required step in the overall performance improvement process is not yet a reality.

Performance improvement professionals have traditionally focused on providing solutions (instructional or beyond) and have not done much in the way of objective needs assessments that allow them to identify the best solution set or evaluations of such solutions. Kaufman and Clark (1999) argue that the actions and deliverables of performance improvement professionals are frequently questionable in terms of value added—the increase in worth and contribution to shared clients and stakeholders. Because of this, the future success of the profession is in jeopardy.

Moreover, Kaufman and Clark (1999) argue that many in our field provide only comfortable solutions to assumed problems, all in a context where people still demand professional help, while the professionals' ability to prove that they have made a measurable contribution to our clients is suspect. Ferrington and Clark (2000) stress that rather than being in the business of creating training or other solutions, human performance technologists should be in the business of improving results. They go on to recommend that to help individuals, organizations, or societies meet their goals, performance consultants must follow a systematic and systemic process and select solutions that actually work, warning that many popular solutions do not work and some even make situations worse.

One reason often heard for not conducting such fundamental performance improvement processes as needs assessments and evaluations is the lack of resources: the funding and time are simply not there. Yet neither needs assessment nor evaluation should be seen as isolated interventions in and of themselves. Rather, they are the basis for solution identification, design, development, implementation, and continual improvement.

EVALUATION AND MEASUREMENT IN PERFORMANCE IMPROVEMENT TODAY

Rigorous evaluation research and practice in the performance improvement literature is scarce. One indicator is the content of the *Handbook of Human Performance Technology* (Pershing, 2006). Pershing identifies performance improvement as a systematic combination of three fundamental processes—performance analysis, cause analysis, and intervention selection—leaving evaluation of such selections out of the equation. Now in its third edition, this handbook has at least sixteen chapters on preset performance improvement solutions versus three chapters on evaluation. Although an entire section is devoted to performance measurement, the topics addressed are limited to selected data collection and analysis methods (for example, quantitative versus qualitative methods, construction questionnaires, interviewing, observations, content analysis, and qualitative data analysis), with only one chapter devoted to evidence-based practice.

If we look at other key performance improvement publications—*Performance Improvement Journal* (PIJ) and *Performance Improvement Quarterly* (PIQ)—over roughly the past decade as an indication of our attention to evaluation and performance measurement, we find mixed signals about the focus on evaluation and performance measurement. Roughly one-tenth of the articles in PIJ (57 of 545 articles reviewed) focus on evaluation, as compared to 44 percent of articles in PIQ (108 of 247 articles). These numbers look better if we expand our view to a broader range of performance measurement, such as needs assessment, analysis, evaluation, and measurement techniques. Thirty-four percent of PIJ's articles touched on some aspect of measurement, and 74 percent of PIQ's journal did the same (Guerra-López & Andrei, 2007). If we go back to the ADDIE model (analysis, design, development, implementation, and evaluation) or A²DDIE (assessment, analysis, design, development, implementation, and evaluation) (Guerra, 2003a), all things being equal, based on five to six phases of performance improvement, a balanced literature would reflect 20 percent of articles focused on evaluation alone. With assessment and analysis in the mix, we should expect roughly 33 percent of the literature to be focused on some aspect of performance measurement.

In this context, we can say that although PIJ, the practitioner-oriented journal, is not presenting a balanced focus on evaluation, it does appear to have a reasonable focus on performance measurement. Its research-based counterpart, PIQ, perhaps predictably, given its research nature, represents a heavy focus on both performance evaluation and performance measurement overall.

WHAT DOES THE FUTURE HOLD?

The field of performance improvement continues to be in transition and continuing development, as previous contributors to the field have indicated (Clark & Estes, 1999; Ferrington & Clark, 2000). As we face a disconnect between what must be evaluated in programs and organizations and the evaluation tools and models that have traditionally dominated the performance improvement field, the requirement to expand evaluation frameworks and models will become more pressing. Thus, the literature on evaluation research and practice should increase modestly but steadily. Action research will merge the line between evaluation and research. We must be open to this evolution by expanding our definitions, conceptualization, and perspectives on evaluation and measurement.

As clients and employers demand accountability for resources consumed, evaluation and performance measurement will move even further up the priority list of performance improvement professionals, clients, and other decision makers. Evaluation continues to evolve as both a process within performance improvement and as a discipline and field in and of itself.

As the demand for evaluations and evaluators increases, evaluation courses and programs within educational institutions, as well as professional workshops, will increase. We should expect that along with an increase in quantity, we will also experience an increase in quality as stakeholders become better informed and develop higher expectations.

As the world continues to develop, giving rise to new organizations, programs, initiatives, and solutions, evaluation will also emerge in more parts of the world, as one prerequisite for accounting for the promised benefits and the resources consumed. Evaluation will be intricately linked to ethical practices demanded by society.

With the integration of technology into much of what we do, not only in the field but in the world, the use of performance measurement systems will grow. Technology has already changed the way data are collected and analyzed, and this impact will continue to grow. This growth in performance measurement systems will have to be accompanied by quality measures to ensure the appropriate design, implementation, and use of performance measurement systems. Guidance, education, and positive consequences will also have to accompany the use of the performance measurement systems—in the context of a broader performance management system—and the information they produce. This will be a prerequisite for ensuring that these systems meet their potential of facilitating decision making that results in continual and measurable performance improvement.

CONCLUSION

Perhaps the dominant theme in this book has been improvement. For improvement to occur, we must be willing and able to learn, accept valuable feedback, and use feedback to adapt as required for the performer and performance system to thrive. Much research has highlighted the power of feedback in improving performance. Evaluation is a central mechanism by which we can obtain purposeful feedback. It is in this context that I hope readers will see the value of evaluation and that all will see evaluation as an integral and required part of everything we do rather than as an isolated and unnecessary use of resources.

KEY POINTS

- There is scarce and inconclusive evidence about the state of evaluation in the performance improvement field today.

- Evaluation, as an important step in the basic performance improvement model, will become increasingly important for people in the performance improvement field, as well as for stakeholders in all organizations.

- Technology can help facilitate many steps and processes within evaluation, thereby also contributing to an increase in evaluations.

REFLECTION QUESTIONS

1. How do you see the current state of evaluation in the field?

2. What are the consequences of dismissing evaluation as an important factor in performance improvement?

3. What do you foresee for evaluation in the future?

Ackoff, Russell L. (2000). Interview. *Technos: Quarterly for Education and Technology.* Retrieved February, 8, 2006, from http://www.findarticles.com/p/articles/mi_m0HKV/is_3_9/ai_66408220.

Adler, P. A., & Adler, P. (1994). Observational techniques. In N. K. Denzin & Y. S. Lincoln (Eds.), *Handbook of qualitative research* (pp. 377–392). Thousand Oaks, CA: Sage.

Alliger, G. M., & Janak, E. A. (1989). Kirkpatrick's levels of training criteria: Thirty years later. *Personnel Psychology, 42*(2), 331–342.

American Evaluation Association. (2004). *American Evaluation Association guiding principles for evaluators.* Retrieved August 20, 2007, from http://www.eval.org/Publications/GuidingPrinciples.asp.

Baldwin, T. T., & Ford, J. K. (1988). Transfer of training: A review and directions for future research. *Personnel Psychology, 41,* 63–105.

Barker, J. A. (1990). *The business of paradigms* [Videorecording]. Burnsville, MN: Charthouse Learning Corp.

Barker, J. A. (1992). *Future edge: Discovering the new paradigms of success.* New York: Morrow.

Bassi, L. J., Benson, G., & Cheney, S. (1996). The top ten trends. *Training and Development, 50*(11), 28–42.

Bates, R. (2004). A critical analysis of evaluation practice: The Kirkpatrick model and the principle of beneficence. *Evaluation and Program Planning, 27*(3), 341–347.

Beer, S. (1979). *The heart of enterprise.* Hoboken, NJ: Wiley.

Berk, R. A. (1980). *Criterion-referenced measurement: The state of the art.* Baltimore, MD: Johns Hopkins University Press.

Berrah, L., Mauris, G., & Montmain, J. (2008). Monitoring the improvement of an overall industrial performance based on a Choquet integral aggregation. *Omega, 36*(3), 340–351.

Bititci, U. (1995). Modelling of performance measurement systems in manufacturing enterprises. *International Journal of Production Economics, 42,* 137–147.

Bititci, U. S., Turner, T., & Begemann, C. (2000). Dynamics of performance measurement systems. *International Journal of Operations and Production Management, 20,* 692–704.

Blake, B. E. (1999). *Development of a plan to measure return on investment for educational programs at Providence Hospital.* Unpublished doctoral dissertation, Nova Southeastern University.

Blenkinsop, S. A. (1993). *Organisational aspects of information processing systems.* Unpublished doctoral dissertation, University of Loughborough.

Bloom, B. S. (1956). *Taxonomy of educational objectives, Handbook I: The cognitive domain.* New York: McKay.

Borg, W. R., & Gall, M. D. (1989). *Educational research: An introduction* (5th ed.). New York: Longman.

Branson, R. K. (1975). *Interservice procedures for instructional systems development.* Tallahassee: Center for Educational Technology, Florida State University.

Brethower, D. M. (2005). Yes we can: A rejoinder to Don Winiecki's rejoinder about saving the world with HPT. *Performance Improvement, 44*(2), 19–24.

Brethower, D. M. (2006). *How time series designs your work: Why they are practical and powerful, and why you should care.* Retrieved January 30, 2006, from http://performanc express.org/0601.

Brethower, D. M., & Dams, P.-C. (1999). Systems thinking (and systems doing). *Performance Improvement, 38*(1), 37–52.

Brewer, J., & Hunter, A. (1989). *Multimethod research: A synthesis of styles.* Thousand Oaks, CA: Sage.

Brinkerhoff, R. (1981). Making evaluation more useful. *Training and Development Journal, 35*(12), 66–70.

Brinkerhoff, R. O. (1983). The success case: A low-cost, high-yield evaluation. *Training and Development Journal, 37*(8), 58–61.

Brinkerhoff, R. O. (1988). An integrated evaluation model for HRD. *Training and Development Journal, 427*(2), 66–68.

Brinkerhoff, R. O. (2003). *The success case method: Find out quickly what's working and what's not.* San Francisco: Berrett-Koehler.

Brinkerhoff, R. (2005). The success case method: A strategic evaluation approach to increasing the value and effect of training. *Advances in Developing Human Resources, 7,* 86–101.

Brinkerhoff, R. O., & Apking, A. M. (2001). *High impact learning: Strategies for leveraging business results from training.* Cambridge, MA: Perseus.

Brinkerhoff, R. O., & Jackson, G. (2003, October). Managing education to maximize impact. *Chief learning office.* Retrieved May 2, 2007, from http://www.clomedia.com/content/ templates/clo_feature.asp?articleid=269&zoneid=32.

Campbell, D. T., Stanley, J. C., & Gage, N. L. (1966). *Experimental and quasi-experimental designs for research.* Skokie, IL: Rand McNally.

Carroll, A. (2000). Conceptual and consulting aspects of stakeholder theory, thinking, and management. In R. Golebiewski (Ed.), *Handbook of organizational consulting* (2nd ed., pp. 169–181). New York: Dekker.

Cascio, W. F. (1987). *Applied psychology in personnel management* (3rd ed). Upper Saddle River, NJ: Prentice Hall.

Clark, R., & Estes, F. (1998). Technology or craft: What are we doing? *Educational Technology, 38*(5), 5–11.

Clark, R. E., & Estes, F. (2000). A proposal for the collaborative development of authentic performance technology. *Performance Improvement, 38*(4), 48–53.

Clark, R. E., & Estes, F. (2002). *Turning research into results: A guide to selecting the right performance solutions.* Atlanta, GA: CEP Press.

Coghlan, D. (2000). Perceiving, evaluating, and responding to change: An interlevel approach. In R. Golebiewski (Ed.), *Handbook of organizational consulting* (2nd ed., pp. 213–217). New York: Marcel Dekker.

Converse, J. M., & Presser, S. (1986). *Survey questions: Handcrafting the standardized questionnaire.* Thousand Oaks, CA: Sage.

Cooley, W. W., & Lohnes, P. R. (1976). *Evaluation research in education.* New York: Irvington.

Cooperrider, D. L., & Srivastva, S. (1987). Appreciative inquiry in organizational life. In R. W. Woodman & W. A. Pasmore (Eds.), *Research in organizational change and development* (Vol. 1, pp. 129–169). Greenwich, CT: JAI Press.

Corcoran, C. (1997). IS managers need to put a price tag on productivity [Electronic version]. *InfoWorld, 19.*

Cowan, D. A. (1986). Developing a process model of problem recognition. *Academy of Management Review, 11*(4), 763–776.

Cowan, D. A. (1990). Developing a classification structure of organizational problems: An empirical investigation. *Academy of Management Journal, 33*(2), 366–390.

Cresswell, A., & LaVigne, M. (2003). ROI analyses for IT projects must focus on strategic objectives. *PA Times, 26*(8), 3. Retrieved May, 6, 2007, from http://www.slu.edu/libraries/pius/databases/dbdesc/bussprem.html.

Cronbach, L. (1963). Course improvement through evaluation. *Teachers College Record, 64,* 672–683.

Cronbach, L. (1980). *Toward reform of program evaluation: Aims, methods, and institutional arrangements.* San Francisco: Jossey-Bass.

Cronbach, L. J. (1982). *Designing evaluations of educational and social programs.* San Francisco: Jossey-Bass.

Cummings, T. G., & Worley, C. G. (2005). *Organization development and change* (8th ed.). Mason, OH: Thomson/South-Western.

Da Silveira, G., & Slack, N. (2001). Exploring the trade-off concept. *International Journal of Operations and Production Management, 21,* 949–964.

Davis, I. (2005). The biggest contract. *Economist,* May 28.

Dean, P. (1993). A selected review of the underpinnings of ethics for human performance technology professionals. Part One: Key ethical theories and research. *Performance Improvement Quarterly, 6*(4), 6–32.

Dick, W. (1987). A history of instructional design and its impact on educational psychology. In J. A. Glover & R. R. Ronning (Eds.), *Instructional technology: Foundations.* Mahwah, NJ: Erlbaum.

Dick, W., & Carey, L. (1990). *The systematic design of instruction* (3rd ed.). Glenview, IL: Scott, Foresman.

Dick, W., & King, D. (1994). Formative evaluation in the performance context. *Performance and Instruction, 33*(9), 3–8.

Doucouliagos, C., & Sgro, P. (2000, June 11). *Enterprise return on a training investment: Final report.* Adelaide, Australia: National Centre for Vocational Education Research.

Drucker, P. F. (1993). *The five most important questions you will ever ask about your nonprofit organization.* San Francisco: Jossey-Bass.

Dumas, J. S., & Redish, J. (1999). *A practical guide to usability testing* (Rev. ed.). Portland, OR: Intellect.

Eccles, R. G., & Pyburn, P. J. (1992). Creating a comprehensive system to measure performance. *Management Accounting, 74*(4), 41–44.

Eckerson, W. (2006). *Deploying dashboards and scorecards.* Retrieved February 26, 2007, from http://www.dmreview.com/portals/portal.cfm?topicId=230006.

Eisenhardt, K. (1998). Decision making and all that jazz. In V. Papadakis & P. Barwise (Eds.), *Strategic decisions.* Norwell, MA: Kluwer.

Ferrington, J., & Clark, R. E. (2000). Snake oil, science, and performance products. *Performance Improvement, 39*(10), 5–10.

Filella-Guiu, G., & Blanch-Pana, A. (2002). Imprisonment and career development: An evaluation of a guidance programme for job finding. *Journal of Career Development, 29*(1), 55–68.

Fitzgerald, L., Johnston, R., Brignall, S., Silvestro, R., & Voss, C. (1991). *Performance measurement in service businesses.* London: CIMA Publishing.

Fitzpatrick, J. L., Sanders, J. R., & Worthen, B. R. (2004). *Program evaluation: Alternative approaches and practical guidelines* (3rd ed.). Boston: Pearson/Allyn & Bacon.

Flanagan, J. C. (1954). The critical incident technique. *Psychological Bulletin, 51*(4), 327–359.

Foxon, M. (1993). A process approach to transfer maintenance: Part 1: The impact of motivation and supervisor support on transfer maintenance. *Australian Journal of Educational Technology, 9*(2), 130–143.

Gharajedaghi, J. (1999). *Systems thinking: Managing chaos and complexity, a platform for designing business architecture.* Burlington, MA: Butterworth Heinemann.

Gilbert, T. F. (1978). *Human competence: Engineering worthy performance.* New York: McGraw-Hill.

Grady, M. W. (1991, June). Performance measurement, implementing strategy. *Management Accounting,* 49–53.

Guba, E. (1969). The failure of educational evaluation. *Educational Technology, 9,* 29–38.

Guerra, I. (2003a). Key competencies required of performance improvement professionals. *Performance Improvement Quarterly, 16*(1), 55–72.

Guerra, I. (2003b). Asking and answering the right questions: Collecting relevant and useful data. *Performance Improvement, 42*(10), 24–28.

Guerra, I. (2003c). Identifying and tracking key performance indicators. *ASTD Links.* Retrieved February 8, 2006, from http://www1.astd.org/news_letter/October03/Links/Practice_Identifying.html.

Guerra, I. (2005). Developing useful questionnaires. In M. Silverman & P. Phillips (Eds.), *The 2005 training and performance sourcebook.* Alexandria, VA: ASTD Press.

Guerra, I., Bernardez, M., Jones, M., & Zidan, S. (2005). Government workers adding societal value: The Ohio workforce development program. *Performance Improvement Quarterly, 18*(3), 76–99.

Guerra, I., & Rodriguez, G. (2005). Social responsibility and educational planning. *Performance Improvement Quarterly,* 18(3), 56–64.

Guerra-López, I. (2007a). *Evaluating impact: Evaluation and continual improvement for performance improvement practitioners.* Champaign, IL: Human Resource Development Press.

Guerra-López, I. (2007b). Evaluating impact: Building a case for demonstrating the worth of performance improvement interventions. *Performance Improvement Journal, 46*(7), 33–38.

Guerra-López, I. (2007c). Planning a responsive evaluation: Establishing solid partnerships by clarifying expectations and purpose. *Performance Improvement Journal, 46*(8).

Guerra-López, I. (2007d). A seven-step evaluation process for evaluating performance improvement interventions. *Performance Improvement Express,* no. 10. Retrieved from http://www.performancexpress.org/.

Guerra-López, I., & Andrei, H. (2007). *The current status of evaluation in performance improvement.* Unpublished manuscript.

Gupta, P. (2004). *Six sigma business scorecard: Ensuring performance for profit.* New York: McGraw-Hill.

Harless, J. (1970). *An ounce of analysis is worth a pound of objectives.* Newman, GA: Harless Performance Guild.

Henderson, A., Davies, J., & Willis, M. (2006). The experience of Australian project leaders in encouraging practitioners to adopt research evidence in their clinical practice. *Australian Health Review, 30,* 474–484.

Hofstadter, D. R., & Dennett, D. C. (1981). *The mind's I: Fantasies and reflections on self and soul.* New York: Bantam Books.

Holton, E. (1996). The flawed four-level evaluation model. *Human Resource Development Quarterly, 7*(1), 5–21.

Joint Committee on Standards for Educational Evaluation. (1981). *Standards for evaluations of educational programs, projects, and materials.* New York: McGraw-Hill.

Joint Committee on Standards for Educational Evaluation. (1994). *The program evaluation standards.* Thousand Oaks, CA: Sage

Kaplan, R. S., & Norton, D. P. (1992). The balanced scorecard—measures that drive performance. *Harvard Business Review, 70*(1), 71–79.

Kaplan, R. S., & Norton, D. P. (2001). *The strategy-focused organization: How balanced scorecard companies thrive in the new business environment.* Boston: Harvard Business School Press.

Kaufman, R. (1992). *Strategic planning plus: An organizational guide* (Rev. ed.). Thousand Oaks, CA: Sage.

Kaufman, R. A. (2000). *Mega planning: Practical tools for organizational success.* Thousand Oaks, CA: Sage.

Kaufman, R. A. (2006a). *Change, choices and consequences: A guide to mega thinking and planning.* Amherst, MA: HRD Press.

Kaufman, R. A. (2006b). *Thirty seconds that can change your life: A decision-making guide for those who refuse to be mediocre.* Amherst, MA: HRD Press.

Kaufman, R. A., & Clark, R. (1999). Re-establishing performance improvement as a legitimate area of inquiry, activity, and contribution: Rules of the road. *Performance Improvement 38*(9), 13–18.

Kaufman, R. A., Guerra, I., & Platt, W. A. (2006). *Practical evaluation for educators: Finding what works and what doesn't.* Thousand Oaks, CA: Corwin Press.

Kaufman, R., & Keller, J. M. (1994). Levels of evaluation: Beyond Kirkpatrick. *Human Resources Development Quarterly, 5*(4), 371–380.

Kaufman, R. A., & Lick, D. (2004). How to get your organization balanced through change creation. In M. L. Silberman & P. Philips (Eds.), *The 2004 team and organizational development sourcebook* (pp. 255–267). Poughkeepsie, NY: Inkwell Publishing.

Kirkpatrick, D. L. (1959). Techniques for evaluating training programs. *Journal of ASTD, 13*(11), 21–26.

Kirkpatrick, D. L. (1987). Evaluation. In R. L. Craig (Ed.), *Training and development handbook* (pp. 301–310). New York: McGraw-Hill.

Kirkpatrick, D. L. (1994). *Evaluating training programs: The four levels.* San Francisco: Berrett-Koehler.

Kirkpatrick, D. L. (2006). Seven keys to unlock the four levels of evaluation. *Performance Improvement Journal, 45*(7), 5–8

Liston, C. (1999). *Managing quality and standards.* Buckingham, UK: Open University Press.

Lynch, R. L., & Cross, K. F. (1991). *Measure up! How to measure corporate performance.* Cambridge, MA: Blackwell.

Lynch, D., Greer, A., Larson, L., Cummings, D., Harriett, B., Springer Dreyfus, K., & Clay, M. (2003). Descriptive metaevaluation: Case study of an interdisciplinary curriculum. *Evaluation and the Health Professions, 26*(4), 447–461.

Madaus, G., & Stufflebeam, D. (1989). *Educational evaluation: Classic works of Ralph W. Tyler.* Norwell, MA: Kluwer.

Mager, R. F. (1997). *Preparing instructional objectives: A critical tool in the development of effective instruction* (3rd ed.). Atlanta, GA: Center for Effective Performance.

Maskell, B. (1992). *Performance measurement for world class manufacturing: A model for American companies.* New York: Productivity Press.

McMillan, J. H. (1992). *Educational research: Fundamentals for the consumer.* New York: HarperCollins.

Miles, M. B., & Huberman, A. M. (1994). *Qualitative data analysis: An expanded sourcebook* (2nd ed.). Thousand Oaks, CA: Sage.

Mohr, L. B. (1992). *Impact analysis for program evaluation.* Thousand Oaks, CA: Sage.

Neely, A. (1999). The performance measurement revolution: Why now and what next? *International Journal of Operations and Production Management, 19,* 205–228.

Neely, A., Adams, C., & Kennerley, M. (2002). *The performance prism: The scorecard for measuring and managing business success.* Upper Saddle River, NJ: Prentice Hall.

Neely, A. D., Mills, J. F., Platts, K. W., Gregory, M. J., & Richards, A. H. (1991). Realizing strategy. *Management Accounting,* 49–53.

Nevo, D. (1981). The evaluation of a multi-dimensional project. In A. Lewy & S. Kugelmass (Eds.), *Decision oriented evaluation in education: The case of Israel* (pp. 169–194.). Philadelphia: International Science Services.

Newby, A. (1992). *Training evaluation handbook.* San Francisco: Jossey-Bass/Pfeiffer.

Niven, P. R. (2002). *Balanced scorecard step by step: Maximizing performance and maintaining results.* Hoboken, NJ: Wiley.

Noe, R. A. (1986). Trainees' attributes and attitudes: Neglected influences on training effectiveness. *Academy of Management Review, 11*(4), 736–749.

Nutt, P. (1979). Calling out and calling off the dogs: Managerial diagnoses in organizations. *Academy of Management Review, 4*(2), 203–214.

Nutt, P. (2007). Intelligence gathering for decision making. *Omega,* no. 35, 604–622.

Patton, M. (1980). *Qualitative evaluation methods.* Thousand Oaks, CA: Sage.

Patton, M. (1984). An alternative evaluation approach for the problem-solving training program: A utilization-focused evaluation program. *Evaluation and Program Planning, 7,* 189–192.

Patton, M. Q. (1997). *Utilization-focused evaluation: The new century text* (3rd ed.). Thousand Oaks, CA: Sage.

Patton, M. Q. (2003). Utilization-focused evaluation. In T. Kellaghan & D. L. Stufflebeam (Eds.), *International handbook of educational evaluation* (pp. 223–244). Norwell, MA: Kluwer.

Pershing, J. (2006). *Handbook of human performance technology: Principles, practices, potential.* San Francisco: Jossey-Bass.

Peters, T. J., & Waterman, R. H. (1982). *In search of excellence: Lessons from America's best-run companies.* New York: HarperCollins.

Phillips, J. (1997a). *Handbook of training evaluation and measurement methods* (3rd ed.). Houston: Gulf Publishing.

Phillips, J. (1997b). *Return on investment in training and performance improvement programs.* Burlington, MA: Butterworth-Heinemann.

Phillips, J. (1997c). *Measuring return on investment in action.* Alexandria, VA: American Society for Training and Development.

Popcorn, F. (1991). *The Popcorn report: Faith Popcorn on the future of your company, your world, your life.* New York: Doubleday.

Popham, W. J. (1975). *Educational evaluation.* Upper Saddle River, NJ: Prentice Hall.

Pounds, W. (1969). The process of problem finding. *Industrial Management Review, 11,* 1–19.

Provus, M. (1971). *The discrepancy model: For educational program improvement and assessment.* Berkeley, CA: McCutchan.

Pyzdek, T. (2003). *The six sigma handbook: A complete guide for green belts, black belts, and managers at all levels.* New York: McGraw-Hill.

Rea, L. M., & Parker, R. A. (1997). *Designing and conducting survey research: A comprehensive guide* (2nd ed.). San Francisco: Jossey-Bass.

Richards, T., & Richards, L. (1994). Using computers in qualitative analysis. In N. K. Denzin & Y. S. Lincoln (Eds.), *Handbook of qualitative research.* Thousand Oaks, CA: Sage.

Rossett, A. (1987). *Training needs assessment.* Upper Saddle River, NJ: Educational Technology.

Rossett, A. (1999). Analysis for human performance technology. In H. D. Stolovitch & E. J. Keeps (Eds.), *Handbook for human performance technology* (2nd ed.). San Francisco. Jossey-Bass/Pfeiffer.

Rothwell, W. (1996). *ASTD models for human performance improvement: Roles, competencies, and outputs.* Alexandria, VA: American Society for Training and Development.

Rummler, G. A. (2004). *Serious performance consulting: According to Rummler.* Silver Spring, MD: International Society for Performance Improvement.

Rummler, G. A., & Brache, A. P. (1995). *Improving performance: How to manage the white space on the organization chart* (2nd ed.). San Francisco: Jossey-Bass.

Saari, L. M., Johnson, T. R., McLaughlin, S. D., & Zimmerle, D. M. (1988). A survey of management training and education practices in U.S. companies. *Personnel Psychology, 41,* 731–743.

Sanders, J. R. (1979). The technology and art of evaluation: A review of seven evaluation primers. *Evaluation News, 12,* 2–7.

Santos, S., Belton, V., & Howick, S. (2002). Adding value to performance measurement by using system dynamics and multicriteria analysis. *International Journal of Operations and Production Management, 22*(1), 1246–1272.

Scriven, M. (1967). The methodology of evaluation. In R. Tyler, R. Gagne, & M. Scriven (Eds.), *Perspectives on curriculum evaluation.* New York: McGraw-Hill.

Scriven, M. (1968). An introduction to metaevaluation. *Educational Products Report, 2*(5), 36–38.

Scriven, M. (1972). Pros and cons about goal-free evaluation. *Evaluation Comment, 13,* 1–7.

Scriven, M. (1973). Goal-free evaluation. In E. R. House (Ed.), *School evaluation: The politics and process* (pp. 319–328). Berkeley, CA: McCutchan.

Scriven, M. (1974). Standards for the evaluation of educational programs and products. In G. D. Borich (Ed.), *Evaluating educational programs and products.* Upper Saddle River, NJ: Educational Technology.

Scriven, M. (1991). *Evaluation thesaurus* (4th ed). Thousand Oaks, CA: Sage.

Scriven, M. (2002). *Key evaluation checklist.* Retrieved May 8, 2007, from http://www.wmich. edu/evalctr/checklists.

Skinner, W. (1974, May/June). The focused factory. *Harvard Business Review, 113–121.*

Stake, R. (1967). The countenance of education evaluation. *Teachers College Record, 68,* 523–540.

Stake, R. (1970). Objectives, priorities, and other judgment data. *Review of Education Research, 40,* 181–212.

Stake, R. E. (1973). Evaluation design, instrumentation, data collection, and analysis of data. In B. R. Worthen & J. R. Sanders (Eds.), *Educational evaluation: Theory and practice.* Worthington, OH: Charles A. Jones.

Stake, R. (1975). *Program evaluation, particularly responsive evaluation.* Kalamazoo: Evaluation Center, Western Michigan University.

Stake, R. E. (2004). *Standards-based and responsive evaluation.* Retrieved April 17, 2007, from http://www.loc.gov/catdir/toc/ecip046/2003014865.html.

Stolovitch, H. D., Keeps, E. J., & Rodrigue, D. (1999). Skill sets for the human performance technologist. In H. D. Stolovitch & E. J. Keeps (Eds.), *Handbook of human performance technology: Improving individual and organizational performance worldwide* (2nd ed.). San Francisco: Jossey-Bass/Pfeiffer.

Stufflebeam, D. (1967). *The evaluation of context, input, process, and product in elementary and secondary education.* Paper commissioned by and presented to the U.S. Office of Education.

Stufflebeam, D. L. (1968). *Evaluation as enlightenment for decision-making.* Washington, DC: Association for Supervision and Curriculum Development.

Stufflebeam, D. (1971). The use of experimental design in educational evaluation. *Journal of Educational Measurement, 8,* 267–274

Stufflebeam, D. L. (2003). The CIPP model for evaluation. In D. L. Stufflebeam & T. Kellaghan (Eds.), *The international handbook of educational evaluation.* Norwell, MA: Kluwer.

Stufflebeam, D., Foley, W., Gephart, W., Guba, E., Hammond, R., Merriman, H., et al. (1971). *Educational evaluation and decision making.* Itasca, IL: Peacock.

Stufflebeam, D. L., McKee B., & McKee, H. (2003). *The CIPP model for evaluation.* Paper presented at the 2003 Annual Conference of the Oregon Program Evaluators Network, Portland, OR.

Stufflebeam, D., & Shinkfield, A. (2007). *Evaluation theory, models, and applications.* San Francisco: Jossey-Bass.

Stufflebeam, D. L., & Webster, W. J. (1980). An analysis of alternative approaches to evaluation. *Educational Evaluation and Policy Analysis, 2*(3), 5–19.

Suwignjo, P., Bititci, U. S., & Carrie, A. S. (2000). Quantitative models for performance measurement system. *International Journal of Production Economics, 64,* 231–241.

Tyler, R. (1949). *Basic principles of curriculum and instruction.* Chicago: University of Chicago Press.

Wagner, R. (1995). *Research on the effectiveness of outdoor management training.* Washington, DC: U.S. Department of Education.

Watkins, R. (2007). *Performance by design: The systematic selection, design, and development of performance technologies that produce useful results.* Amherst, MA: HRD Press and Silver Spring, MD: International Society for Performance Improvement.

Watkins, R., & Guerra, I. (2003). Assessing or evaluating: Determining which approach is required. In M. L. Silberman (Ed.), *The 2003 training and performance sourcebook.* Princeton, NJ: Active Training.

Weitzman, E. A., & Miles, M. B. (1995). *Computer programs for qualitative data analysis: A software sourcebook.* Thousand Oaks, CA: Sage.

Witkin, B. R., & Altschuld, J. W. (1995). *Planning and conducting needs assessments: A practical guide.* Thousand Oaks, CA: Sage.

A

AB design, 189
ABC . . . D . . . design, 189
Accuracy standards
    analysis of qualitative information, 129
    analysis of quantitative information, 128
    context analysis, 127
    justified conclusions, 129
    reliable information, 128
    valid information, 127–128
Ackoff, Russell L., 160
Action recommendations.
    See Recommendations
Adams, C., 142
ADDIE model, 9, 274, 281
Adjusting performance, 253–254
Adler, P. A., 161
Alliger, G. M., 48
Altschuld, J. W., 93
American Evaluation Association (AEA),
    120, 122
Andrei, H., 281
ANOVA (analysis of variance), 214
Apking, A. M., 77
Artifacts
    data collection using, 192
    error of the, 245
Assessment
    needs, 12*t*–13*t*, 25, 33
    standard for complete and fair, 126
    See also Evaluation
Association error, 243
Average performer error, 246

B

Bache, A. P., 49
Baldwin, T. T., 53
Bar graphs, 210, 211*fig*
Bassi, L. J., 49
Bates, R., 54, 69
BCR (benefits-cost ratio), 67
Beer, S., 275
Begemann, C., 276
Behavioral engineering model, 271–272
Bell curve, 209*fig*
Belton, V., 275
Benson, G., 49
Berk, R. A., 180, 181

Berrah, L., 272
Bias (observation), 163–164
Bititci, U. S., 276
Blake, B. E., 70
Blenkinsop, S. A., 275
Blind spot error, 245
Bloom, B. S., 180, 181
Bloom's taxonomy, 181
Borg, W. R., 171
Brethower, D. M., 8, 189
Brewer, J., 128
Brignall, S., 142
Brinkerhoff, R., 42, 52, 69, 75, 76, 77
    See also SCM (case success model)

C

Campbell, D. T., 189
Carrie, A. S., 276
Carroll, A., 9
Cascio, W. F., 47
Center for Instructional Research and
    Curriculum Evaluation (University of
    Illinois), 228
Cheney, S., 49
CIPP model
    applicability in formative/summative
        evaluations, 110*t*
    articulating program core values/solutions,
        111–112
    on context evaluation, 108
    on input evaluation, 109
    introduction to, 5, 43, 107–108
    methods used in, 112
    PORO application example of, 113–115
    on process evaluation, 109
    on product evaluation, 109–111
    strengths and limitations of, 113
    See also Stufflebeam, D.
Clark, R., 280, 282
Clark, R. E., 280, 282
Closed-ended questions, 176–177
Coghlan, D., 253
Communicating findings
    developing the report for, 226–235
    importance of, 221–222
    recommendations component of, 96,
        216*fig*, 222–226
Complete and fair assessment standard, 126

Concoran, C., 62
Confidentiality agreement, 268
Conflict of interest standard, 126–127
Construct validity, 183
Consulting retainer contract, 260
Consumer-oriented evaluation model, 40, 82
Content-related validity, 182
Context analysis standard, 127
Context evaluation, 108
Context standards
    analysis of qualitative information, 129
    analysis of quantitative information, 128
    context analysis, 127
    justified conclusions, 129
    reliable information, 128
    valid information, 127–128
Continual improvement
    adjusting performance for, 253–254
    definition of, 250
    monitoring performance for, 250–253
    role of leadership in, 254–255
Contracting. *See* Evaluation contract
Converse, J. M., 175
Cooperrider, D. L., 6
Correlation coefficient, 212–213
Cost-benefit evaluation, 20
Cost-effectiveness evaluation, 20
Cost-effectiveness standard, 125
Cost-plus-fixed-fee contract, 259
"Course Improvement Through Evaluation"
    (Cronbach), 5
Cowan, D. A., 272
Cresswell, A., 62
Criterion-references tests, 180–182
Criterion-related validity, 183
Critical incident technique, 171–172
Cronbach, L., 4, 5, 43
Cronbach's alpha, 128
Cross, K. F., 142
Cummings, T. G., 254
Customer satisfaction, 90–91

D

Da Silveira, G., 277
Data
    collecting postporgram, 63
    converting to monetary values, 65–66
    defining from performance objectives,
        139, 141
    definition of, 134
    graphical representations of, 210–212*fig*
    hard, 135
    linkages between results and required,
        145*t*–147*t*
    qualitative, 95, 129, 136–137, 171, 196–197

quantitative, 95, 128–129, 136–137
relevance, reliability, validity of, 135–137
scales of measurement for, 137–138*t*
soft, 136
See also Evaluation questions; Information;
    Measurable indicators
Data analysis
    graphical representations used in, 210–212*fig*
    inferential statistics used in, 214–217
    interpretation component of, 217–218
    linking recommendations, findings,
        interpretations and, 234–235
    measures of relationship in, 212–214
    progression to recommendations for action
        from, 216*fig*
    qualitative, 196–197
    quantitative, 199–210*fig*
    selecting tools for, 93–96
    standard for, 128–129
    structured discussion, 197–199
Data collection
    document-centered methods, 191–192
    error of the instrument, 244
    experimental research, 186–190
    importance of, 159–160
    instrument-centered methods, 172–178
    person-centered direct observation methods,
        161–166
    person-centered indirect observation tech-
        niques, 166–172
    plan flow for, 140*t*
    selecting methods of, 92–93
    standards on, 123–124
    traditional knowledge testing, 179–184
    treatment-centered methods, 184–186
Data sources
    finding, 152–155
    identifying, 92
    for specific data categories, 154*t*–155*t*
Davies, J., 20
Davis, I., 21
Decision making
    evaluation question decision string for, 29–30
    performance gap reduced through, 272–273
    performance measurement systems (PMSs)
        tool for, 273–277
    performance monitoring role in, 271–273
Delivery and acceptance, 262
Delphi technique, 169–170
Deming, W. E., 94
Demonstration, 233
Dennett, D. C., 48
Descriptive statistics
    described, 200
    measures of central tendency, 201–204

measures of dispersion (variability),
204–210*fig*
"Development of a Plan to Measure Return on
Investment of Educational Programs at
Providence Hospital" (Blake), 70–73
Dick, W., 54
Direct observation. *See* Person-centered direct
observation methods
Discrepancy evaluation model, 5, 41, 83
Displacement shift error, 245
Dissemination. *See* Communicating findings
Division of Blind Services (DBS) case study,
148–151
Document-centered methods
artifacts and work products, 192
extant data review, 191
literature review, 192
Doucouliagos, C., 68, 69
Drucker, P., 24
Dumas, J. S., 227

Eccles, R. G., 275
Eckerson, W., 253
Educational Evaluation and Decision Making
(Stufflebeam et al.), 107
Efficiency (or process) evaluation, described, 19
Eisenhardt, K., 272
Employee satisfaction, 91
Ends
definition of, 25, 32
definition of societal, 22
evaluation comparison of intentions
with, 32–33
Environmental Protection Agency, 152
"Equivalent of alternate forms" method, 184
Errors of logic, 242–243
Errors of procedure, 244–246
Errors of system mapping, 240–242
Estes, F., 282
Ethical issues, 262
Evaluation
benefits of, 24–25
brief overview of history of, 4–5
communicating findings of, 96, 216*fig*,
221–236
definition of, 240
ensuring ownership and commitment to, 23–24
ensuring stakeholders' buy-in, 9–10
experimental research relationship to,
185–186
formative, 15, 17, 18, 110*t*
performance improvement role of, 281–282
purpose and definition of, 5–8

reasons for conducting, 7
relationship to other investigative processes,
11–15
simulation and gaming used for, 190
standards used for, 119–120
summative, 15, 17, 18–20, 110*t*
terminology related to, 25–26
timing of, 15, 17–18
See also Assessment; Meta-evaluation;
Performance-based evaluation
Evaluation contract
consulting retainer, 260
controls included in, 260–262
cost-plus-fixed-fee, 259
ethics and professionalism
elements of, 262
fixed-price, 258–259
overview of, 258
time-and-materials, 259–260
Evaluation contract controls
delivery and acceptance, 262
management plan, 261
other contract clauses, 261
program review, 261–262
schedule and work breakdown
structure, 262
scope of work, 260–261
statement of work, 261, 262–268
Evaluation errors
logic, 242–243
procedure, 244–246
system mapping, 240–242
Evaluation impact standard, 124
Evaluation models
Brinkerhoff's SCM (case success
evaluation), 42, 75–80
conceptualizing fit between situation and,
44–45
error of, 244–245
Guerra-López's impact, 42, 81–104
historic overview of, 5
Kirkpatrick's four levels, 42, 47–58
Patton's utilization-focused, 42
Phillips's ROI methodology, 42, 61–73
Provus's discrepancy, 5, 41, 83
Scriven's consumer-oriented, 40, 82
Scriven's goal-free, 5, 15, 41, 162
selecting, 43
self-evaluation framework, 250–253
Stake's responsive/client-centered, 5, 41
Stufflebeam's CIPP, 5, 43, 107–115
Tyler's objective-based, 40
Evaluation Network, 120
Evaluation questions
asking the right, 28–32

Evaluation questions (*continued*)
  coming from various perspectives and
    stakeholders, 87–88
  decision string of, 29–30
  evaluation study are driven by, 35
  follow-up, 155–157
  open- and closed-ended, 176–177
  process string of, 29
  societal string of, 29
  system string of, 30
  See also Data; Questionnaires/surveys
Evaluation Research Society, 120
Evaluators
  AEA principles for, 120, 122
  challenges faced by, 20–22
  competencies of, 11
  contracting with, 257–268
  ethics and professionalism of, 262
  functions of, 13
  as job versus role, 10–11
  observation bias by, 163–164
  recommendation implementation role of,
    235–236
  See also Meta-evaluators
Executive briefing, 232–233
Experimental design
  basis of, 186–187
  examples of typical, 187*t*–188
  variations of time-series, 189
Experimental research
  designing, 186–188, 189
  problems with classic, 188
  relationship between evaluation and, 185–186
  time-series, 188–190
Expert error, 242
Explanation creep error, 243
Extant data review, 191

F

Face validity, 182–183
Fair assessment standard, 126
False conclusion error, 242
Feasibility standards
  cost-effectiveness, 125
  meeting propriety, 125
  political viability, 124–125
  service orientation, 125–126
Ferrington, J., 280, 282
Findings. *See* Communicating findings
Fitzgerald, L., 142
Fitzpatrick, J. L., 4, 5, 39, 40, 119, 120
Fixed-price contract, 258–259
Focus groups
  conducting, 166–167
  samples used for, 167–168

Follow-up evaluation questions, 155–157
Ford, J. K., 53
Forked path error, 246
Formative evaluations
  CIPP model applicability to, 110*t*
  described, 15, 17, 18
  timing and issues of, 17
Foxon, M., 52
Freedman, M., 21

G

Gage, N. L., 189
Gall, M. D., 171
Games, 189–190
Gharajedaghi, J., 83
Gilbert, T. F., 8, 49, 92, 271
Gilbert's behavioral engineering
  model, 271–272
Goal-free evaluation model, 5, 15, 41, 82, 162
Goals
  based on valid organization
    needs, 33–34
  definition of, 26
  needs assessment to determine, 33
  See also Objectives
Grady, M. W., 275
Graphical data representations, 210–212*fig*
GRE (Graduate Record Examination), 183
Guba, E., 5, 6, 185
Guerra, I., 13, 50, 86, 91, 92, 93, 135, 138, 148,
    170, 257, 262, 281
Guerra-López, I., 6, 41, 42, 81, 84, 96, 112, 281
  See also Impact evaluation process

H

Handbook of Human Performance Technology
    (Pershing), 281
Hard data, 135
Harless, J., 8, 272
Henderson, A., 20
Hofstadter, D. R., 48
Holton, E., 54
Howick, S., 275
Huberman, A. M., 197
Human Competence: Engineering Worthy
    Performance (Gilbert), 8
Human subject rights standard, 126
Hunter, A., 128

I

Impact evaluation
  definition of, 19
  impact evaluation process model, 42, 81–104
Impact evaluation process
  comments on, 96

elements of the, 83–96
illustrated diagram of, 84*fig*
introduction to, 42, 81–83
strengths and limitations of, 97
TVC (Visionary Corporation) application example of, 97–104
See also Guerra-López, I.
Impact evaluation process steps
  1: identify stakeholders and expectations, 84–86
  2: determine key decisions and objectives, 86–91
  3: deriving measurable indicators, 91–92
  4: identifying data sources, 92
  5: selecting data collection methods, 92–93
  6: selecting data analysis tools, 93–96
  7: communication of results and recommendations, 96
Indirect observation. *See* Person-centered indirect observation methods
Inferential statistics
  described, 201
  parametric and nonparametric, 214–217
Information
  definition of, 134
  included in written reports, 229–230
  standards for, 127–129
  standards for collecting, 123–124
  See also Data
Input evaluation, 109
Instructor-made tests, 179–180
Instrument errors, 244
Instrument-centered methods
  choosing the right instrument, 172–174
  overview of, 172
  questionnaires and surveys, 174–178
International Society for Performance Improvement (ISPI), 9, 279
Interpretation
  data analysis, 217–218
  linking recommendations, findings, data analysis and, 234–235
Interval measurement level, 137, 138*t*
Interview methods, 170–171
Investigative processes
  common elements of all, 14–15
  dimensions of, 16*t*
  evaluation relationship to other, 11–15
  needs assessment, 12*t*–13*t*, 25
IRHTP (Interdisciplinary Rural Health Training Program) evaluation case
  background information on, 122
  findings of, 123–129
  methodology used in, 122–123
"Item-objective congruence," 181

J

Janak, E. A., 48
Johnson, T. R., 49
Johnston, R., 142
Joint Committee on Standards for Educational Evaluation, 119–120
Juran, J., 94
Justified conclusions standard, 129

K

Kaplan, R. S., 142, 276
Kaufman, R. A., 13, 21, 22, 25, 55, 82, 88, 90, 92, 93, 94, 109, 112, 135, 138, 139, 170, 254, 257, 262, 280
Kaufman's organizational elements model, 82
Keller, J. M., 55
Kennerly, M., 142
Key Evaluation Checklist, 40
King, D., 54
Kirkpatrick, D., 42, 47, 49, 50, 52, 53
Kirkpatrick's four levels of evaluation
  application example of, 56–58
  comments regarding, 54–55
  introduction to, 42, 47–49
  Kaufman and Keller's variation of, 55
  level 1: reactions, 47, 48*fig*, 49–50
  level 2: learning, 48*fig*
  level 3: behavior transfer, 48*fig*, 52–53
  level 4: results, 48*fig*, 53–54
  Phillips's expansion of, 61–62
  "reactionnaires" forms used in, 174
  strengths and limitations of, 55–56
Knowledge of Health Care Disciplines Questionnaire, 128
Kuder-Richardson formula, 184

L

Lavigne, M., 62
Leadership
  accountability demands by, 282
  continual improvement and role of, 254–255
Levels of result, 25
Lick, D., 254
Likert scales
  attitudinal surveys using, 137, 184
  Kirkpatrick's level 1 reactions using, 49
  mean of, 202
  median of, 203
  questionnaire items, 136
Lincoln, Y., 5
Line charts, 210–211*fig*
Liston, C., 4
Literature review, 192
local value error, 241–242

Logic errors
of association, 243
of the expert, 242
of explanation creep, 243
false conclusion, 242
of the quick fix, 243
wishful thinking, 243
Lynch, D., 122
Lynch, R. L., 142

M

Madaus, G., 40
Mager, R. F., 139
Management by walking around, 161
Management plan, 261
Market share increase, 90
Maskell, B., 1424
Mauris, G., 272
McKinsey, 21
McLaughlin, S. D., 49
McMillan, J. H., 136
Mean, 201–202
Means
definition of, 25, 32
of evaluation process, 32–33
Measurable indicators
CIPP framework of, 114t
commonly used financial, 142–143
definition of, 141–142
deriving, 91–92, 141–152
general categories of commonly used, 143t–144t
vocational rehabilitation case study on, 148–151
See also Data
Measurement
central tendency, 201–204
data analysis of relationship, 212–214
dispersion (variability), 204–210fig
error of, 244
levels of, 137, 138t
Likert scales, 49, 136, 137, 184, 202, 203
observation methodology and purpose of, 160–186
performance, 271–277
performance improvement role of, 281–282
See also Statistics
Measures of central tendency
the mean, 201–202
the median, 202–203
the mode, 203–204
Measures of dispersion (variability)
the normal curve, 208–210fig
the range, 204–206

the semi-interquartile range, 206
the standard deviation (SD), 206–208
Median, 202–203
Merit (CIPP model), 108
Meta-evaluation
AEA principles for evaluators, 120, 122
definition of, 118–119
importance of, 118
IRHTP application example on, 122–129
standards used for, 119–120, 121t
See also Evaluation
Meta-evaluators
essential qualifications for, 119
See also Evaluators
Miles, M. B., 197
Minnesota Multiphasic Personality Inventory, 183
Misattribution error, 241
Missing player error, 241
Mode, 203–204
Mohr, L. B., 139
Monitoring performance
continual improvement by, 250–251
organizational decision making and role of, 271–277
self-evaluation framework for, 251–253
Montmain, J., 272
Myers-Briggs test, 183

N

National Centre for Vocational Education Research (Australia), 68
Needs
definition of, 22, 25
organization goals/objectives based on valid, 33–34
using top-down approach to derive valid, 34
Needs assessment
definition of, 25
objectives/goals determined by, 33
unique perspectives of, 12t–13t
Needs assessors, 13
Neely, A., 142, 275, 276
Negatively skewed distribution, 210fig
Nevo, D., 44
Newby, A., 174
Niven, P. R., 144, 152, 155
Noe, R. A., 53
Nominal group technique, 168–169, 170t
Nominal measurement level, 137, 138t
Nondisclosure agreement, 268
Nonparametric inferential statistics, 214–217
Nonstructured direct observations, 163
Norm-referenced tests, 182
Normal curve, 208–210fig
Norton, D. P., 142, 276
Nutt, P., 272, 273, 275

Objective-based evaluation model, 40
Objectives
  based on valid organization needs, 33–34
  congruence between test items and, 181
  defining required data from
    performance, 139, 141
  definition of, 26
  determining key decision and, 86–91
  needs assessment to determine, 33
  See also Goals
Observation bias, 163–164
Observation methodology
  instrument-centered, 172–178
  person-centered direct, 161–166
  person-centered indirect observation
    techniques, 166–172
  reliability and validity of tests, 182–184
  rules for, 161
  traditional knowledge testing, 179–182
  treatment-centered, 184–185
Obtrusive direct observations, 162–163
OMT (outdoor management training) programs
  description of, 56–57
  evaluation of, 57–58
Open-ended questions, 176, 177
Oral reports/presentations, 232–233
Ordinal measurement level, 137, 138t
Organizational elements model, 82
Organizational mission, 34
Organizational vision
  definition of, 34
  Kaufman's ideal, 112
  value-added, 89–90
An Ounce of Analysis Is Worth a Pound of
  Objectives (Harless), 8, 272

Parametric inferential statistics, 214–217
Parker, R. A., 174
Participant observation, 164–166
Patton, M. Q., 5, 42, 75, 123
Patton's utilization-focused evaluation
  model, 42
Performance
  adjusting, 253–254
  definition of, 25
  monitoring, 250–253
  role of leadership in improving, 254–255
Performance dashboards, 274
Performance gaps, 272–273
Performance improvement
  ADDIE model for, 9, 274, 281
  a conceptual framework for, 8–9
  definition of, 9, 25

evaluation and measurement in, 281–282
  future of evaluation, 279–283
  ISPI definition of, 279–280
Performance Improvement Journal (PIJ),
  281, 282
Performance Improvement Quarterly
  (PIQ), 281, 282
Performance measurement systems (PMSs)
  ADDIE approach adopted for, 274
  description of, 273
  Gilbert's approach to, 273
  issues and challenges of, 275–277
  performance dashboards for, 274
Performance pyramid, 142
Performance-based evaluation
  overview of, 27–28
  principles of, 27–35
  See also Evaluation
Performance-based evaluation principles
  1: asking the right questions, 28–32
  2: evaluation as function of obtained
    results, 32–33
  3: organizations objectives should be based
    on valid needs, 33–34
  4: derive valid needs using top-down
    approach, 34
  5: every organization should aim for the
    best, 34–35
  6: evaluation questions drive the evaluation
    study, 35
Pershing, J., 8, 9, 280, 281
Person-centered direct observation methods
  acceptance by the group, 165
  bias problem of, 163–164
  effects of participation, 165–166
  obtrusive versus unobtrusive, 162–163
  overview of, 161–162
  participant, 164–165
  structured versus nonstructured, 163
  "surplus meaning" problem of, 164
Person-centered indirect
    observation methods
  critical incident technique, 171–172
  Delphi technique, 169–170
  focus groups, 166–168
  interview methods used for, 170–171
  nominal group technique, 168–169, 170t
Peters, T. J., 161
Phi Delta Kappa National Study Committee on
  Evaluation, 6, 107
Phillips, J., 42, 61, 62, 63
  See also ROI methodology
Pie charts, 212fig
Platt, W. A., 92, 135, 138, 170, 257, 262
Political viability standard, 124–125
Popham, W. J., 43

Population masking error, 246
PORO (Guidance Program for Job Search) evaluation case, 113–115
Positively skewed distribution, 210*fig*
Postprogram testing, 54*fig*, 96
Pre-program testing, 54*fig*
Presser, S., 175
Problem solving assumptions, 7
Procedure errors, 244–246
Process (or efficiency) evaluation, 19, 109
Product evaluation, 109–111
Professional ethics, 262
Program review, 261–262
Propriety standards
    complete and fair assessment, 126
    conflict of interest, 126–127
    rights of human subjects, 126
    service orientation, 125–126
Provus, M., 5, 41, 83
Provus's discrepancy evaluation model, 5, 41, 83
Public forum, 233
Pyburn, P. J., 275

Q

Qualitative data
    critical incident technique for collecting, 171
    data analysis of, 196–197
    description of, 95, 136–137
    standard on analysis of, 129
Quantitative data
    analysis of, 199–210*fig*
    description of, 95, 136–137
    standard on analysis of, 128
Quantitative data analysis
    examples of purposes of, 199–200
    measures of central tendency, 201–204
    measures of dispersion (variability), 204–210*fig*
    statistics used in, 200–210*fig*
Questionnaires/surveys
    basic types of items used in, 175–176
    as data collection instrument, 174–175
    length of, 178
    Likert-scale, 137
    open- and closed-ended questions used in, 176–177
    other types of question formats used in, 177
    structure of, 177–178
    See also Evaluation questions
Quick fix error, 243

R

Range (or spread), 204–206
Ratio measurement level, 137, 138*t*
Rea, L. M., 174

"Reactionnaires," 174
Recommendations
    communicating findings and, 222–223
    considerations for implementing, 225–226
    evaluator's possible role in implementing, 235–236
    framework for identifying and presenting, 223*t*–224*t*
    impact evaluation process on communicating, 96
    linking to interpretations, findings, data analysis and, 234–235
    progression from analyzed data to, 216*fig*
    reporting the, 226–235
Redish, J., 227
Relationship measures, 212–214
Relevant data, 135
Reliability
    of data, 135
    standard for information, 128
    testing, 182–184
Reliable information standard, 128
Repeated AB design, 189
Report development
    clarifying stakeholders' responsibilities, 235
    evaluator's role after the report, 235–236
    format decisions, 228
    identifying the key message, 233–234
    knowing the audience, 227–233
    language elements of, 227–228
    linking evaluation components, 234–235
    oral reports, 232–233
    overview of, 226–227
    written reports, 229–232
Research. *See* Experimental research
Responsive/client-centered evaluation model, 5, 41
Results evaluation, 19
Reversal/ABA designs, 189
Richards, L., 197
Richards, T., 197
ROI methodology
    application example of, 70–73
    calculating ROI of program, 67
    collecting postprogram data, 63
    comments on the, 67–69
    converting data to monetary values, 65–66
    identifying intangible benefits of program, 67
    introduction to, 42, 62–63
    isolating effects of training, 64–65
    Kirkpatrick's four levels model expanded by, 61–62
    strengths and limitations of, 70
    tabulating program costs, 66–67
    See also Phillips, J.

ROI (return on investment)
    calculation for, 67
    concept and applications of, 68
Rowland, C., 56
Rowland/Diamond, 56
Rummler, G. A., 8, 49

S

Saari, L. M., 49
Sanders, J. R., 4, 5, 11, 39, 119
Santos, S., 275, 277
SAT (Scholastic Assessment Test), 183
Schedule/work breakdown
    structure, 262
SCM (success case model)
    application example of, 79–80
    introduction to, 42, 75–77
    process of, 77–78
    strengths and weaknesses of, 78
    See also Brinkerhoff, R.
Scope of work, 260–261
Scriven, M., 4, 5, 15, 19, 40, 82–83, 95,
    118, 119, 162
Scriven's consumer-oriented evaluation
    model, 40, 82
Scriven's goal-free evaluation model,
    5, 15, 41, 82, 162
SD (standard deviation), 206–208
Self-evaluation framework, 250–253
Semi-interquartile range (SIQR), 206
Service orientation standard, 125–126
Sgro, P., 68, 69
Shinkfield, A., 39, 40, 41, 42, 107,
    118–119, 120
SimPak Computers evaluation case, 79–80
Simulations, 189–190
Sivestro, R., 142
Skinner, B. F., 8, 280
Skinner, W., 277
Slack, N., 277
Society
    core values and ideals held by, 111–112
    ends in context of, 22
    evaluation questions in context of, 29
Socrates, 4
Soft data, 136
Sputnik, 5
Srivastva, S., 6
Stake, R. E., 5, 41, 75, 119, 139, 241
Stakeholders
    clarifying responsibilities of, 235
    core values and ideals held by, 111–112
    definition of, 25
    determining key decisions and objectives
        of, 86–91

ensuring evaluation buy-in by, 9–10
evaluation questions coming
    from, 87–88
identification of, 84–86, 123
pre- and postprogram results reported to,
    54*fig*, 96
test performance comparison reported
    to, 51*fig*
Stake's responsive/client-centered evaluation
    model, 5, 41
Standard deviation (SD), 206–208
Standards
    accuracy, 127–129
    context, 127–129
    development of evaluation, 119–120
    feasibility, 124–125
    listing of program evaluation, 121*t*
    propriety, 125–127
    utility, 123–124
*Standards for Evaluation of Educational
    Programs, Projects, and Materials*
    (Joint Committee), 120, 122
Stanley, J. C., 189
Statement of work
    description of, 261
    sample and example of, 262–268
Statistics
    descriptive, 200
    inferential, 201, 214–217
    measures of central tendency, 201–204
    measures of dispersion (variability),
        204–210*fig*
    See also Measurement
Structured direct observations, 163
Structured discussion
    analysis using, 1979
    controls on, 198–199
    imposing structure on emerging issues of,
        197–198
    relevance of, 198
Stufflebeam, D., 5, 6, 18, 19, 39, 40, 41, 42,
    43, 44, 107, 108, 109, 111, 112, 118–119,
    120, 185
    See also CIPP model
Summative evaluations
    CIPP model applicability to, 110*t*
    described, 15, 17, 18–20
"Surplus meaning" problem, 164
Surveys. *See* Questionnaires/surveys
Suwignjo, P., 276
System mapping errors
    error of causal path, 240–241
    error of local value, 241–242
    error of misattribution, 241
    error of the missing player, 241

T

Technos: Quarterly for Education and Technology (2000), 160
Test-retest method, 184
Testing
 criterion-referenced, 180–182
 data collection through, 179–182
 instructor-made for training, 179–180
 norm-referenced, 182
 reliability and validity of, 182–184
Time-and-material contract, 259–260
Time-series studies
 four design variations of, 189
 overview of, 188–189
 simulations and games, 189–190
Treatment-centered methods, 184–186
Turner, T., 276
TVC (Visionary Corporation) evaluation case
 background information on, 97–98
 findings of, 101–104
 methodology used in, 98–99, 101
 relevant performance indicators, 100*t*
Tyler, R., 4, 40, 41
Tyler's objective-based evaluation model, 40

U

Unobtrusive direct observations, 162–163
Usability testing, definition of, 20
Utility standards
 evaluation impact, 124
 feasibility, 124
 information scope and collection, 123–124
 stakeholder identification, 123
 values identification, 124
Utilization-focused evaluation model, 42
Utilization-Focused Evaluation (Patton), 42

V

Valid data, 135
Valid information standard, 127–128
Validity

criterion-referenced test, 180–181
 data, 135–137
 standard for information, 127–128
 testing, 182–184
Value
 error of local, 241–242
 identification standard for identifying, 124
Value added
 definition of, 26
 organizational vision on, 89–90
Variability. *See* Measures of dispersion (variability)
Vision
 definition of, 34
 Kaufman's ideal, 112
 value-added, 89–90
Vocational rehabilitation measurable indicators, 148–151
Voss, C., 142

W

Wagner, R., 57
Waterman, R. H., 161
Watkins, R., 86, 88
Webster, W. J., 18, 19, 43
Weiss, C., 5
Western Michigan University's Evaluation Center, 119
Willis, M., 20
Wishful thinking error, 243
Witkin, B. R., 93
Work products, 192
Worley, C. G., 254
Worth, 108
Worthen, B. R., 4, 5, 39, 119
Written reports
 information included in, 229–230
 outline for formal, 230–231
 outline for "quick-and-dirty," 231–232

Z

Zimmerle, D. M., 49

Lightning Source UK Ltd.
Milton Keynes UK
UKHW021537041219
354735UK00003B/13/P